THE SLAVES' ECONOMY
INDEPENDENT PRODUCTION BY SLAVES
IN THE AMERICAS

T0330840

THE SLAVES' ECONOMY
Independent Production by Slaves in the Americas

Edited by
Ira Berlin and Philip D. Morgan

Routledge
Taylor & Francis Group
New York   London

First published in Great Britain by
FRANK CASS & CO. LTD.
Newbury House, 900 Eastern Avenue
London IG2 7HH, England

and in the United States by
FRANK CASS & CO. LTD.
c/o ISBS
5804 N.E. Hassalo Street, Portland, Oregon 97213-3644

Copyright © 1991 Frank Cass & Co. Ltd.

First published 1991
Reprinted in paperback 1995 (ISBN 978-0-7146-4172-0)

Library of Congress Cataloging-in-Publication Data

Applied for.

British Library Cataloguing in Publication Data

Applied for.

This group of studies first appeared in a special issue on 'The Slaves' Economy: Independent Production by Slaves in the Americas' in *Slavery and Abolition*, Vol.12, No.1, published by Frank Cass & Co. Ltd.

Contents

Introduction

Ira Berlin and Philip D. Morgan

Slaves worked. When, where, and especially how they worked determined, in large measure, the course of their lives. The centrality of labour in the slaves' experience seems so obvious that it has often been taken for granted. Recent studies of slavery in the Americas have focused on the slaves' social organization, domestic arrangements, religious beliefs, medical practices, along with the music, cuisine, and linguistic and sartorial style that gave Afro-American culture its distinctive form during slavery. For the most part these aspects of slave life have been understood as emanating from the quarter, household and church rather than field and workshop.[1] This emphasis has obscured the activities that dominated slave life. After all, slavery was first and foremost an institution of coerced labor. Work necessarily engaged most slaves, most of the time.

Acknowledging the centrality of work offers a useful beginning, but an understanding of the slaves' labour cannot stop there. Most elementally, the work of slaves can be divided into that done for the master and that for the slave. Slave societies, then, generally involved two interrelated and overlapping economies: one organized by and for masters; the other by and for slaves. The work slaves did for their masters accounted for most of their labouring time, but the independent economic activities of slaves – what has been called the 'internal economy', 'peasant breach', or more simply the slaves' economy – had far-reaching consequences.[2] By producing food for themselves and for others, tending cash crops, raising livestock, manufacturing finished goods, marketing their own products, consuming and saving the proceeds, and bequeathing property to their descendants, slaves took control of a large part of their lives. In many ways the slaves' independent economic endeavours offered a foundation for their domestic and community life, shaping the social structure of slave society and providing a material basis for the slaves' distinctive culture. Moreover, the character of the slaves' economy and the modest economic success black men and women achieved during slavery influenced the hopes and aspirations they carried into freedom, giving direction to the post-emancipation struggle for equality. The legacy of slavery cannot be understood without a full appreciation of the slaves' economy.

To explore how patterns of work shaped the lives of Afro-American

1

slaves a group of some 40 scholars met together at the University of
Maryland in the spring of 1989 under the head of 'Cultivation and
Culture: Labour and Shaping Slave Life in the Americas'. Representing a variety of disciplines, these scholars focused on the ways the
processes of production, especially the demands of particular forms of
agricultural cultivation, influenced the lives of the men and women
who tended the New World's great staple crops. Although attention
naturally focused on the cultivation of sugar, coffee, rice, cotton and
tobacco, careful consideration was also given to the production of other
commodities – cattle, timber, wheat, manioc and arrowroot – as well as
the various forms of non-plantation agriculture and manufacture
that proliferated along the periphery of plantation society. The conference's proceedings outgrew the bounds of a single volume and it was
agreed to publish them in two parts. One, which will appear in 1992, will
examine the influence of staple production – the masters' economy – on
slave life. The other, this special number of *Slavery & Abolition*,
focuses on the labour slaves did for themselves. Obviously, these
are complementary and overlapping subjects, separable only as a
convenience in organizing a great wealth of scholarship. Ultimately,
both volumes reassess the slave experience in the New World from the
perspective of what slaves did most of the time.

*   *   *

At root, slavery was a form of labour organization in which masters
forcibly expropriated the slaves' person, plus the lion's share of the
surplus that slaves produced. In return, the master generally offered
subsistence and protection. But, while slaveowners reaped the benefit
of the slaves' toil, they did not always meet their obligations. Often they
required slaves to provide their own subsistence, requiring them to
feed, clothe, and medicate themselves. Such bad faith burdened slave
men and women, who worked long hours to support themselves and
their families after they had finished doing their owners' bidding. But,
in a manner that characterized so much of the slave experience, slaves
turned the masters' additional demands to their own advantage,
transforming attempts to rivet tighter the bonds of servitude into small
grants of independence – niches or breaches – whereby they controlled
a portion of their own lives. By appropriating their labour for themselves, slaves articulated their own interests and the means of achieving
them. None the less, relations between master and slave remained at
once 'dependent and antagonistic', so that if the slaves' economy stood
apart from the masters' – physically and ideologically – it never formed,
as Dale Tomich notes, 'an independent "peasant breach" with a logic of

it own'.[3] The slaves' economy can be understood only within the context of the struggle between master and slave.

In economy – as in other aspects of that struggle – slaves achieved their greatest success where masters were most vulnerable. The masters' vulnerability increased the slaves' bargaining power, enlarging the niches or breaches in which the slaves' fragile economic independence rested. Such points of vulnerability differed under different productive regimes. Mahogany cutters in Belize derived a degree of economic independence from their ability to roam the forest, armed with axes and guns; cotton pickers in pioneer upcountry South Carolina from the acute shortage of labour; tobacco hands in the Chesapeake from the small size of their productive units; sugar workers throughout the Americas from the necessity to harvest and grind the cane rapidly.[4] Thus in every slave society an understanding of the slaves' economy rests upon an understanding of the masters' economy: the labour requirements of particular crops, their seasonal rhythms, and their susceptibility to drought, frost and disease, among other constraints.

The slaves' economy must also be studied in conjunction with masters' need to subsist their slaves. In the Americas slaveholders employed three broad strategies to feed their slaves: they imported rations from outside the plantation, supervised the production of food as part of estate labour, or allowed or required slaves to feed themselves by ceding them a portion of their time and access to gardens (sometimes called houseplots or yards) and provision grounds (sometimes called *conucos*, *polinks*, or 'negro grounds'). Such practices were not mutually exclusive, and they differed from place to place and changed over time. Thus some slave societies depended almost exclusively on rationing and others relied on slave provision grounds for most of their food requirements; most, however, developed a mix between imported and estate-grown rations and the independent production of food by slaves.

Planters allowed, encouraged, or forced their slaves to subsist themselves when provisions were expensive or difficult to obtain. Such practices reached back to the beginning of plantation production on the island of São Tomé off the west coast of Africa in the sixteenth century. They were carried to the New World by the Portuguese and spread throughout the Caribbean by the Dutch.[5] None the less, the practice of requiring slaves to provision themselves did not rest upon precedent; it developed only under particular circumstances. For example, in non-agricultural operations like mining provisions were generally in short supply and land was readily available and easily given over to slaves. Thus mine owners in many parts of the Americas required their slaves to grow food, often giving them large blocks of time in lieu of rations. In the Colombian Choco a five-day week was the general practice, so that slaves had two days to grow their own provisions. On smaller *cuadrillas* some slaves had three days per week to maintain themselves, but such practices were not universal. In the Minas Gerais region of Brazil mine owners often denied their slaves access to provision grounds and frequently ignored the law granting slaves Sundays and holy days to cultivate their own plots.[6]

The slaves' economy took shape at the confluence of the requirements of staple production and the demands of the established system of subsistence. Understanding the slaves' independent economic activities requires a knowledge of both the labour regimen and method of provisioning imposed by the master. These, in turn, depended upon the geography and demography of particular slave societies, the degree of commitment to staple production, the availability of alternative sources of subsistence, and – most importantly – the stiff-necked refusal of slaves to accept their masters' rule. Like Afro-American religion or language, the slaves' economy was both an exemplar of the continuing struggle between master and slave and a portion of the terrain on which that struggle was fought.

Whereas masters saw the slaves' self-subsistence as a means to lower their expenses and raise their profits, slaves understood their independent economic activity in a different light. Throughout the Americas slaves believed they could enlarge and vary their diet from the produce of their own gardens and provision grounds. Moreover, by marketing their surplus and keeping the proceeds of those sales slaves also earned cash that enabled them to elevate their standard of living, to move freely through the countryside, and to learn about the world beyond the plantation's borders. Finally, with their small accumulations of cash slaves placed their domestic and communal life on a firmer base, offered 'a start' to the next generation and – upon occasion – secured freedom for themselves and their loved ones.

Slaves pushed hard to establish and then to expand the right to produce and market independently, demanding additional land and time to work it and pressing for greater freedom to sell the surplus. Frequently, they – not their owners – had initiated independent economic production. After carving out their own grounds slaves on one St Vincent estate offered their owner a bargain: if he would allow them Saturday afternoon out of crop they would feed themselves and expect him to supply only salt provisions.[7] Moreover, once in place slaves transformed the masters' grant of privileges into entitlements and defended them fiercely. On the sugar plantations neighbouring Vere, Jamaican slaves voted with their feet, refusing to be transferred to a parish where they would have to depend on rations for their food supply. In the Windward Islands the continued presence of plantation yam grounds harked back to earlier days of provision production by estate labour.[8] Claiming a larger and larger share of the produce of their labour, slaves gained *de facto* – and occasionally *de jure* – proprietorship over a portion of what they had created. But, win or lose, the struggle itself taught slaves how they could manipulate their circumstances to their own advantage. In the process slaves developed ideas about the importance of labour, the role of property and the relation of both to their own being; such ideas eventually stood at the centre of the slaves' political cosmos.

* * *

The peculiar demands of staple production – be it sugar, coffee, rice, tobacco or cotton – and the desire of slaveowners to subsist their slaves as cheaply as possible shaped the evolution of the slaves' independent enterprises. The availability of land – particularly land that could not be profitably employed in staple production – often induced masters to allow their slaves to feed themselves. Planters encouraged slaves to develop their own provision grounds in hilly or mountainous land – known as 'gutsides' in the Leeward Islands – that bordered the great estates. The presence of vacant backlands allowed the slaves' economy to thrive in the Windward Islands of St Vincent, Grenada, St Lucia, most parishes or quarters in Jamaica and the Leeward Islands of Montserrat, and, to a lesser extent, St Kitts and Nevis.[9]

Conversely, where land was limited and fertile staple cultivation soon took precedence and independent provisioning by the slaves assumed importance only under special circumstances. Once the commitment to sugar production had been made, a small, low-lying island like Antigua or Barbados essentially became an extensive plantation, where slaves were exclusively foreign-fed, at least through the eighteenth century. Likewise, slaves in the Jamaican parish of Vere, which consisted of one large and exceptionally rich plain, devoted all their attention to sugar production and were fed by rations as long as slavery lasted.[10]

But a surfeit of land did not persuade masters to allow their slaves to provision themselves if greater profits could be secured in employing slaves in staple production or if food could be obtained more cheaply elsewhere. The requirements of commodity production convinced some slaveowners to keep their slaves working the great staples rather than allow them to tend provision grounds. Planters in the extensive coastal plain of Demerara-Essequibo and Berbice refused to provide their slaves with provision grounds, even though nearby backlands were available, because the estates required labour for massive irrigation projects.[11] Similarly, when food could be imported cheaply or purchased easily from non-slaveholding Indians, whites, or even free blacks, planters did little to encourage the slaves' independent production and sometimes actively discouraged it. On mainland North America, for example, the presence of free whites – extending to a majority in most places – limited the development of the slaves' economy. Although there was land aplenty for slave provision grounds, North-American slaveholders generally preferred to control the production of foodstuffs themselves or purchase provisions from the non-slaveholding population. Buying food and necessities from non-slaveholders offered important political rewards, since it tied the non-slaveholding population to the slaveholders' regime.[12]

Moreover, planters found advantages in growing provisions. The growing cycle of some staples, most notably tobacco and cotton, easily accommodated estate production of foodstuffs. Planters dovetailed their operations to keep their slaves employed. Even sugar planters on mainland North America had land and time enough to have their slaves plant one or two crops of corn as well as vegetables. In time, certain regions came to specialize in provisioning. On non-staple producing islands such as Anguilla, the Bahamas, and the Cayman Islands, slaves cultivated food crops as part of estate labor. In certain parts of the Chesapeake where tobacco could no longer be profitably grown, many slaves became farm labourers, not plantation hands. In addition, small-time resident masters, who were firmly committed to their colonies, may have been far more wary of the independence that self-provisioning fostered among their slaves than their grand, absentee counterparts.[13]

The availability of land and dynamics of population thus only partially explain the emergence and growth of the slaves' economy. In the short term, masters continually altered the method by which they provisioned their slaves to assure dominance, meet the requirements of staple cultivation, and maximize profits: when export commodities commanded high prices, slaveowners tended to ration slaves; when exports mustered low prices, masters often obliged slaves to grow their own food. But, over the long run, the development of the slaves' economy was tied directly to the evolution of a slave society and the slaveowners' changing commitment to staple production.

In the earliest years of settlement, when staple production was not yet all-encompassing, planters generally had spare land, which they put into provisions either through regular estate labour or by making it available to slaves to work on their own account. Even Barbados, which at the height of the sugar revolution exemplified a plantation regime that relied upon imported foodstuffs, contained slave provision grounds in the seventeenth and the first decades of the eighteenth centuries. In the early history of St Kitts, sugar planters generally planted prime caneland in yams and provided fallow cane fields for their slaves to cultivate their own food crops. A similar pattern could be found on mainland North America. The slaves' economy took hold during the initial period of settlement in the Chesapeake, the Carolina lowcountry and the lower Mississippi Valley.[14]

As slave societies matured and the commitment to staple production deepened, planters usually began to provision their slaves directly – often on imported foodstuffs. Efforts to maximize staple production resulted in the withdrawal of land and labour from food crops. As the acreage devoted to staples increased, provisioning land for slaves contracted, unless there was sufficient marginal land – usually located in plantations' back lots – to which *polinks* or 'negro grounds' could be relocated. Legislation regulating various aspects of the slaves' economy – trading, ownership of certain kinds of property and travel – signalled the new constraints on independent economic activities by slaves. The planters' desire to limit the slaves' economy was most evident in an island like Barbados, where, by the mid-eighteenth century, planters had wrested provisioning grounds away from their slaves. Barbadian slaves came to depend almost exclusively on imported rations and grew little of their own food. But the pattern was general. During the height of the eighteenth-century sugar expansion in the Caribbean even planters in home-fed colonies supplemented provision-ground supplies with imported food. Sometimes they did so under the pressure of metropolitan authorities. In Martinique French officials required that planters subsist their slaves and limited the growth of slave provision grounds.[15]

With the decline in the commitment to staple production, slave-holders again shifted responsibility for provisioning to their slaves, encouraging – sometimes requiring – slaves to feed themselves. The size of provision grounds and the time slaves had to tend them increased, often under pressure of metropolitan regulation to guarantee the slaves' subsistence. The slaveholders' new policies not only reflected a simple desire to cut costs but also changes in the structure of the labour force, which, in a mature slave society, included large numbers of young and old people. Such changes could be seen in the Caribbean where, by the early nineteenth century, the provision-ground system had become the dominant mode of subsisting slaves. At the time of emancipation some three-quarters of the slaves in the British West Indies subsisted themselves. The surplus they produced fed a large proportion of the free population. On some islands slaves achieved a monopoly over the production of commodities like firewood and fodder.[16]

The evolution of staple production explains a good deal about the origins and growth of independent production by slaves. Still, the development of the slaves' economy did not follow any preordained pattern. Within the same society masters and slaves made different choices, depending, for example, upon the size and topography of their plantations, the character of the plantations' work force, the availability of transportation and, of course, the changing balance of power between master and slave. Moreover, natural and man-made crises, everything from hurricane to revolution – which set in motion sharp changes in commodity prices and the availability of provisions – altered the dynamics of both the masters' and the slaves' economy. Indeed, such crises often became the occasion for the appearance, growth and demise of the slaves' economy. When planters found it difficult or expensive to buy the necessary foodstuffs they gladly gave their slaves the land and time to do the work themselves; when provisions were cheap they tried to limit the slaves' independent activity.

The War for American Independence, which denied Caribbean slaves access to mainland foodstuffs and unleashed a wave of revolutionary activity that culminated with the Haitian Revolution, was the greatest of these traumas. In the Caribbean, where the disruptions caused massive starvation on some islands, planters reverted to estate labour to grow provisions or turned the job over to their slaves, greatly enlarging the amount of land set aside for growing provisions. Between 1750 and 1800 the average size of provision grounds in the British West Indies nearly doubled, increasing from four-tenths of an acre per slave to seven-tenths. By the beginning of the nineteenth century slaves in many Caribbean societies gained Saturdays, as well as Sundays, to work their grounds. The closing of the African slave trade, the disruptions of commerce that accompanied the Napoleonic Wars, and the metropolitan-sponsored campaigns to ameliorate the condition of the slave reinforced the shift toward provisioning in the Caribbean, generally by the slaves themselves.[17]

The revolutionary events of the late eighteenth century had a different effect in the North and South American mainland. Hard times in the Caribbean sent staple prices skyrocketing on the international market, and mainland planters rushed to increase production. Sugar boomed in north-eastern Brazil and southern Louisiana, especially after the fall of slavery in St Domingue. As these mainland slaveholders transferred land and slaves into sugar and pressed their slaves to grow the great staple, the slaves' struggled to maintain their own economies.[18]

*   *   *

The slaves' willingness to work independently derived first from the desire for a richer subsistence. The bounty of the slaves' gardens and provision grounds led many observers to conclude that the quantity and quality of food was better where slaves subsisted themselves than where they relied upon planters' rations. Throughout the Americas slaves created enormous horticultural repertoires in their gardens and grounds, blending native American plants like cassava, European vegetables like *calavance* peas, African trees like *ackees* and Oceanian fruits like mangoes. Able to cultivate their gardens with a minimum of interference, the Saramaka maroons grew a staggering array of crops, but the diversity of vegetables, spices, nuts, fruits and trees grown by Jamaican slaves, to take just one example, astonished all who saw it: *abbay* (or African oil-palm), Angola or pigeon or *gungo* peas, bananas, *bissy* (or African kola nut tree), cabbage (leaves from cabbage tree), calabashes, *calalu* (green vegetable and comprising many different plants), cashews, *chocho*, coconuts, custard apples, maize, *mammee apples* (*mammee* gum was used by slave doctors for chiggers and *mammee* bark against lice), naseberries, *okra*, oranges, palms, varieties of peppers, pimento, pineapples, pumpkins, shaddocks, and sweetsops, to name just a few. Root crops – especially the yellow and the white yam (of which there were many varieties, such as *afu*, *backra*, and *Negro*), together with eddoes and cocos – were the primary staples, with plantains and corn (both American and Guinea) the secondary supplements. The centrality of the yam was symbolized by its linguistic connection to the many African words meaning 'to eat' or 'food', rendered in Jamaican English as *nyam* and *ninyam*. To paraphrase John H. Parry, the history of the West Indies should be the story of yams, no less than that of sugar.[19]

In most parts of North America slaves largely grew crops of European or New World origin – such as corn, turnips, cabbages, and potatoes – but the most distinctive feature of their independent production was the cultivation of the dominant cash crop of their region. Many Chesapeake slaves produced small amounts of tobacco, the region's primary staple. In the South Carolina and Georgia lowcountry slaves grew rice on their own grounds, while in the upcountry they turned to the production of 'Mexican' short-staple cotton on a large scale, producing, in one upcountry South Carolina district, about seven per cent of all the area's cotton in the mid-nineteenth century. Although the commercial orientation of slave production in the antebellum South may testify to the confidence of the mainland's slaveholding class, slaves in the Caribbean also cultivated crops for export: ginger, arrowroot, gums and oil nuts – although never sugar.[20]

As the prohibition of sugar cultivation suggests, slaveholders disliked and generally discouraged the direct competition of slaves, fearful that slaves would steal from their fields. Although the belief that slaves were naturally thieves was rooted as much in the masters' ideology as in the slaves' reality, thievery played an important role in the slaves' economy. Many slaves held, as a matter of principle, that their masters' property was their own, or in the slaves' idiom: 'me no thief him; me take him from massa'. Goods removed from the masters' field and house commonly found their way to market and added to the slaves' resources.[21]

Skills in animal husbandry also enriched the slaves' economy – and their diet. Throughout the Americas slaves raised a variety of barnyard fowl. In fact, in almost all New-World slave societies slaves became the ubiquitous 'Chicken Merchants', as one eighteenth-century Virginian put it. The slaves' poultry-raising varied from place to place. Barbadian slaves reared Guinea fowls, ducks and pigeons as well as chickens; Louisiana slaves raised geese, ducks and turkeys alongside their chickens. As Roderick McDonald explains, '[r]aising poultry was ideally suited to the economy of the slave community, since it demanded little investment of time or effort, required minimal capital outlay and provided a steady income through marketing both eggs and the birds themselves'. Perhaps, too, chickens were important in ritual ceremonies elsewhere in the New World as they were for the Saramakas. The significance of this form of property ownership was well captured by a visitor to the Leeward Islands who observed that a slave's 'poultry and little stock ... are his wealth'. A 'negro without stock', he continued, was 'miserable'.[22]

In many parts of the Americas slaves also gained access to cattle and other livestock during the initial periods of settlement. But the freedom of movement such stock allowed incurred the planters' wrath and planter-controlled legislatures soon barred slave ownership of cattle and horses. These laws curbed livestock ownership by slaves in many slave societies; in others, however, repeated passage of the same legislation indicates that slaves maintained control over their cattle and larger stock. Indeed, in those societies where slaves participated in an extensive internal economy – like Jamaica – livestock ownership became quite widespread. By the nineteenth century, if not before, Jamaican slaves sold their cowhides, goatskins and animal horns in foreign markets. Similar developments could be found in other places.

At the end of the eighteenth century 'small stock, goats, and hogs' – which were 'for the most part the property of the Negroes' – supplied Antigua's shipping. Extensive woodlands and pastures facilitated stock raising by slaves on the North-American mainland, particularly in lowcountry South Carolina and Georgia, where ownership of cattle by slaves approached or even exceeded Caribbean levels. Of the nearly 90 former slaves in Liberty County, Georgia, who lost property to federal troops during the Civil War (and who later applied for compensation), nearly all – 97 per cent – testified to a loss of hogs and more than half to horses, mules and cows. After emancipation a South-Carolina planter who recollected that 'a good many' slaves owned livestock seems not to have been exaggerating. The lowcountry slaves' 'passion for ownership of horses or some other animal' became worthy of comment.[23]

But there was much more to the slaves' economy than the raising of animals, theft, or the cultivation of crops. Once given the time, slaves proved adept exploiters of the New World's natural resources. They hunted and fished, blending techniques they and their ancestors brought from Africa with those learned from Native Americans and Europeans. The creativity of Saramaka maroons – with bow and various arrows, fishtraps, and drugging techniques – was singular, but Afro-American slaves in general were inventive hunters and fishermen. Slaves also gathered nuts, berries, kept bees and used wild plants to supplement their diet, decorate their households, supply their furnishings and cure their ills. In Carolina, Janet Schaw observed, 'the Negroes are the only people who seem to pay any attention to the various uses that the wild vegetables may be put to'. Of the 160 species of medicinal plants identified in Jamaica, over a third of them seemed to be of African origin. Throughout the New World slaves employed gourds and calabashes as containers, eating utensils and musical instruments. Slaves also used local clays to make their own pottery, called *yabbas* in Jamaica and colonoware in the South Carolina and Georgia lowcountry.[24]

In addition to making the land work for them, slaves manufactured many valuable items. Skills in woodworking, basketmaking, straw-plaiting and other crafts allowed slaves to fashion bed-mats, bark-ropes, wicker-chairs, baskets, brooms, horse collars, canoes and earthen jars. Slave shoemakers produced extra shoes in their own time, coopers barrels, carpenters carts and furniture, blacksmiths tools and so on. Such products enriched slave life and provided slaves with vital commodities to trade.[25]

Given the opportunity to work for themselves, slaves marketed the product of their labour to their masters, fellow slaves and neighbouring non-slaveholders. Occasionally they exported their produce. Slave-controlled markets – generally called Sunday markets no matter what day of the week they convened – became significant social and economic institutions in nearly every slave society. This was particularly true in the Caribbean, where the prevalence of urban places and the sheer proportion of slaves engaged in independent economic production joined to make the Sunday market the essential mechanism of provisioning. From 'day cut', as Jamaican slaves termed it, slaves began streaming toward the town centre, carrying their produce on their heads, or, if more well-to-do, riding mules or leading asses. By the late eighteenth century some 10,000 Jamaican slaves attended the market at Kingston and 15,000 St Domingue slaves gathered at the Clugny market at Cap François each Sunday morning. On smaller islands like Barbados and Antigua, where the commitment to staple production and the available land limited the slaves' economy, slave markets were neither as well attended nor as well supplied. But they were always significant institutions, for in the words of physician George Pinckard, Barbadian markets in the early nineteenth century 'depend almost entirely' on the slaves' enterprise, while the produce grown by Antiguan slaves, according to another estimate, prevented the island's whites from 'starving'.[26]

Marketing by slaves was generally more limited in mainland North America. The vastness of the land, the absence of towns, and – most significantly – the competition of non-slaveholding whites constrained the slaves' ability to trade independently. Only in towns – like the rice ports of the Carolina and Georgia lowcountry or the small riverine villages of the Louisiana sugar country – did mainland North-American slaves create Sunday markets approximating those further south. Instead, the plantation itself became the great entrepôt for slave-grown produce on the mainland, with planters buying the slaves' produce for their own use, factoring the slaves' sales and purchases, or establishing stores at which slaves could buy and sell. Beyond the boundaries of the plantation itinerant peddlers – often immigrants – and white store keepers became the most important trading partners for mainland slaves, purchasing their produce and selling them liquor and other contraband goods.[27]

No matter what its form or extent, trading – through regularly scheduled markets or clandestine rendezvous with peddlers and shopkeepers – became an important element in the lives of New-World slaves. In selling and bartering their produce and handicrafts slaves acquired small amounts of cash to buy extra food, clothing, tobacco, alcohol and an assortment of 'luxuries'. Perhaps because their lives were similarly impoverished, the slaves' shopping list varied little from place to place. In the Leeward Islands slaves purchased 'tobacco and other little conveniences, and some finery too'; Jamaican slaves, salted meat and fish; Louisiana slaves, a wide range of foodstuffs and cloth as well as pocket knives, combs, fiddles, umbrellas and, in at least one case, a watch. Almost everywhere, tobacco, alcohol, and cloth and clothing, usually of higher quality than the planters' allocations, were important items of consumption, as were bowls, pots and other utensils. Jewellery and ornamental items were occasional purchases. Purchases of larger pieces of furniture, horses and cattle, and, in special circumstances, even other slaves, required long-term savings and were accordingly rare events.[28]

Market day was also a social occasion of the first rank. Slaves dressed in their best to attend market and their neat, even natty, attire impressed visitors. For the average field hand, as Elsa Goveia observed, participation 'in the Sunday market released them temporarily from the isolation and confinement of the plantations, and helped to make their hard life more tolerable'. It was 'the one occasion', Goveia continues, 'on which he was permitted to share in the greater freedom of the town slaves; and it enabled him to modify, in some degree, his heavy dependence on the master, by acquiring a little money of his own to use as he wished'. Once the haggling had ended, market day became a time of great merriment, and slaves turned to more joyful pursuits from religious observance to drinking, dancing and gaming. Slaveholders and local officials emphasized the latter, denouncing the immorality that accompanied both markets and clandestine meetings with peddlers. But the planters' persistent efforts to regulate independent trading by slaves revealed deeper fears. Market day became the occasion for slaves – sometimes joined by free blacks and non-slaveholding whites – to review their own standing and plan ways to improve their lot, generally to the disadvantage of the planter class. The process of redefining their own interests, which began in their gardens and provision grounds, crystallized in market day banter. Even when slaves left the market with no more in their pockets than when they arrived, they carried ideas of incalculable worth.[29]

Material benefits, however paltry from the planters' perspective, added considerably to the slaves' estate. Slaves supplemented these with payments for overwork and 'wages' earned from hiring their own time, both of which were also important elements in the slaves' economy. Once the boundaries between the masters' time and the slaves' time had been established masters crossed it at their own risk, for breaking the carefully negotiated rules of the game could put the game itself into question. Slaves could be forced to work on their own time only under great duress. When extra work had to be done –

during planting and harvest, for example – slaveowners generally
compensated their slaves, paying them for overwork on Sunday, in the
evening, or on special holidays with equivalent amounts of time or with
cash. Overwork payments became standard for labor in the ceaseless
grinding and processing of cane, as did the onerous labor of digging and
clearing canals. Slaves also received incentive payments for picking
cotton above a targeted quota in upcountry South Carolina. In almost
every slave society some slaves won the right to hire themselves out on
'free' days and in the evening, time otherwise given over to working
their gardens or provision grounds. In Louisiana, for example, slaves
accumulated considerable sums cutting wood and gathering moss, and
smaller amounts by, among other tasks, ditching, sugar-potting,
collecting fodder and serving as watchmen on their own time.[30]

If most of the proceeds of the slaves' independent economic activity
went to meet immediate needs for food and clothing, some slaves
managed to save and accumulate substantial estates, at times equal to
that of a moderately successful free artisan or farmer. At death,
according to Edward Long, Jamaican slaves had property valued at
between £50 and £200; 'few among them', he added, 'that are at all
industrious and frugal lay up less than £20 or £30'. In the Windward
Islands slaves saved similar sums, and some mainland slaves did equally
as well. During the nineteenth century slaves growing their own cotton
in upcountry South Carolina put away about a sixth of their earnings.
Their savings became the basis of a complex system of credit arrangements within the slave community, whereby slaves financed each
other's purchases and, in the process, knit their community together.[31]

Such striking circumstances – slaves as bankers – made it easy to
exaggerate the size of the internal economy and the wealth of the
participants. By the best accounts most slaves earned only pocket
change. None the less, both abolitionists and slaveholders found
reason – albeit different ones – to emphasize the slaves' prosperity.
Edward Long estimated that a fifth of the money circulating in Jamaica
was in slave hands; Alexander Campbell, a Grenadian planter,
reckoned that one half of 'the current specie' in the Windward Islands
was 'the property of Negroes'; and a South Carolina planter thought
that 'in a small way a good deal of money circulated among the negroes,
both in the country and in the towns'.[32] Although the success of a
minority could overshadow the desperate poverty of the majority, and
the persistence of the slaves' economy could obviate its fragility, the
few dollars that slaves earned played a large role in Afro-American life.

* * *

Much of the independence Afro-Americans secured during slavery – which manifested itself in the slaves' domestic, religious and community life – derived from the slaves' economy. The extent that slaves wrested control of a portion of their lives from their masters owed directly to their own independent production. That independence began with the slaves' choice of how they would organize their gardens and provision grounds. For, unlike work in their masters' fields, slaves decided what they would plant in their gardens and grounds, when they would plant it, where they would market it and how they would employ the profits that accrued. Working outside the watchful eye of the master and his minions, slaves laboured with great intensity, demonstrating initiative and ingenuity in squeezing profits out of marginal land. Few observers failed to compare the difference between the desultory manner slaves worked in their owners' fields with the energy and care they applied to their own crops.

Slaves worked in a variety of ways, but almost always the slaves' economy was a family economy. In Jamaica, scouting out the mountain land – not too different from Saramaka maroons 'examining the site' of their prospective gardens – devolved on family heads, generally men. Women, however, did much of the marketing, and children and old people worked in the garden. Although the slaves' economy provided a basis for a sexual division of labour within the slave household, independent production remained the concern of the entire family. House plots involved all members of the household, as best evidenced in the memorials they contained to dead relatives. Jamaican slaves, according to one account, formed themselves into 'distinct parties' as they began work in their grounds, 'mov[ing], with all their family, into the place of cultivation'. Likewise, an ex-slave from Chatham County, Georgia, recollected how his family of nine had 'all worked together' on their corn crop. Since slave families pooled their resources and worked in concert, they also made collective decisions on how they would consume their profits. Although funds earned by families on Louisiana sugar estates accumulated in the account of the head of the household – almost always a man, 'married' women rarely had accounts in their own names – all family members drew upon them, although not equally. The symbolic basis of family life also had roots in the material one. In Jamaica the connection between independent economic activity and family life was symbolized by the *cotta* (derived from the Twi *kata* (to cover)), a circular headpad traditionally made of plantain-leaf or a twisted cloth which was used to protect the head when carrying goods to market. What better way for slaves to signify a divorce then to cut the *cotta* into two, allowing each party to take their half.[33]

Wealth accumulated from independent economic production reached beyond individual households, supporting communal as well as domestic institutions. Slave-grown produce and slave-crafted goods allowed for small exchanges within the Afro-American community, thus providing a basis for sociability that encouraged co-operation and mutuality between households. With their earnings slaves purchased small gifts for one another, placed a few coins in the collection plate on Sunday and assured a respected elder a proper burial. Slaves also pooled their scant resources for the benefit of the entire community. Labor exchanges were doubtless more numerous and significant than monetary ones, and reinforced the co-operative ethos within the slave community. The wealth that slaves earned helped build churches and pay ministers and teachers. The arrival of the Union army in the American South unleashed a variety of complicated disputes over the ownership of antebellum African churches. Although white trustees held the legal deeds to these buildings and their contents, slaves claimed that their contributions had built them and maintained them. When the disputes entered the offices of the Freedmen's Bureau and local courts, slaves generally proved their case.[34]

Funds accumulated by the slaves' independent economic production also secured the future of children, providing 'a start' for the next generation. Slaves developed complex systems of inheritance. In Jamaica, a family head when nearing death nominated a trustee or executor from among his kin to distribute his personal property to his legatees. Jamaican masters even permitted their slaves, Bryan Edwards claimed, to will their gardens or grounds; and if a master decided to convert the slaves' grounds to estate use he compensated them. In the early nineteenth century slaves on the Codrington plantations began to bequeath their cottages, gardens and personal belongings to other slaves, and in the Windward Islands slaves bequeathed rights of occupancy along with movable property. 'They pass them on from father to son, from mother to daughter, and, if they do not have any children, they bequeath them to their nearest kin or even their friends', wrote one observer of the inheritance practices of Martinique slaves. Lowcountry South Carolina and Georgia slaves employed guardians to facilitate the transfer of property across plantation lines as well as generational lines.[35]

The slaves' economy reached deep into all aspects of Afro-American culture. Gardens and provision grounds, Barry Higman suggests, permitted the elaboration of African-influenced conceptions of spatial order. Here boundaries could be fluid and irregular, as against the geometric and rigidly ordered notions of Europeans. Moreover, slaves infused their gardens and grounds with magical beliefs, many carried from Africa. Saramaka maroons closely examined potential garden sites in order to avoid forest spirits and snake-gods and to placate the god responsible for their chosen location. In lowcountry South Carolina and Georgia slaves planted sesame or *benne* at the end of rows in their private fields, because it was thought to help ward off intruders. When one visiting absentee owner first saw sesame in Jamaica 'it was growing in a negro's plantation'. Known as *wangla*, it was used in *obeah* practices. Jamaican slaves also planted the 'cut-eye' or 'overlook' bean at the borders of their provision grounds to protect them from the evil eye. Thus, when the Intendant of Saint Domingue described the slaves' provision ground as '*une petite Guinée*', he was more perceptive than he knew.[36]

*   *   *

Although slaves garnered numerous benefits from independent economic production, they understood that their participation benefited the planter class. From the owners' perspective the slaves' participation signalled acceptance of the legitimacy of the master–slave relationship. For some slaves that price was too high to pay. They refused to participate, not merely because of the extra work independent production entailed or because masters reduced rations to the extent slaves could feed themselves, but because participation acknowledged the owners' authority.

Slaves may have also understood the divisive effect independent economic production had on their own community. The scramble for modest wealth could be no less mean and demeaning than the scramble for great wealth. It unleashed a variety of conflicts, great and petty, among slaves, as some tried to gain advantages at the expense of others. These conflicts sometimes grew from the opposing roles of farmer and merchant, buyer and seller, even 'employer' and 'employee'. When plantation slaves took their goods to market they often found their produce engrossed by savvy urban hucksters – generally slave and free blacks – who controlled the trade, took the lion's share of the profit and left country folks with but small returns on their labour. Where the slave trade remained open and provision grounds constituted the dominant mode of subsistence slaveholders often assigned newly arrived Africans to creole families, for whom they laboured in return for subsistence until they could establish grounds of their own. While some creoles took seriously their mentoring responsibilities – often forming life-long friendships with the newly arrived – others shamelessly exploited the initiates. Creoles forced newly arrived Africans to work long hours in their gardens and provision grounds, even while the newcomers had to labour in the owners' fields, so that the newly arrived faced a double servitude. Such exploitation characterized other portions of the slaves' economy. Privileged slaves – overseers, drivers and artisans, for example – employed their elevated status to raise themselves at the expense of field hands. Those who controlled more extensive grounds hired the less fortunate to assist them, paying them just a small portion of what their labour was worth. Family members, especially children and old people, were not immune from such abuse, as household heads pressed them hard to assure group survival.[37]

Much of this exploitation was the self-exploitation of desperate people, pressed to the wall to survive. The self-exploitation that drove petty producers the world over was also the lot of New-World slaves. But no matter what the source, it deeply affected the slave community, turning slave against slave. The padlocks slaves purchased to protect their possessions and the guards stationed at provision grounds suggest the extent of these tensions. So too did the denunciations of those slaves who refused to participate in the slaves' economy by their more industrious compatriots. According to a public prosecutor in Martinique, such attacks left non-participants so 'ashamed' that they refused to accept rations. Independent economic production could divide as well as unite.[38]

It was not so much sloth but the lack of results that led many slaves to eschew independent economic production. No matter how hard they laboured, participation in the slaves' economy did not guarantee a better life. Given time and the right circumstances an industrious slave might gain a more varied and nutritious diet from gardens and grounds, but time was always short and agricultural conditions less than ideal. Provision grounds, by their very nature, were located on waste land, far from the slave quarters. The slaves' crops, no less than the masters', were subject to the ravages of drought, storm and vermin. If Saramaka maroons quite often faced famine because of the failures of their gardens, it is hardly surprising that plantation slaves, exhausted by estate labour, experienced shortfalls from their plots.[39]

Participation in the slaves' economy thus did not necessarily make slaves healthier, longer lived, or more fecund. Much evidence suggests just the opposite. The natural increase of a slave population cannot be linked directly to the slaves' participation in a system of independent economic production. Barbados, where rationing was always central to subsistence, was the one British Caribbean sugar colony to have a slave population that maintained a positive natural increase, a position it achieved by about 1810; the one Jamaican sugar parish to have a naturally increasing slave population before emancipation was Vere, and it too had few provision grounds. In fact, an experienced observer maintained that Vere slaves were 'the most comfortable' in Jamaica and claimed to be able to 'tell a Vere Negro almost in a Hundred others from his fat, sleek Appearance'. On the mainland Virginia's slave population achieved natural increase much earlier than that of South Carolina, although the slaves' economy was more active in lowcountry Carolina than in Virginia. Slave heights also seem to correspond inversely with self-subsistence. Thus creole-born slaves in the Caribbean were significantly shorter than those of the United States and, within the Caribbean, creole slaves living on islands devoted to intense sugar cultivation were shorter than non-sugar island slaves.[40]

Slaveowners appreciated the slaves' desire for economic independence and turned it to their advantage as they could. By shifting part or all of the burden of subsisting their slaves onto the slaves themselves, owners reduced the time, effort and cost of maintaining their slaves. Although slaves theoretically received compensation in time for producing their own food, the best calculations indicate that slaves worked longer where they subsisted themselves than where they received rations.[41] Many masters also believed slaves would labour more efficiently if they were given time to themselves after they had finished their daily tasks. Allowing slaves time for independent economic enterprise not only operated against malingering, but it also armed slaveowners with another means of disciplining their slaves.

The slaves' economy could be made to support the masters' economy in less tangible ways as well. 'The negro who has acquired by his own labor a property in his master's land', asserted Bryan Edwards, 'has much to lose, and is therefore less inclined to desert his work'. Other slaveholders concurred with Edward's judgement. A Grenadan proprietor argued that 'the more money the Negroes got for themselves, the more attached they were to the property', and a South Carolina planter proclaimed that no lowcountry 'Negro with a well-stocked poultry house, a small crop advancing, a canoe partly finished or a few tubs unsold, all of which he calculates soon to enjoy, will ever run away'. And even when slaves did run away masters frequently echoed another lowland Carolina slaveholder who was 'convinced [his] runaways would not go far, being connected at home, and having too much property to leave'. By extending or withholding from their slaves the 'rights' to enlarge their gardens, attend markets, or trade with neighbours, slaveholders found another way to bend slaves to their will. By masking the raw, coercive nature of chattel bondage behind the seemingly consensual exchange of the opportunity to subsist in return for labour in staple production, slaveholders cloaked the violent exploitive character of their regime. Thus, if the slaves' economy fell short of producing the 'obedient, property-respecting, and hard-working' Negroes masters' so coveted but never possessed, slave-holders still had good reason to encourage slaves to provision them-selves, to pay for overwork, to attend slave-operated markets, to factor the slaves' purchases and to respect the slaves' property rights.[42]

*   *   *

No matter how fulsome the benefits, slaveowners remained deeply suspicious of the slaves' independent economic activities. They feared that the slaves' preoccupation with their own enterprises and their dealings with free blacks and non-slaveholding whites could dissipate their energy and undermine their dependence – material and psycho-logical – on the owning class. For if the slaves' economy made slaves complicit in their own oppression it also set limits on the masters' rights. Transforming the master–slave relation to one approximating that of buyer and seller or employer and employee – where negotiation and consent replaced fiat and coercion – undermined the basis of the slave regime. At base, slaveholders understood that no matter what short-term advantages they reaped, the slaves' independent economic activities sowed the seeds of subversion and threatened their rule by allowing slaves to articulate an interest of their own.

Slaveholders thus not only worked hard to limit the benefits that accrued to slaves as a result of their independent activity, but to integrate the slaves' economy into their own. At every opportunity they tried to maximize the time slaves spent growing the great staples and to limit the time slaves worked their gardens and grounds. They proscribed the goods slaves could buy and sell freely, constrained their right to hire their own time and collect overwork and, if given the opportunity, denied slaves the property they had earned on their own, thus enforcing their claim to the slaves' entire being and its product. To the extent slaves succeeded in feeding themselves and earning a surplus, masters reduced rations and added to the slaves' responsi-bilities for supplying shelter, clothing and medication. In short, slave-owners recognized the slaves' rights only to the extent those rights affirmed their own domination.

Such actions deny Bryan Edwards's claim that the slaves' economy manifested a happy 'coalition of interests' between master and slave and strengthen Sidney Mintz's contention that the slaves' independent economic production represented a 'temporary resolution' of the 'social contradiction arising from exploitation ... that served the interests of both parties, oppressor and oppressed'.[43] Like all such resolutions, the slaves' economy was inherently unstable. As soon as slaves found a way to eke out a little more independence, masters sought new methods to drive them back into greater dependence. As masters tightened bonds of servitude, slaves sought new avenues to enlarge their independence. If its outer limits remained fixed, the day-to-day dynamics of the master–slave relationship was constantly being negotiated and renegotiated. The struggle had no end.

The contest took various forms. In some places, at some time, the internal marketing system stood at the centre and masters and slaves disputed the terms of participation. In a place like the Jamaican parish of Vere, where rations constituted the dominant means of feeding the slaves, the struggle for subsistence revolved not about labour time, but about allowances. Elsewhere master and slave fought over the appropriation of free time; the size, quality and placement of gardens and provision grounds; the organization of labour; the very composition of the labour force. Each of these was itself a matter of great complexity. On the question of time, for example, master and slave contested free Sundays and Saturdays, night work and holidays. Labour organization brought into dispute various advantages and disadvantages of gang and task work, as well as the composition of the gang and the definition of the task. Moreover, complex as they were such matters rarely stood alone. Instead they became fused together in inseparable compounds. When slaves in Martinique appropriated more time to themselves masters tried to reorganize the system of production from the gang to the task system so that when slaves failed to complete their assignments slaveholders could reclaim their free Saturdays.[44] The slaves' initiative, in short, provoked a response from the owners which shifted the terrain on which the struggle was contested but not the nature of the struggle itself.

The constantly shifting terrain also took no single form. During the early years of settlement in upcountry South Carolina shortages of labour and capital restricted the slaves' ability to cultivate their own land but allowed them to work for wages – a most unusual form of independent economy activity. Rather than just trading their own products on Sunday, as did slaves elsewhere in the Americas, upcountry Carolina slaves also participated in a Sunday labour market. The maturation of upcountry society, and especially the introduction of a high-yield strain of cotton, transformed the slaves' economy. Deprived of the opportunity to work for wages, upcountry slaves grew their own cotton. The advent of independent cotton production transformed the conflict between master and slave. While slaves gained larger material benefits over time, they lost much of their freedom to travel and bargain for themselves. As Woodville Marshall shrewdly observes of the struggles in the Windward Islands, 'much of what is termed resistance may have been subsumed under a competition and scramble for land and labor resources'.[45]

Others joined the contest between master and slave. Metropolitan authorities, local officials, non-slaveholding whites and free people of colour – all of whom saw the struggle between master and slaves impinging on their own liberty – added their voice to the continuing conflict. Men of the cloth were alternately horrified that masters forced their slaves to work on Sunday and that slaves used the Lord's day for their own labour. Regulation of Sunday markets also involved great merchants (always white) and small shop keepers (white and coloured) as well as local authorities and metropolitan overlords. The number of participants and the complexity of the contest can be measured in the struggle over the Barbados market in which some white hucksters profited by trading with or even robbing slaves, while others saw their interests threatened by slave competition. Bridgetown merchants, meanwhile, feared competiton from both black and white peddlers, while urban masters could not seem to decide where to stand: they profited from their slaves' ability to market, yet worried about the losses suffered from slave theft. Small planters fretted at the slaves' production of crops like cotton and ginger in which small-holders specialized, while the grandees desired to prohibit the slaves' trade in sugar cane even while they encouraged the slaves' market in firewood and grass. Among the slaves plantation and town hucksters found mutually advantageous relations, each providing markets for the other's goods; yet urban slave hucksters also engrossed at the expense of their rural counterparts.[46] These cross-cutting interests suggest how the slaves' economy became everyone's business and the resolution of any contest between master and slave required the concurrence – silent or active – of all members of slave society, high and low.

From the constant struggle over the appropriation of space in gardens and grounds and time to work them, the slaves' world took shape. Their most cherished beliefs about the centrality of labour to their own worth and the significance of property to their own independence grew out of their experience as workers, particularly their independent labour. Such beliefs were given full voice in 1789 by a group of Bahian rebels who, after killing their overseer and flee- ing to the forest, stipulated that they would return to the plantation if their former master gave them 'Friday and Saturday to work for ourselves', supplied them with nets and boats to fish on their own and provided them with land 'to plant our rice wherever we wish, and in any marsh, without asking permission'. They also wanted a large boat to market their goods. Once their economy was assured these former slaves felt certain their freedom would be secure and that they would then 'be able to play, relax and sing any time we wish without your hindrance'.[47]

Such notions of freedom, forged in the crucible of slavery, informed the aspirations of black people once slavery ended. The time slaves secured to work their own land became a kind of 'rehearsal for reconstruction' during which slaves established their priorities, ordered their lives and developed their own conceptions of freedom. With emancipation, freedpeople throughout the Americas made it clear that they wanted, above all, access to land and other material resources that they could work in family and communal groups. They wanted no part of gang labour or any system which limited their control over what they could grow, what they could rear, and what they could sell. They understood these rights – the right to work on their own and control their own resources – to be coincident with their independence. In short, they desired most to build upon the independent economic activity in which they had engaged as slaves.

NOTES

The editors would like to acknowledge the critical assistance of Sidney Mintz, Joseph P. Reidy and Stuart Schwartz who, along with the contributors to this special number, made numerous suggestions which assisted in the preparation of this essay. We are grateful to them all.

1. These generalizations are most evident in the studies of North American slavery, for example Eugene D. Genovese, *Roll, Jordan, Roll: The World the Slaves Made* (New York, 1974), although see Genovese's discussion of 'Gardens', pp.535–40; Herbert G. Gutman, *The Black Family in Slavery and Freedom, 1750–1925* (New York, 1976); John W. Blassingame, *The Slave Community: Plantation Life in the Antebellum South*, rev. edn. (New York, 1979); Lawrence W. Levine, *Black Culture and Black Consciousness: Afro-American Folk Thought from Slavery to Freedom* (New York, 1977); Albert J. Raboteau, *Slave Religion: The 'Invisible Institution' in the Antebellum South* (New York, 1978); but for the Caribbean see Mary Turner, *Slaves and Missionaries: The Disintegration of Jamaican Slave Society, 1787–1834* (Urbana, 1982) and Richard B. Sheridan, *Doctors and Slaves: A Medical and Demographic History of Slavery in the British West Indies, 1680–1834* (Cambridge, 1985).
2. For the pioneering and still invaluable work on the slaves' economy, see Sidney W. Mintz and Douglas Hall, *The Origins of the Jamaican Internal Marketing System*, Yale University Publications in Anthropology No. 57 (New Haven, 1960), 3–26, and Mintz, 'The Jamaican Internal Marketing Pattern: Some Notes and Hypotheses', *Social and Economic Studies*, 4 (1955), 95–103; 'The Role of the Middleman in the Internal Distribution System of a Caribbean Peasant Economy', *Human Organization*, 15 (1956), 18–23; 'Internal Marketing Systems as Mechanism of Social Articulation', *Proceedings of the American Ethnological Society* (1959), 20–30. The debate over the 'peasant breach' in Brazil is summarized by Ciro Flamarion S. Cardoso, 'The Peasant Breach in the Slave System: New Developments in Brazil', *Luso-Brazilian Review*, 25 (1988), 49–57. Cardoso's own point of view is stated more fully in *Agricultura, escravidão e capitalismo* (Petropolis, Brazil, 1979), ch. 4 and *Escravo ou Campones. O proto-campesinato*

24 THE SLAVES' ECONOMY

negro nas Américas (São Paulo, 1987). For the British Caribbean, see B.W. Higman's encyclopedic *Slave Populations of the British Caribbean 1807–1834* (Baltimore, 1984), esp. 53, 56, 60, 204–18. Other important statements on the subject can be found in Robert Dirks, *The Black Saturnalia: Conflict and Its Ritual Expression on British West Indian Slave Plantations* (Gainesville, 1987) and Tadeusz Lepkowski, *Haiti*, 2 vols. (Havana, 1968–9), 1: 59–60. Nothing of a similar nature exists from the mainland American South, but Philip D. Morgan, 'Work and Culture: The Task System and the World of Lowcountry Blacks', *William and Mary Quarterly*, 3rd series, 39 (1982), 563–99, 'The Ownership of Property by Slaves in the Mid-Nineteenth Century Low Country', *Journal of Southern History*, 49 (1983), 399–420, and Leslie S. Rowland, 'The Politics of Task Labor and Independent Production in Lowcountry South Carolina and Georgia' (unpublished essay courtesy of the author) explore the subject for the South Carolina and Georgia lowcountry. Also useful is Lawrence T. McDonnell, 'Money Knows No Master: Market Relations and the American Slave Community', in Winfred B. Moore Jr *et al.* (eds.), *Developing Dixie: Modernization in a Traditional Society* (New York, 1988), 31–44.

3. See Tomich's essay in this volume.
4. O. Nigel Bolland, 'The Extraction of Timber in the Slave Society of Belize' and Lorena Walsh, 'Slave Life, Slave Society, and Tobacco Production in the Tidewater Chesapeake' in Ira Berlin and Philip D. Morgan (eds.), *Cultivation and Culture: Labor and the Shaping of Slave Life in the America* (forthcoming); and the essays by Campbell, Schlotterbeck, and McDonald, below.
5. See the essay by Tomich in this volume. Also Stuart B. Schwartz, 'The Plantations of St. Benedict: The Benedictine Sugar Mills of Colonial Brazil', *Americas*, 39 (1982), 1–22.
6. William Frederick Sharp, *Slavery on the Spanish Frontier: The Colombian Choco 1680–1810* (Norman, Okl., 1976), 133–5; A.J.R. Russell-Wood, *The Black Man in Slavery and Freedom in Colonial Brazil* (New York, 1982), 118.
7. See Marshall's essay, below.
8. See the essays by Turner and Marshall in this volume.
9. Elsa V. Goveia, *Slave Society in the British Leeward Islands at the End of the Eighteenth Century* (New Haven, 1965), 137; Higman, *Slave Populations*, 53, 56, 210–12.
10. Higman, *Slave Populations*, 52–3; Orlando Patterson, *Sociology of Slavery: An Analysis of the Origins, Development and Structure of Negro Slave Society in Jamaica* (London, 1967), 66, 218; and the essay by Turner in this volume.
11. Higman, *Slave Populations*, 208.
12. Although historians and economists admit regional differences, the debate over self-sufficiency in foodstuffs in the mainland American South has generally been decided in favour of self-sufficiency. William K. Hutchinson and Samuel H. Williamson, 'The Self-Sufficiency of the Antebellum South: Estimates of the Food Supply', *Journal of Economic History* 31 (1971), 591–612; Sam Bowers Hilliard, *Hog Meat and Hoecake: Food Supply in the Old South, 1840–1860* (Carondale, Ill., 1972); Robert E. Gallman, 'Self-Sufficiency in the Cotton Economy of the Antebellum South' and Diane L. Lindstrom, 'Southern Dependence upon Interregional Grain Supplies: A Review of Trade Flows, 1840–1860' both in William N. Parker (ed.), *The Structure of the Cotton Economy in the Antebellum South* (Washington DC, 1970); and Ralph V. Anderson and Robert E. Gallman, 'Slaves as Fixed Capital: Slave Labor and Southern Economic Development', *Journal of American History*, 64 (1977), esp. 29–39. To our knowledge, no scholar has systematically explored the social as well as the economic implications of the purchase of provisions by slaveowners from non-slaveowners.
13. Higman, *Slave Populations*, 205; Anderson and Gallman, 'Slaves as Fixed Capital', 24–46; Robert William Fogel, *Without Consent or Contract: The Rise and Fall of American Slavery* (New York, 1989), 192; see also the essays by McDonald and Campbell in this volume.

14. J. Harry Bennett Jr, *Bondsmen and Bishops: Slavery and Apprenticeship on the Codrington Plantations of Barbados, 1710–1838*, (Berkeley, 1958), 37; Goveia, *Slave Society in the British Leeward Islands*, 136–9; Patterson, *Sociology of Slavery*, 217; J.R. Ward, *British West Indian Slavery, 1750–1834: The Process of Amelioration* (Oxford, 1988), 19, 65, 76; Peter H. Wood, *Black Majority: Negroes in Colonial South Carolina from 1670 through the Stone Rebellion* (New York, 1974), esp. ch. 7; James T. McGowan, 'Creation of a Slave Society: Louisiana Plantations in the Eighteenth Century', Ph.D. Diss. (University of Rochester), 1976, 139–45; Edmund Morgan, *American Slavery – American Freedom: The Ordeal of Colonial Virginia* (New York, 1975), 154–7.
15. Goveia, *Slave Society in the British Leeward Islands*, 136–9; Ward, *British West Indian Slavery*, 18. For the French Caribbean, see, in addition to Tomich's essay, Gabriel Debien, 'La Nourriture des esclaves sur les plantations des Antilles francaises aux XVIIe et XVIIIe siecles', *Caribbean Studies*, 4 (1964), 3–28.
16. Higman, *Slave Populations*, 41, 210; and the essays by Beckles and Marshall in this volume.
17. Richard B. Sheridan, 'The Crisis of Slave Subsistence in the British West Indies during and after the American Revolution', *WMQ*, 3rd series, 33 (1976), 615–41, and *Doctors and Slaves*, 154–62; Richard Pares, *A West-India Fortune* (London, 1950), 106, 126–7; Bennett, *Bondsmen and Bishops*, 101–2; Ward, *British West Indian Slavery*, 41, 108–9, 113, 117; David Barry Gaspar, 'Slavery, Amelioration, and Sunday Markets in Antigua, 1823–1831', *Slavery and Abolition*, 9 (1988), 1–26.
18. J. Carlyle Sitterson, *Sugar Country: The Cane Sugar Industry in the South, 1753–1950* (Lexington, Ky., 1953), ch.1; Stuart B. Schwartz, *Sugar Plantations in the Formation of Brazilian Society: Bahia, 1550–1835* (New York, 1985), 343–4, 351, 423, 428, 449.
19. Frederic G. Cassidy, *Jamaica Talk: Three Hundred Years of the English Language in Jamaica* (London, 1961), 43, 334–90; F.G. Cassidy and R.B. Le Page (eds.), *Dictionary of Jamaican English*, 2nd edn (London, 1980); John H. Parry, 'Plantation and Provision Ground: An Historical Sketch of the Introduction of Food Crops into Jamaica', *Revista de Historia de America*, 39 (1955), 1–20 (quote on p.1). For the variety of slave crops, see, for example, Dirks, *The Black Saturnalia*, 70; Higman, *Slave Populations*, 212; Jerome S. Handler, 'The History of Arrowroot and the Origin of Peasantries in the British West Indies', *Journal of Caribbean History*, 2 (1971), 46–93; Joseph William Jordan, *An Account of the Management of Certain Estates in the Island of Barbados* (London, 1826), 4; Henry Nelson Coleridge, *Six Months in the West Indies, in 1825* (London, 1832), 125–6; and the essays by Beckles, Marshall, Price, and Tomich in this volume.
20. Genovese, *Roll, Jordan, Roll*, 535; Fogel, *Without Consent or Contract*, 192; Mintz and Hall, *Origins*, 17; and the essay by Campbell in this volume.
21. See especially Alex Lichtenstein, ' "That Disposition to Theft, With Which They have Been Branded": Moral Economy, Slave Management, and the Law', *Journal of Social History*, 21 (1989), 413–40. Also see essays by Beckles, Campbell, and McDonald, below.
22. James Mercer to B. Muse, 8 April and 9 Jan. 1779, Battaille Muse Papers, Duke University, Durham; Sir William Young, *Tour through the Several Islands of Barbados, St. Vincent, Antigua, Tobago, and Grenada, in the Years 1791 and 1792*, in Bryan Edwards, *History of the British Colonies ...* (Philadelphia, 1806), 4: 266, 271; Dirks, *Black Saturnalia*, 70–72; and the essays by McDonald, Price, and Schlotterbeck, below.
23. Mintz and Hall, *Origins of the Jamaican Internal Marketing System*, 15, 17; Ward, *British West Indian Slavery*, 115, 199–200, 284–5; B.W. Higman, *Slave Population and Economy in Jamaica, 1807–1834* (Cambridge, 1976), 228; Patterson, *Sociology of Slavery*, 221; Goveia, *Slave Society in the British Leeward Islands*, 226; Pares, *West-Indian Fortune*, 122; Michael Craton, *Testing the Chains: Resistance to Slavery in the British West Indies* (Ithaca, NY, 1982), 257–8; Morgan, 'The Ownership of Property', 399–420.

24. In addition to his essay in this volume, see Richard Price, 'Caribbean Fishing and Fishermen: A Historical Sketch', *American Anthropologist*, 68 (1966), 1363–83; Evangeline Walker Andrews and Charles McLean Andrews (eds.), *Journal of a Lady of Quality* ... (New Haven, 1923), 176–7; Sheridan, *Doctors and Slaves*, 95; Cassidy and Le Page (eds.), *Dictionary of Jamaican English*, 483; Leland Ferguson, 'Looking for the "Afro" in Colono-Indian Pottery' in Robert L. Schuyler (ed.), *Archaeological Perspective on Ethnicity in America* (Farmingdale, NY, 1980), 14–28. Archaeological investigations of slave sites reveal much evidence of slave hunting and fishing.

25. The literature is vast, but see, for example, the essays by Campbell, Schlotterbeck and McDonald, below.

26. Patterson, *Sociology of Slavery*, 225–6; Sidney W. Mintz, 'Was the Plantation Slave a Proletarian?', *Review*, 2 (1978), 95; George Pinckard, *Notes on the West Indies* ..., 3 vols. (London, 1806), 1: 369–70; John Luffman, *A Brief Account of the Island of Antigua* ... (London, 1788), 94–5; Higman, *Slave Populations*, 208. See also Sidney W. Mintz, 'Caribbean Marketplaces and Caribbean History', *Nova Americana*, 1 (1980–1981), 333–44; Daniel McKinnen, *A Tour through the British West Indies, in the Years 1802 and 1803: Giving a Particular Account of the Bahama Islands* (London, 1804), 68–9; the essays by Beckles and Tomich, below.

27. See the essays by Campbell, Schlotterbeck, and McDonald, below. For marketing in one mainland town, see Philip D. Morgan, 'Black Life in Eighteenth-Century Charleston', *Perspectives in American History*, new series, 1 (1984), 191, 194–7, 202–3.

28. Young, *A Tour through the Several Islands* in Edwards, *History of the British Colonies*, 4: 271; Charles Leslie, *A New and Exact History of Jamaica* (Edinburgh, 1739), 306; and the essay by McDonald.

29. Goveia, *Slave Society in the British Leeward Islands*, 239.

30. Overwork was especially prevalent in various industrial work, see Robert S. Starobin, *Industrial Slavery in the Old South* (New York, 1970) and Charles B. Dew, 'Disciplining Slave Ironworkers in the Antebellum American South: Coercion, Conciliation, and Accommodation', *American Historical Review*, 79 (1974), 393–418; also see below the essays by Campbell and McDonald.

31. Long, *History of Jamaica*, 2: 410; and the essays by Marshall and Campbell, below. See, however, Orlando Patterson's critique of Long, *Sociology of Slavery*, 229. For other examples of spectacular savings, see Sidney W. Mintz, 'Currency Problems in Eighteenth-Century Jamaica and Gresham's Law' in Robert A. Manners (ed.), *Process and Pattern in Culture* (Chicago, 1964), 253.

32. Long, *History of Jamaica*, 2: 562; Campbell is quoted in Marshall's essay; Alice R. Huger Smith, *A Carolina Rice Plantation of the Fifties* (New York, 1936), 72.

33. William Beckford, *A Descriptive Account of the Island of Jamaica*, 2 vols. (London, 1790), 2: 155; Morgan, 'The Ownership of Property', 403; J. Stewart, *A View of the Past and Present State of the Island of Jamaica* (Edinburgh, 1823), 267; Jerome S. Handler and Frederick W. Lange, *Plantation Slavery in Barbados: An Archaeological and Historical Investigation* (Cambridge, Mass., 1978), 173–4; Cassidy and LePage (eds.), *Dictionary of Jamaican English*, 123; Long, *History of Jamaica*, 2: 413. Also see below, the essay by McDonald.

34. See, for example, Petition of Colored Men of Mobile, Ala., to the Congress of the United States of America, Jan.1866, Unregistered Letters Received, series, 9, Alabama Asst. Comr., RG 105, National Archives, Freedmen and Southern Society Project file number A-1735.

35. Long, *History of Jamaica*, 2: 410–11; Edwards, *History of the British Colonies*, 2: 133; Bennett, *Bondsmen and Bishops*, 105; see Tomich's essay in this volume; Morgan, 'Work and Culture', 535.

36. B.W. Higman, *Jamaica Surveyed: Plantation Maps and Plans of the Eighteenth and Nineteenth Centuries* (Kingston, 1988), 262–76, 291; Barham is quoted in Cassidy, *Jamaica Talk*, 345; Cassidy and LePage (eds.), *Dictionary of Jamaican English*, 139, 462; the intendant of St Domingue is quoted in Tomich's essay.

37. Ward, *British West Indian Slavery*, 18, 110–11; Higman, *Slave Populations*, 207 and 237–42 for relations between urban sellers and plantation slaves; for an excellent example of the individual differentiation in provision ground allotments, see Higman, *Jamaica Surveyed*, 269–73; and the essay by Marshall, below.
38. See the essays by Campbell and Tomich, below.
39. For the best data on the distances between estate and mountain grounds, see Higman, *Jamaica Surveyed*, 266. For other good information on the drawbacks of the provision ground system, see Kenneth F. Kiple, *The Caribbean Slave: A Biological History* (New York, 1984), 69–76 and Sheridan, *Doctors and Slaves*, 164–9.
40. Higman, *Slave Population and Economy*, 129 and *Slave Populations*, 307; Ward, *British West Indian Slavery*, 254; Sheridan, *Doctors and Slaves*, 174–7; the differences between Virginia and South Carolina come from Philip Morgan's research. For slave heights, see Fogel, *Without Consent or Contract*, 138–41; Barry Higman, 'Growth in Afro-Caribbean Slave Population', *American Journal of Physical Anthropology* 50 (1979), 373–85; and Gerald Friedman, 'The Heights of Slaves in Trinidad', *Social Science History*, 6 (1982), 482–515.
41. Higman, *Slave Populations*, 188.
42. Edwards, *History of the British Colonies*, 2: 131; Pinckard, *Notes on the West Indies*, 1: 368; the Grenadan is quoted in Marshall's essay; Rufus King Jr to William Washington, 13 Sept. 1828, *American Farmer*, 10 (1828), 346; William Read to Jacob Read, 22 March 1800, Read Family Papers, South Carolina Historical Society, Charleston.
43. Edwards, *History*, 2: 161; Mintz, 'Caribbean Marketplaces and Caribbean History', 336.
44. See the essays by Tomich and Turner.
45. See the essays by Campbell and Marshall.
46. See the essay by Beckles.
47. Stuart B. Schwartz, 'Resistance and Accommodation in Eighteenth-Century Brazil: The Slaves' View of Slavery', *Hispanic American Historical Review*, 57 (1977), 69–81, esp. 77–9.

THE CARIBBEAN

An Economic Life of Their Own: Slaves as Commodity Producers and Distributors in Barbados

Hilary McD. Beckles

Studies of patterns of property ownership and resource use in the Caribbean slave societies have generally focused on the nature of economic conditions within the free, mostly white, communities. Particular attention has been given, for example, to the manner in which economic relations developed between the dominant mercantile and planting communities. Scholars who have examined the economic experiences of free people of colour have reinforced opinions held about the tendencies of the white elite to monopolize the market. The slaves' independent economic behaviour, especially for the English colonies, has received less attention. The neglect of this subject is surprising, since slave hucksters had great influence over the informal commercial sector of most island economies. Comprehending the economic role of slave marketing practices will provide both a more realistic understanding of slave life and a firmer basis for interpreting the nature of master–slave relations in the economic sphere of plantation culture.

Much evidence exists to illustrate that slaves, like free persons, sought to increase their share of colonial wealth by participating in the market economy as commodity producers and distributors, with and without their owners' permission. Although they were undoubtedly the primary victims of colonial economies, in which they were defined and used as property, generations of slaves managed, none the less, to identify and pursue their own material interests.[1] By combining their work as fieldhands, artisans, domestics, or whatever with their own productive and commercial activities, slaves made economic decisions as 'free' persons. At least such was the case on the island of Barbados.

For slave owners, the largely independent activities of slaves at times complicated the generally understood terms and conditions of chattel slavery. In nearly all instances, property owning whites, who dominated colonial governments in the Caribbean, objected to market competition from slaves and enacted legislation that gradually proscribed their economic activities.[2] Since slave owners considered the slaves' subordination critical to the island's system of control, they

31

sought to assert their dominance in all economic relations, no matter how petty. On Barbados, slaves tenaciously resisted such legislative assaults upon this aspect of their independent economic activities and made from the outset a determined effort to maintain their market participation. At times, Barbadian slave owners adopted concessionary policies, prompted generally by their desire to secure the wider goals of social stability and high levels of labor productivity. Slaves, in turn, converted the most limited concessions into customary rights and defended them adamantly.

Huckstering, the distributive dimension of small-scale productive domestic activity, was familiar to Africans. It was certainly as much part of their culture as other more well-known aspects of Afro-American life, such as religion and the arts. Its attractiveness to slaves, however, had much to do with the social and material conditions of their enslavement. Huckstering afforded slaves the opportunity to improve the quantity and quality of their nutrition in environments where malnutrition was the norm.[3] It allowed them to possess and later own property, which in itself represented an important symbolic offensive against the established order. It enabled them to make profitable use of their leisure time. And it afforded them the chance to travel and normalize their social lives as much as possible under highly restrictive circumstances.

The relations between slaves' independent production and huckstering provides the context in which the development of the internal marketing systems can be understood. In what accounts to a typology of food production, Sidney Mintz and Douglas Hall[4] have shown how the autonomous economic life of slaves in Barbados, and other smaller sugar monoculture plantation colonies, differed from that of their Jamaican counterparts. Within this analysis, they divided plantation systems into two basic categories: first, those in which slaves were fed by their masters, such as Barbados; and, second, those in which slaves were largely responsible for producing their own subsistence, such as Jamaica.

In Barbados especially, planters allotted 'land to food cultivation only by impinging on areas which, generally, could be more profitably planted in cane'. The planters' policy was to 'restrict the land at the disposal of the slaves to small house plots', import food for the slaves, and include 'some food production in the general estate program'.[5] In Jamaica, owners allotted their slaves large tracts of land unsuited to cane production in the foothill of the mountain ranges and there encouraged slaves to produce their own food. These provision grounds or polinks represented the primary form of food cultivation, and slaves were given managerial authority in this activity. In addition to these provision grounds, which were generally located miles from their homes, Jamaican slaves also cultivated little 'house spots'.

The provision grounds on which Jamaican slaves became experienced proto-peasants constituted the basis of their entry into, and subsequent domination of, the internal marketing system. White society came to depend heavily upon the slaves' produce. There was, as a result, no persistent legislative attempt to arrest and eradicate the slaves' commercial activities and, by the mid-eighteenth century, the slaves' domination of the provisions market was institutionalized.[6]

The experience of slaves in Barbados was somewhat different in scale and character than that of those in Jamaica. Barbadian slaves had no provision grounds. They were fed from the masters' stocks, which were both imported and locally produced. Imported salted meat and plantation grown grain were allocated to slaves by their overseers, sometimes on Friday night, but mostly on Sunday morning. Slaves possessed only little house spots, generally no more than 25 yards square, on which to root their independent production and marketing activity. They could not therefore be defined as anything more than 'petty proto-peasants', and yet the vibrancy of their huckstering activities was no less developed than that in Jamaica where slaves cultivated acres of land.

Several visitors to Barbados paid attention to the relationship between slaves' receipt of food allowances and their huckstering. Dr George Pinckard, who toured the island during the mid-1790s, was especially perceptive. He noted that slaves received their subsistence on a weekly basis, 'mostly guinea corn, with a small bit of salt meat or salt fish', which served for 'breakfast, dinner and supper'. This diet, he added, was 'for the most part the same throughout the year', though 'rice, maize, yams, eddoes, and sweet potatoes form an occasional change'. But the slaves, 'in order to obtain some variety of food', were often seen 'offering guinea corn for sale' and using the proceeds obtained to 'buy salt meat or vegetables'. When slaves were asked why they preferred to sell or barter their food allocations, Pinckard declared, they would commonly

> 'express themselves: "me no like for have guinea corn always! Massa gib me guinea corn too much – guinea corn today – guinea corn tomorrow – guinea corn eb'ry day – Me no like him guinea corn – him guinea corn no good for guhyaam"'.

In his 1808 *History of Barbados*, John Poyer, a white creole social commentator, agreed with Pinckard that slaves would generally 'barter the crude, unsavory, substantial allowance of the plantations for more palatable and nutritious food'.[8]

Pinckard, however, recognized that slaves did not rely fully on food rations in creating supplies of marketable goods. Rather, he observed, 'those who are industrious have little additions of their own, either from vegetables grown on the spot of ground allotted to them, or purchased with money obtained for the pig, the goat, or other stock raised about their huts in the negro yard'.[9] He regarded it as 'common for the slaves to plant fruit and vegetables, and to raise stocks'. At one hut on the Spendlove estate Pinckard 'saw a pig, a goat, a young kid, some pigeons, and some chickens, all the property of an individual slave'. He observed the advantages of these activities for both slave and master, for he thought garden plots and livestock afforded slaves 'occupation and amusement for their leisure moments', and created 'a degree of interest in the spot'.[10]

Thirty years later F.W. Bayley's account of the slaves' domestic economy, like that of Pinckard's, emphasized the raising of poultry and animals, as well as the cultivation of roots, vegetables and fruits. He described as 'pretty well cultivated' the 'small gardens' attached to slave huts. For him, 'slaves have always time' to cultivate their 'yams, tannias, plantains, bananas, sweet potatoes, okras, pineapples, and Indian corn'. To shade their homes from the 'burning rays and scorching heat of the tropic sun', noted Bayley, slaves planted a 'luxuriant foliage' of trees that bear 'sweet and pleasant fruits', such as the 'mango, the Java plum, the breadfruit, the soursop, the sabadilla and the pomegranate'. In 'every garden' could be found 'a hen coop' for some 'half dozen of fowls' and, in many, 'a pigsty', and 'goats tied under the shade of some tree'. Bayley also observed that while the animals were 'grazing or taking a nap' a watchful 'old negro woman was stationed near' to ensure that 'they were not kidnapped'.[11]

Retailing was the slaves' principal means of raising the cash necessary for their purchases, and many produced commodities specifically for sale. Sunday was their main market day (until 1826, when it became Saturday), although it was customary for 'respectable overseers and managers' to grant slaves time off during the week when 'work was not pressing' in order to market 'valuable articles of property'.[12] The established Anglican Church was never happy with Sunday marketing. In 1725 the catechist at Codrington Plantation informed the Bishop of London, under whose See Barbados fell: 'In this Island the Negroes work all week for their masters, and on the Lord's Day they work and merchandize for themselves; in the latter of which they are assisted, not only by the Jews, but many of those who call themselves Christians'.[13] Efforts made by the estate's managers to prevent Sunday trading were unsuccessful, and many insubordinate slaves went to their beds 'with very sore backsides unmercifully laid on'. The catechist suggested that the 'force of custom' among slaves in this regard would inevitably break through 'managerial resolve'.[14]

Descriptions of slave huckstering illustrate the extent to which these fettered entrepreneurs made inroads into the colony's internal economy. William Dickson reported in the late eighteenth century that slaves were seen all over the island on Sundays walking 'several miles to market with a few roots, or fruits, or canes, sometimes a fowl or a kid, or a pig from their little spots of ground which have been dignified with the illusive name of gardens'.[15] J.A. Thome and J. H. Kimball, who witnessed the disintegration of Barbados slavery in the nineteenth century, had much to say about the role of black people – slave and free – in the internal marketing system. Thome and Kimball were impressed by the spectacle of these 'busy marketeers', both 'men and women', 'pouring into the highways' at the 'crosspaths leading through the estates'. These plantation hucksters were seen 'strung' all along the road 'moving peaceably forward'. Thome and Kimball described as 'amusing' the 'almost infinite diversity of products' being transported, such as 'sweet potatoes, yams, eddoes, Guinea and Indian corn, various fruits and berries, vegetables, nuts, cakes, bundles of fire wood and bundles of sugar canes'. The women, as elsewhere, were in the majority. They mentioned one woman with 'a small black pig doubled up under her arm'; two girls, one with 'a brood of chickens, with a nest coop and all, on her head', and another with 'an immense turkey' also elevated on her head. Thome and Kimball were not only impressed with the 'spectacle' of this march to the Bridgetown market, but also with the hucksters' commercial organization, especially the manner in which their information network conveyed 'news concerning the state of the market'.[16]

Huckster slaves dominated the sale of food provisions in the Bridgetown market. Numerous urban slaves, however, retailed for their owners, mainly in the supply of non-agricultural foodstuffs, such as cakes, drinks, and a range of imported goods. According to Bayley, many Bridgetown inhabitants gained a livelihood by sending slaves about the town and suburbs with articles of various kinds for sale. These hucksters, mostly women, carried 'on their heads in wooden trays' all sorts of 'eatables, wearables, jewelry and dry goods'. Bayley also commented on the social origins of free persons who directed huckster slaves. Most, he stated, were less fortunate whites, but it was common for members of 'the higher classes of society' to 'endeavour to turn a penny by sending their slaves on such money-making excursions'.[17] Such slaves retailed exotic items such as 'pickles and preserves, oil, noyau, anisette, eau-de-cologne, toys, ribbons, handkerchiefs, and other little nick-knacks', most of which were imported from the neighbouring French island of Martinique.

Town slaves, who sold on their own account, marketed items such as 'sweets and sugar cakes'. Bayley described these items as 'about the most unwholesome eatables that the West Indies produce'. Hucksters could be found 'at the corner of almost every street' in Bridgetown, 'sitting on little stools' with their goods neatly displayed on trays. Plantation hucksters, then, posed no competition for their urban counterparts. There was a mutually beneficial relationship in which each provided a market for the other's goods.[18]

From the early eighteenth century, government policies respecting slave hucksters were informed by the planters' beliefs that a significant proportion of the goods sold at the Sunday markets were stolen from their estates. The assumptions that the tiny garden plots cultivated by slaves could not support the quantity of produce marketed and that hucksters were not sufficiently diligent and organized to sustain an honest trade throughout the year underpinned the debates in the Assemblies and Legislative Councils. It was more in the slaves' nature, planters argued, to seek the easier option of appropriating plantation stocks. The charge of theft, therefore, featured prominently in the planter's opinions and policies towards slave hucksters.

The acquisition of plantation stocks by slaves was one likely way to obtain items for the Sunday markets, though such acts of appropriation were difficult to separate from scavenging by malnourished slaves looking to improve their diet. There was little planters could do to eradicate the leakage of stocks into slave villages. In spite of the employment of numerous watchmen and guards to protect their property, they complained constantly about the cunning and devious-ness of slaves in this regard.

Contrary to the planters, Pinckard found evidence of a sort of moral economy in which slaves asserted a legitimate right over a satisfactory share of the produce of their labor. Many slaves, he stated, were firm in the opinion that it was not immoral to appropriate plantation stock, but rather it was the master's inhumanity that denied them what was rightfully theirs, an adequate proportion of estate production. Slaves, he said, 'have no remorse in stealing whensoever and wheresoever' and do not accept the notion of 'robbing their masters'. They would commonly respond to the charge of theft, Pinckard added, with the expression: 'me no tief him; me take him from massa'.[19] The slaves' perception of the planter as the guilty party may have fuelled the highly organized system through which they sought redress by the clandestine redistribution of resources. The lavish over-consumption by the planter elite also enhanced the moral imperative implicit in the slaves' responses.

A case illustrative of the slaves' determination to increase their share of estate produce can be extracted from events on the Newton plantation between 1795 and 1797. During this time the manager, Mr Wood, made several references to the confiscation of stocks by slaves and considered it a major problem. Wood's account of the slaves' organized appropriation under the management of his predecessor, Mr Yard, provides a detailed view of extensive contact between plantation thief and huckstering. Dolly, the daughter of Old Doll, the estate's retired housekeeper, was brought into the house by Yard and kept as his mistress. On account of their intimate relations, Dolly obtained access to all stores, and it was believed that she 'pilfered' for the enrichment of her family. Sir John Alleyne, the estate's attorney, discovered the sexual relation between Yard and Dolly on a surprise visit to the property, and Yard's services were terminated. Dolly was removed from the household, but the flow of goods continued. When Wood conducted his investigation he realized that Billy Thomas, Dolly's cousin, who worked for Yard and was held 'in great confidence' and 'trusted with everything', was the culprit. Billy, noted Wood, 'had an opportunity of stealing the key of the box which held the key of the building'. This gave him and his family access to 'the rum, sugar, corn, and everything else which lay at their mercy'. Billy's aunt, Betsy, also a plantation slave, was married to a free black huckster who, 'through these connections', was 'supplied plentifully with everything'. Old Doll also did some huckstering and her home was described by Wood as a 'perfect out-shop for dry goods, rum, sugar, and other commodities'.[20]

A greater problem was posed for planters, however, when their slaves plundered the property of other persons, which was also another way of obtaining articles – especially fresh meat – for sale. Such cases involved more than estate discipline, and at times required criminal litigation. The records of Codrington Estate, for example, show that neighbouring planters commonly sought compensation outside of court when Codrington slaves were presumed guilty of theft. In some instances, however, courts settled such matters. In 1746, for example, Richard Coombs was paid £1 by the estate 'for a hog of his kill'd by the plantation negroes'. The following year James Toppin was paid 3s 9d 'for a turkey stolen from him by the negro John', and in 1779 the manager paid William Gall £8 when he agreed not to sue at law 'for a bull stolen' from him by a group of field slaves.[21] It was suspected that these stocks found their way onto the market through white intermediaries who worked in league with slaves.

Most contemporaries believed that the typical huckster's income, outside of what was earned from the occasional sale of high priced fresh meats, was meagre.[22] Bayley offered an account of their annual earnings by estimating the values of produce sold. In normal times, he noted, 'a tray of vegetables, fruits, calabashes, etc.' brought in gross annual receipts of six or seven shillings. The sale of poultry and animals, in addition to 'cane, cloth, and sugar', would increase receipts to about 'ten shillings'.[23] Such an income level, Bayley suggested, could not sustain a slave's life without plantation allowances. Free blacks or poor whites with such an income would have had to resort to the parish for relief.

Bayley, however, considered such modest incomes the result of the slave huckster's lack of the accumulationist spirit. Slavery, he believed, was responsible for the suppression of their acquisitive impulse. He made reference to slaves who had 'the power of earning' but 'frequently neglected it'. He attributed this to 'the cursed spirit of slavery' which 'leaves too many contented with what they deem sufficient for nature, without spurring them to exert themselves to gain an overplus'. Such persons, he added, would 'only cultivate sufficient ground to yield them as much fruit, as many vegetables as they require for their own consumption'. As a result, according to Bayley 'they have none to sell'.[24]

Bayley believed a minority of 'more enterprising' hucksters, who 'strive to make as much as they can', generally do very well. Some even accumulated enough cash to purchase their freedom. Most financially successful slaves in Bayley's opinion, however, lacked the appetite for freedom. 'I have known several negroes', he averred, who had

> 'accumulated large sums of money, more than enough to pur-
> chase their emancipation, but that as they saw no necessity for
> changing their condition, and were very well contented with
> a state of slavery, they preferred remaining in that state and
> allowing their money to increase'.[25]

Bayley's belief was tempered by his recognition that many slaves realized that the free black's material and social life was frequently not an improvement over their own. Consequently, for some slaves it made more sense to seek the amelioration of their condition by the purchase of a 'host of comforts'. The use of cash to facilitate the education of their children was as important as the purchase of a 'few luxuries for their huts', Bayley concluded.[26] Plantation hucksters, who were mostly field slaves, did not live as well as the mechanics, artisans, domestics and drivers or other members of the slave elite. One was more likely to find a driver in a position to offer a visitor 'a glass of wine and a bit of plumcake' than a huckster.[27]

The poor white, living on the margins of plantation society, developed the most noticeable contacts with slave hucksters. From the seven-teenth century, many white women labourers, mostly former indentured servants and their descendants, made a living by selling home-grown vegetables and poultry in the urban market. Largely Irish Catholics, they were discriminated against in the predominantly English Protestant community. They formed their own communities in back country areas of the St Lucy, St John, St Andrew, St Joseph, and St Philip parishes, where they cultivated crops as subsistence peasants on a variety of rocky, wet and sandy, non-sugar lands. Descriptions of their huckstering activity differ little from those of the slaves.

William Dickson, who studied the poor whites closely, offered a detailed account of their huckstering culture. Labouring Europeans, both men and women, he stated, 'till the ground without any assistance from negroes', and the 'women often walk many miles loaded with the produce of their little spots, which they exchange in the towns for such European goods as they can afford to purchase'.[28] Their gardens were generally larger than those utilized by slaves, as was the volume of commodities they traded. But in spite of their disadvantage, slaves offered their white counterparts stiff competition especially at the Sunday markets.

The relationship between slave and white hucksters was complex. Both Dickson and Pinckard commented that the marketing patterns and customs of the two showed similarities. White women hucksters were typically seen carrying baskets on their heads and children strapped to the hip in a typical African manner, which suggests some degree of cultural transfer. Dickson stated that some white hucksters owned small stores in the towns and most of these depended upon the exchange of goods with slaves. These hucksters, he said, 'make a practice of buying stolen goods from the negroes, whom they encourage to plunder their owners of everything that is portable'.[29]

Dickson made a strong moral plea for the protection of slave hucksters in their unequal relationship with their white counterparts. Until 1826 slaves had no legal right to own property, and they suffered frequent injustices in their transactions with whites. Many white hucksters, Dickson stated, 'depend for a subsistence on robbing the slaves' by taking their goods 'at their own price' or simply 'by seizing and illegally converting to their own use, articles of greater value', which the 'poor things may be carrying to market'. 'For such usage', he added, 'the injured party has no redress' and so 'a poor field negro, after having travelled eight or ten miles, on Sunday, is frequently robbed, by some town plunderer, within a short distance of his or her market, and returns home fatigued by the journey, and chagrined from having lost a precious day's labor'.[30] Slave owners were not prepared to offer huckster slaves – even those who sold on their account – protection from these white 'plunderers'. Many saw the matter as nothing more than thieves stealing from thieves, from which honest folk should distance themselves.

The detailed descriptions and accounts of slave huckstering offered by visitors to Barbados present a static image which underestimates the social and political tension and conflict that surrounded it. Concealed in these reports was an important social crisis. However common, huckstering was never fully accepted, and slaves struggled to maintain their marketing rights against hostile legislation. From the mid-seventeenth century Barbadian lawmakers designed legislation to prevent slave huckstering by linking it directly to a range of illicit activities. In addition, authorities formulated policies to mobilize the entire white community against the slaves' involvement in marketing by stereotyping slaves as thieves and receivers of stolen goods. Against this background of persistent efforts to criminalize huckstering, slaves attempted to maintain an economic life of their own.

Initially, legislators considered it possible to prevent slaves going from 'house to house' with their 'goods and wares'. But a difficulty was recognized in that so many whites declared a willingness to accept slave hucksters. Legislators, therefore, had to differentiate this 'deviant' element within the white community and target it for legal consideration. The 1688 Slave Code provided, for instance, that justices of the peace were required to identify such whites and warn them against transacting business with slave hucksters.[31] The law also empowered justices to take legal action against persistent offenders.

In 1694 an assemblyman who considered the 1688 provisions insufficient introduced two bills designed to remove slaves from the internal market economy. The first bill prohibited 'the sale of goods to negroes' and the second barred 'the employment of negroes in selling'.[32] The debate over this legislation focused on the need to prevent the employment of slaves in activities other than those related to plantations. Some planters, however, expressed concern that a curtailment of slaves' 'leisure' would impair already fragile labour relations on the estates. Slaves had grown accustomed to considerable freedom of movement during non-labouring hours and marketing was a direct consequence of this independent use of leisure time. The implementation of the proposed restrictions would entail closer surveillance of slaves – undoubtedly a major administrative task for local officials and slave owners alike.

The legislation never became law, but persistent complaints from small-scale white cash-crop producers, urban shopkeepers, and other of the slaves' competitors kept the subject at the forefront of discussion concerning the 'governing' of slaves. In 1708 the first of many eighteenth-century laws was finally passed attempting to undermine the huckstering culture of slaves. This 1708 law tackled every aspect of slave huckstering, both as a planter-controlled enterprise and as an independent slave activity. The preamble to the act linked huckstering to slave insubordination and criminality, stating that 'sundry persons do daily send their negroes and other slaves to the several towns in this island to sell and dispose of all sorts of Quick stock, corn, fruit, and pulse, and other things', with the result that slaves 'traffick among themselves, and buy, receive and dispose of all sorts of stolen goods'. The 1708 law, therefore, flatly disallowed any white person from sending or employing a slave to sell, barter, or dispose 'of any goods, wares, merchandize, stocks, poultry, corn, fruit, roots, or other effects, or things whatsoever'.[33]

While provisions were made for the punishment of whites – who either transacted with or employed slave hucksters, as well as for the hucksters themselves, the law of 1708 also implicitly recognized the hucksters' existence by stating conditions and terms under which they could legally function. Offending white persons found guilty could be fined £5, while slaves convicted for selling or bartering could receive 'one and 20 stripes on his or her bare back upon proof thereof made by any white person'. Exempted hucksters were allowed to sell 'stocks' to their masters, overseers and managers, and 'milk, horse meat or firewood' to any person. But this concession was also granted on terms that dehumanized the huckster and symbolized criminality, for the huckster had to wear 'a metaled collar' locked about his or her neck or legs. The collar had to display the master's and maker's name and place of residence.[34]

Legislators were concerned specifically with plantation slaves huckstering in Bridgetown, as they had suspected collusion between these slaves, white hucksters and shopkeepers. The 1708 law thus required 'the clerk of the market' to hire annually two able men to apprehend slaves that 'come into the said town to sell' without 'a metal collar' or accompanied by a white person. Magistrates were also empowered to remove all slaves from 'tippling houses, huckstering shops, markets, and all other suspected place' where they might trade with whites.[35]

During the eighteenth century elements in the white community and their elected representatives remained dissatisfied with the ineffectual nature of the 1708 law. Bridgetown continued to attract large numbers of hucksters from the countryside, who, like the residents in the town, appeared determined to ignore the law. During the 20 years after 1708 reports reaching the government confirmed the continued expansion of huckstering in Bridgetown. In 1733 the island's assembly passed a new law to strengthen and expand the provisions of the 1708 act. This time the law enumerated the foodstuffs and other items that hucksters were allowed to sell. It also enlarged the range of commodities which slaves could not trade, either on their own or their masters' account.[36]

The 1733 law was undoubtedly a response to the growing number of slave hucksters in the years after 1708. It suggests that the planter-controlled government saw hucksters as a threat to efficient slave control and its own economic dominance. The list of commodities that constables and market clerks were empowered to confiscate from slave hucksters now included sugar cane, 'whole or in pieces, syrup, molasses, cotton, ginger, copper, pewter, brass, tin, corn and grain'. Particular concern was expressed for the welfare of petit white and small planters, whose profits were adversely affected by intense slave competition. In order to protect these persons, the act made it unlawful for slaves to plant crops for the use of anyone but their masters. Cotton and ginger were singled out, and any slave found selling these two crops could be charged for selling 'stolen goods'.[37] In addition, white persons who purchased such items from slave hucksters could be prosecuted for receiving stolen goods. The 1733 Act was amended in 1749, making it illegal for slaves to assemble 'together at Huckster shops' for any reason.[38] Still slaves refused to comply, rendering these provisions ineffective. For example, in 1741 the manager of Codrington plantation, reporting on his slaves' attitudes towards these laws, stated that nothing short of 'locking them up' could keep slaves away from the markets, and such an action would probably result in a riot.[39]

In spite of these laws, then, slaves continued to participate actively in the internal marketing system. In 1773 the legislature came under pressure from Bridgetown merchants who claimed that slave and white hucksters posed unfair competition for their businesses and a public nuisance on account of the noise and litter the slaves' created. The legislative Assembly responded by appointing a committee to 'settle and bring in a bill for putting a stop to the Traffick of Huckster Negroes'.[40] The committee's bill became law in 1774, proscribing 'free mulattos and negroes', who hitherto were not singled out for legal discrimination, from the marketplace.[41]

The 1774 act sought to diffuse three decades of accumulated grievances among the island's merchants. This time, however, the legislature's emphasis was not to attempt the impossible – that is, eradicate huckstering – but to seek its containment. Provisions were made for the punishment of slaves and free people of colour who sold meat to butchers and who operated on 'Sunday, on Christmas Day and Good Friday'. The 1774 law also outlawed slave huckstering 'in or about any of the streets, alleys, passages, or wharfs of any of the towns' and on 'any of the highways, broad-paths and bays'.[42] Slaves found guilty of these offences were to be imprisoned and have their goods confiscated.

The small measure of legitimacy given 'country' hucksters by the 1733 Act was retained in 1774. Such slave hucksters could 'sell firewood and horse meat', items which posed no competition to small white merchants and planters. No mention was made of milk, the sale of which had been allowed under the 1708 Act. To those enterprising hucksters, however, who were accused of creating commodity shortages and inflating prices, legislators were particularly hostile. They singled out slave hucksters 'who go on board vessels' and who 'go a considerable way out of the respective towns to meet' country hucksters, in order to 'buy up and engross' produce with the result that 'the price of stock and provisions are greatly advanced'. Such attempts by slaves to manipulate, even corner, the market were outlawed. Offending slave hucksters were liable to receive 21 lashes. Since some offenders were likely to be women, law makers, sensitive to the ameliorative spirit of the time, included a provision that 'the punishment of slaves with child may, in all cases, be respited'.[43]

Established Bridgetown merchants remained dissatisfied with these legal provisions and they lobbied for still tougher measures. In 1779 the 1774 Act, like its predecessors, was amended.[44] The new law aimed to end the 'traffick carried on by slaves' and limit the number of free hucksters – white, coloured, and black. For the first time white hucksters were subject to official regulation, and categorized with free coloureds and free blacks. All free hucksters were now required to obtain a trade licence from the treasurer at an annual cost of £10, in addition to a processing fee of 25 shillings. This levy, which also served as a revenue measure, sought to eliminate marginal hucksters. In 1784 an amendment to the 1779 act provided for a penalty of up to three months imprisonment for white persons convicted of buying 'cotton or ginger' from slaves.[45] In November 1784, shortly after the 1779 act was amended, the *Barbados Mercury* reported that the number of hucksters on the streets of Bridgetown continued to increase.[46] The Court of Quarter Session subsequently urged the government to adopt a policy towards huckstering which emphasized formal organization and legitimization rather than opposition. The government agreed, and hucksters in Bridgetown were instructed to confine themselves to the 'public market place called the Shambles adjoining the Old Church Yard'.[47]

John Poyer, a local historian, opposed the reasoning behind the legislative provisions of 1774, 1779 and 1784, and welcomed the institutionalization of the huckster market. Attempts to eradicate slave hucksters and penalize free hucksters, he argued, reflected the monopolistic thinking and tendencies of the commercial elite, which ultimately burdened the majority of the island's inhabitants. Both free and slave hucksters, he insisted, displayed survival skills and energy under adverse circumstances which should be encouraged. White hucksters, he stated, were in great part 'aged and infirm' and women whose capital 'in very few instances' was equal to the 'sum required for a licence'. These persons, he added, could not afford to pay such a levy, and would be forced out of business, resulting in their families becoming 'burdensome to their parish'.[49] As for the slaves, the huckster trade allowed them an income with which they could vary their nutrition. 'Let not the hapless slave', he argued, 'be denied these needful comforts by absurd and unnatural policies.'[50] Poyer led the lobby which in 1794 succeeded in repealing the 1774 and 1779 laws. As a result, huckster markets, such as the Shambles, became accepted in law, and a victory against discriminatory legislation partly won.

During the June 1811 sittings of the Assembly, members were informed that 'Roebuck (a central Bridgetown street) was as much crowded as ever by country negroes selling their goods'.[51] Reportedly, hucksters refused to be confined to the Shambles, which they considered out of the way of pedestrians. From their perspective, Roebuck Street was ideally situated, and it attracted hucksters in spite of stiff penalties attached to street vending. The Assembly also learned that slave hucksters 'do not like to go there [Shambles] because the persons about the market set whatever price upon their commodities and the poor negroes are compelled to take that price'. Hucksters associated the old market with consumer domination, something they were determined to destroy. Freedom of movement, they believed, was the most effective way of gaining some measure of control over prices.

The Shambles became a place of open hostility between hucksters and constables. Disagreements among hucksters and between hucksters and customers sometimes resulted in affrays. In these instances the clerk of the market would instruct constables to arrest offending hucksters and confine them to the stocks. Stocks were eventually fixed adjoining the market where 'disorderly' hucksters were imprisoned and flogged. In 1811 the Grand Session was notified that the Shambles had become a public flogging place to the great disgust and annoyance of all who go there and buy and sell.

By the beginning of the nineteenth century the huckster market had become an entrenched institution within the colony, commonly described by visitors as colourful, exciting and attractive. Alongside this formal arrangement, street vending proliferated, and each was an important part of the internal marketing system. In 1826 the 'Sunday and Marriage Act', designed to accelerate the pace of slave Christianization, finally outlawed Sunday markets and Saturday became the major market day until the present time. After emancipation hucksters continued to dominate in the marketing of food provisions, although plantations sometimes sold food directly to the public. As in other Caribbean colonies, former slaves took to other types of work, but huckstering remained an attractive occupation.[52] It was an economic niche which they had identified and protected during slavery, and which, in freedom, became a cornerstone in the survival strategies for many households.[53]

During slavery the Barbadian internal marketing system revealed the slaves' struggle to achieve an economic life of their own. Unlike their Jamaican counterparts, Barbadian slaves pursued this objective within the context of persistently hostile legislative interventions from their owners. Evidence confirms the aspect of the Mintz and Hall account which shows that in the sugar monoculture colonies of the English Caribbean slave owners did not or could not make provisions that would enable slaves to produce their own subsistence. A close look at slave huckstering in Barbados, however, requires an important revision of the Mintz and Hall analysis by demonstrating that, in spite of the land handicap suffered by 'small island' slaves, they too were able to establish their own vibrant economic culture based upon the exchange of food allocations, the raising of poultry and stocks, and the intensive cultivation of lands that surrounded their huts.

NOTES

1. Hilary Beckles, *Natural Rebels: A Social History of Enslaved Black Women in Barbados* (New Brunswick, NJ, 1989), 72–7; Robert Dirks, *The Black Saturnalia: Conflict and Its Ritual Expression on British West Indian Slave Plantations* (Gainesville, 1987), 69–80; Jerome S. Handler, *The Unappropriated People: Freedom in the Slave Society of Barbados* (Baltimore, 1974), 125–33; Hilary Beckles and Karl Watson, 'Social Protest and Labor Bargaining: The Changing Nature of Slaves' Responses to Plantation Life in 18th Century Barbados', *Slavery and Abolition*, 8 (1987), 272–93; Edward Brathwaite, *Contradictory Omens: Cultural Diversity and Integration in the Caribbean* (Kingston, 1974), 41–3; Sidney W. Mintz and Douglas Hall, *The Origins of the Jamaican Internal Marketing System*, Yale University Publications in Anthropology No. 57 (New Haven, 1960); Sidney W. Mintz, 'Caribbean Market Places and Caribbean History', *Nova Americana*, 1, (1980–81), 333–44; John H. Parry, 'Plantation and Provision Ground: An Historical Sketch of the Introduction of Food Crops in Jamaica', *Revista de Historia de America*, 39 (1955), 15–18.
2. In 1711, the Jamaican Assembly prohibited slaves from owning livestock, or from selling meat, fish, sugar cane, or any manufactured items without their masters' permission. In 1734 and 1735, the St Lucian Assembly prevented slaves from selling coffee or cotton. Between 1744 and 1765, the French Antillean slave owners passed laws prohibiting slaves from huckstering in towns or trading in coffee. In 1767, the St Vincent Assembly forbade slaves to plant or sell any commodities that whites export from the colony. See Franklin Knight, *The Caribbean: the Genesis of a Fragmented Nationalism* (New York, 1978), 92; Hilary Beckles, *Black Rebellion in*

Barbados: The Struggle Against Slavery, 1727–1838 (Bridgetown, 1984), 71–2;
Edward Long, *The History of Jamaica* ... 3 vols. (London, 1974 [1774]), 2: 486–7;
Woodville Marshall's essay in this volume.

3. For an account of slave nutrition, see Kenneth F. Kiple, *The Caribbean Slave: A Biological History* (Cambridge, 1984). On the impact of malnutrition upon mortality levels, see Richard B. Sheridan, *Doctors and Slaves: A Medical and Demographic History of Slavery in the British West Indies, 1680–1834* (Cambridge, 1985); 'The Crisis of Slave Subsistence in the British West Indies during and after the American Revolution', *William and Mary Quarterly*, 3rd series, 23 (1976), 615–43.

4. Mintz and Hall, *Origins*, 23.

5. Ibid., 10.

6. Mintz and Hall note that the laws in force during the seventeenth century 'make plain that a number of markets were established, formalized, and maintained under government provision ...', and that 'formal legal acknowledgement of the slaves' right to market had been in negative form at least, as early as 1711'. Restrictions were applied to the slaves' sale of beef, veal and mutton, but they were allowed to market provisions, fruits, fish, milk, poultry and small stocks. Ibid., 15.

7. George Pinckard, *Notes on the West Indies* ..., 3 vols. (London, 1806), 2: 116.

8. John Poyer, *The History of Barbados* ... (London, 1971 [1808]), 400.

9. Pinckard, *Notes,* 2: 116–17.

10. Ibid., 1: 368.

11. F.W. Bayley, *Four Years Residence in the West Indies* (London, 1830), 92.

12. *Report of a Debate in Council on a Dispatch from Lord Bathurst* (Bridgetown, 1822), 8.

13. J. Harry Bennett Jr, *Bondsmen and Bishops: Slavery and Apprenticeship on the Codrington Plantations of Barbados, 1710–1838*, University of California Publications in History, 62 (Berkeley, 1958), 26.

14. Ibid., 24–5.

15. William Dickson, *Letters on Slavery* (London, 1814), 11.

16. J.A. Thome and J.H. Kimball, *Emancipation in the West Indies: A Six Month's Tour in Antigua, Barbados, and Jamaica in the Year 1837* (New York, 1838), 66.

17. Bayley, *Four Years Residence*, 60–61.

18. Ibid.

19. Pinckard, *Notes*, 2: 118.

20. Sampson Wood to Thomas Lane, 1796, M523/288, Newton Papers, Senate House Library, University of London.

21. Bennett, *Bondsmen and Bishops*, 25.

22. In 1822, Mr Hamden, a member of the Legislative Council, reported, 'The goods which they have to take to market are comparatively insignificant; nor are the supplies which they procure from thence less so. The poultry which they raise with the superfluity of their allowance, or the surplus of allowance in kind, which can never be considerable, are the only objects of honest traffic which they have', *Report of a Debate in Council*, 8.

23. Bayley, *Four Years Residence*, 422.

24. Ibid., 423.

25. Ibid., 424.

26. Ibid., 425. See also Hilary Beckles, 'The Literate Few: An Historical Sketch of the Slavery Origins of Black Elites in the English West Indies', *Caribbean Journal of Education*, 11 (1984), 19–35; Claude Levy, *Emancipation, Sugar, and Federalism: Barbados and the West Indies, 1838–1876* (Gainesville, 1980), 19.

27. Bayley, *Four Years Residence*, 425.

28. Dickson, *Letters*, 41.

29. Ibid., 41–2. In 1741, Abel Alleyne, manager of Codrington Plantation informed the estate owner that the white hucksters are 'often worse than the negroes, by receiving all stolen goods'. Alleyne to the Society for the Propagation of the Gospel in Foreign Parts, 9 Dec. 1741, Letter Book, Vol. B8, 51, SPGFP Archives, London. Whites

were protected by law from slaves' evidence; also, white hucksters could not be prosecuted if their slave suppliers informed legal authorities. In 1788, Joshua Steele informed Governor Parry that 'under the disqualification of Negro evidence the crime of *receiver of stolen goods* cannot be proven against' white hucksters, and that this acts as an encouragement to them. Reply of Joshua Steele to Governor Parry, 1788, *Parliamentary Papers*, 1789, Vol. 26, 33 (italics in original).

30. Dickson, *Letters*, 41–2.
31. An Act for the Governing of Negroes, 1688, in Richard Hall, *Acts Passed in the Island of Barbados from 1643–1762 inclusive* (London, 1764), 70–71.
32. Journal of the Assembly of Barbados, 17 Oct. 1694, Colonial Entry Book, Vol. 12, 484–6, Public Record Office, London. Also, *Calendar of State Papers, Colonial Series*, 1693–6, 381.
33. An Act to Prohibit the Inhabitants of this Island from employing their Negroes and other slaves in selling and Bartering; passed 6 Jan. 1708. See Hall, *Laws*, 185–7.
34. Ibid., 185–6.
35. Ibid., 187.
36. An Act for the Better Governing of Negroes, and the more Effectual Preventing the Inhabitants of this Island from Employing their Negroes or Other Slaves in Selling and Bartering, Passed 22 May 1733, Hall, *Laws*, 295–9.
37. Ibid., 298.
38. An Act for Governing Negroes, 1749, in Hall, *Laws*, 355–6.
39. Bennett, *Bondsmen and Bishops*, 24–5.
40. Minutes of the House of Assembly, 6 July 1773, HA 3/15, 1772–4, Barbados Archives.
41. 'An Act for the better to Prohibit Goods, Wares, and Merchandize, and other things from being carried from House to House, or about the roads or streets in this Island, to be sold, bartered, or dispose of ... and to remedy the mischief and inconveniences arising to the Inhabitants of this Island from the Traffic of Huckster Slaves, Free Mulattos, and Negroes', passed 15 March 1774, in Samuel Moore, *The Public Acts in Force, Passed by the Legislature of Barbados, from May 11th, 1762 to April 8th, 1800, inclusive* (London, 1801), 154–71.
42. Ibid., 164.
43. Ibid., 167.
44. Ibid., 212–7.
45. Ibid., 251–5.
46. *Barbados Mercury*, 20 Nov. 1784.
47. Ibid.
48. Poyer, *History of Barbados*, 398–419.
49. Ibid., 400–401.
50. Ibid., 400.
51. Minutes of the House of Assembly, 14 June 1811, CO 31/45, PRO.
52. See Handler, *The Unappropriated People*, 125.

Provision Ground and Plantation Labour in Four Windward Islands: Competition for Resources during Slavery

Woodville K. Marshall

The role of the provision ground and internal marketing system in the context of plantation slavery has been a subject of increased interest during the last generation. Recent findings have greatly enriched comprehension of slave subsistence patterns, internal markets, the slaves' 'proto-peasant' activities, and even the quality of the slaves' diet.[1] However, no scholar has yet provided a full description of the provision-ground system, and only Sidney Mintz has attempted to link slaves' proto-peasant activities with post-slavery developments.[2]

A description and analysis of the provision-ground system in the four Windward Islands of Grenada, St Lucia, St Vincent and Tobago during the last 50 years of slavery offer insight into these large subjects. Three tentative conclusions are reached: first, echoing Mintz, that the provision-ground and internal marketing system provided an extensive stage, as in Jamaica, for slaves' participation in independent activities; second, that the slaves' attempts to exploit the potential of these activities inevitably created intense competition between themselves and plantation owners and managers for labour services and land resources;[3] third, that slaves' success in creating and defending corners of independent existence fostered the growth of attitudes to plantation labour and to independent activities which affected labour relations in the post-slavery period.[4]

* * *

The four Windward Islands were, like Jamaica, 'home fed' colonies.[5] Most of the slaves subsisted not on rations of imported or locally grown food but on the produce of own-account cultivation of provision grounds, supplemented by weekly allowances of salt provisions – mackerel, cod, shad, or herring – provided by their owners. In emergencies caused by flood and drought or depletion of soil of the provision grounds, masters were usually expected (and often

48

compelled by law) to supply weekly food rations of imported food-stuffs (grains, cornmeal or plantains), the amounts of which were not specified until the amelioration of slavery in the 1820s.[6] This pattern of slave feeding was firmly in place in Grenada, St Vincent, and Tobago by 1790; witnesses before the parliamentary committee said it was 'universally the custom'.[7]

However, the four Windwards adopted provision-ground system at different times, reflecting the differential rates of conversion to full slave-plantation economies. In general, it would appear that the first stage of plantation establishment (as well as the seasoning of all slaves) involved the feeding of slaves from rations of either imported food or a combination of imported food and ground provisions produced by gang labour. When land for the staples was cleared and planted, the provision-ground system took root, and continued to co-exist with other methods of slave feeding. In Grenada, where the plantation economy was well established by the 1750s, the provision-ground system was being subjected to legal regulation by 1766, suggesting that law was catching up with practice.[8] From St Vincent, where the plantation was established after 1763, the governor, James Seton, indicated that by 1789 the provision-ground system was the dominant method of slave feeding among others.[9] In both Tobago and St Lucia, where full plantation exploitation was constrained by frequent exchanges of ownership between England and France, the remnants of the original method of slave feeding could be found in slave laws as late as 1794 for Tobago and 1825 for St Lucia. In both cases the law directed planters to produce a quantity of provisions by gang labour in a fixed proportion to their slave population.[10]

Several factors influenced the adoption of the system. First, as Mintz points out, slaveowners had an obvious interest in maximizing 'their returns from the slave labour' in a situation where the demand for slave labour was not constant all year round and where the cost of imported provisions represented a significant and regular outlay of capital.[11] Planter witnesses before the parliamentary committees of 1789–91 often linked the existence of provision grounds to reduced importation of foodstuffs, indicating that they were aware of the savings they had achieved.[12] Second, such savings became most important during the crisis of slave subsistence between 1776 and 1783, and again between 1794 and 1815. Wars and the effects of wars on established trading arrangements triggered a steep rise in the price of imported food, caused malnutrition and starvation, increased slave mortality, and forced planters to allocate more estate land to the production of food supplies.[13] Provision grounds therefore saved money and reduced the planters' risks.[14]

Third, slaves' preference for provision grounds also merged with masters' self-interest. For slaves, the advantages of a more secure and plentiful food supply, cash from the sale of surpluses and periods of unsupervised activity were apparent. Indeed, slaves may have taken the initiative in modifying the patterns of feeding on some estates. In 1789 Ashton Warner Byam, a leading judicial official in Grenada and a proprietor in St Vincent, told the parliamentary committee that when his slaves had made complete provision grounds for themselves '*they of their own accord offered to me that if I would give them the Saturday afternoon, out of crop time, they would require nothing but salt provisions from me*'.[15] Such an expressed preference enabled masters to perceive quickly the value of provision grounds as a mechanism for control. One year later Alexander Campbell, one of the leading proprietors in Grenada, observed that it was 'the custom' in Grenada to grant slaves as much land as they could work because it had been 'universally considered the greatest benefit to a planter that his Negroes should have a sufficient quantity of provisions, and the more money the Negroes got for themselves, the more attached they were to the property'.[16]

The topography of the Windwards was perhaps the most important factor in the planters' adoption and the slaves' consolidation of the provision-ground system. Grenada, St Vincent, and St Lucia were mountainous and Tobago at least hilly; all possessed wooded, mountainous interiors which restricted settlement to the coasts and coral lowlands, to the volcanic foothills, and to well-watered valleys leading to the sea.[17] The plantations, usually located in shore-facing valleys, often possessed land which ran into the foothills and 'new ground' or 'mountain runs' that were marginal or unsuited to sugar or other staple cultivation.[18] Lowland plantations, which were not so well endowed, often possessed 'little vacant spots' on which, as David Collins, a St Vincent physician, said, slaves were permitted to cultivate on their own account.[19] In those few cases where these vacant spots proved inadequate planters purchased mountain land 'for the purpose of negro ground'.[20] Allocation of this type of land for provision cultivation was sometimes justified by the disingenuous argument that 'these broken and steep places' did 'answer very well for provisions'.[21] But this inversion of the laws of husbandry could neither fully deflect criticism of the adequacy of slave feeding methods nor obscure the fact that planters recognized that such an allocation advanced their vital interests in low production costs and social control.

Provision grounds could consist of three different types of land allowance – yam grounds, gardens and mountain land or mountain ground. Yam grounds, apparently distributed only in St Vincent as customary allowances, may have been a remnant of earlier slave feeding methods, which featured provision production by gang labour. These grounds were small portions, not exceeding 40 square feet, of cane land being prepared for planting. Allotments were distributed to slaves on a declining scale according to age, and on these allotments slaves were expected to raise a yam crop before the new cane crop was planted. The allowance therefore served a dual purpose. It increased the slave's subsistence by assuring him of 'a fair crop' out of the cultivation of good land and it reduced the planter's labour costs by providing him with a 'clean and ameliorated surface to plant first crop canes'.[22]

Gardens, which can be confused with provision grounds because contemporaries sometimes used the terms interchangeably, were in the main not a land allowance at all.[23] In general, slaves created gardens from the land surrounding their houses, but sometimes garden allotments were provided by planters as partial substitutes for provision grounds. In Grenada, a 1788 law directed planters, who were prevented by the nature of soil or the 'particular situation' of estates from providing provision grounds, to allot each adult slave at least one-fortieth of an acre 'contiguous to the Negro Houses for the purpose of cultivating gardens for their sole use and benefit'.[24]

Sketchy and contradictory contemporary comment makes difficult any assessment of the size, exploitation and value of these gardens. Mrs Carmichael, the wife of a West Indian planter, and John Bowen Colthurst, a special magistrate on St Vincent, both of whom seemed intent on proving that slaves and apprentices were 'plentifully maintained' by their own-account activities, described the St Vincent gardens as of 'a very comfortable size'. For them, the gardens offered space for raising poultry and small stock and for cultivating tree crops, vines and vegetables, which could meet the short-term food needs of the cultivators.[25] Another observer, John Anderson, noted that these gardens were generally neglected and unappreciated.[26] The point turns, no doubt, on the size and quality of this land. Since broken ground of the estate would most likely be the site planters' preferred for slave villages, as abolitionist James Stephen argued, the garden's main utility would be to provide yards and passages between houses.[27] Gardens, therefore, had value to the extent that they contained conveniently located space for raising small stock and poultry.

Mountain ground was the characteristic provision ground, and its location created problems for optimal cultivation. Distance between the grounds and slaves' residences was one problem. No direct information exists on the distance slaves had to walk to their grounds, but the inference may be drawn from various estate papers, slave codes and local abolition acts that it was often 'considerable', probably as much as ten miles.[28] Such distances posed problems for the most efficient use of labour time and for the security of growing crops. Time consumed in a long trek to and from provision grounds meant loss of labour and under-exploitation of the grounds; distant residence from growing crops also reduced the possibility of effective policing and increased the risk of theft.

More important, difficulties with mountain grounds arose from the natural constraints on cultivation which such a location imposed. As the name suggests, such land was mainly forest and mountain: difficult of access because of steep slopes, difficult to clear because of virgin forests, difficult to cultivate because of boulders and stones, and impossible to protect against threats of land slippage and erosion. No doubt, as John Bowen Colthurst suggested, some provision grounds were established in 'deep rocky glens' containing some of the richest deposits of soil in St Vincent, but the search for these locations could consume valuable time.[29] Moreover, success in the search might compound the problem of inconvenient distance from residence.

Planters apparently cared little about the selection of the actual location of provision grounds. Only two contemporary commentators suggest that any criteria were applied in its selection. James Baillie, proprietor of estates in Grenada and St Vincent, allotted 50 acres of 'the most valuable seasonable part' of his Grenada estate for provision grounds; Sir William Young 'set apart' 46 acres of 'the richest ground' on his St Vincent estate for 'the negro gardens'.[30] Those planters who possessed mountain runs, which automatically recommended themselves as provision grounds, seem to have left the exact locations to drivers and field slaves. The viability of the soil for provision grounds did not have to be pre-tested because of the presumed fitness of the land for the purpose. It was the slaves' responsibility to check its possibilities, identify its deficiencies, and indicate when new ground was required.[31] On lowland and smaller estates inattention could not be the rule. Choices had to be made: how much land could be spared, whether gardens should substitute for provision grounds, and whether a specific quantity and quality of mountain land should be leased. No doubt planters in general paid more attention to the distribution of individual lots, but that attention was probably misplaced because the location of the ground could determine the adequacy of the provisions to be derived from the individual lot.

The law did not define the size of the individual allotments until the last years of slavery. Late eighteenth-century legislation in Grenada directed that adult slaves (over 14 years) should receive 'his or her proper ground', but the assessment of its size and adequacy for maintenance was left to a loose inspection procedure controlled by planters themselves.[32] In the 1820s, under abolitionist pressure for greater precision, 'a sufficient portion of land adapted to the growth of provisions' was stipulated and the size of allotment was fixed at one-quarter acre for adult slaves in Grenada and Tobago.[33] The greatest precision and most liberal provisions were achieved in St Lucia: land *'properly'* adapted for provision cultivation and a half acre in size became the legal requirement.[34] This was a consequence of the island's constitutional position; direct British rule made possible by Crown Colony status prevented planters from obstructing the will of the British government to an extent that was impossible in the other islands. The local abolition legislation generally echoed these provisions, though the Tobago legislature found it 'desirable' to follow St Lucia's example and increase the size of the allotment to a half acre for adult slaves.[35] Only in St Vincent did vagueness about the allowance persist until the end of slavery. On St Vincent the local abolition act defined the size of the acreage and its quality in negative terms: the 'sufficient portion' of provision ground would be 'deemed adequate and proper for maintenance and support of every praedial apprentice *unless good and sufficient cause be shown to the contrary'.*[36]

Customary practices undoubtedly influenced the legal definition of the allowance. Some planters, eager to exonerate themselves from charges of underfeeding their slaves, loosely suggested that the islands' topographical variety ensured that slaves had access to 'great quantity' of ground and to 'considerable tracts' which they cultivated 'for their own benefit'.[37] It is probable that planters recognized that a restrictive policy could be self-defeating; they could hardly spare the resources of personnel and time to enforce it. In any event, they could resume possession or restrict the size of the allotment whenever the imperatives of plantation expansion or slave discipline warranted. Moreover, the brute fact remained that the size of the allotment was effectively limited by its location, the quality of its soil, the available labour time and the labour requirements of the particular cultigens.[38] Therefore, the amount of land that individual slaves managed to cultivate was probably no more than a quarter acre. In 1790 Alexander Campbell told the parliamentary committee that the provision-ground allowance in Grenada was never less than one acre for a family of six; two years later Sir William Young reported that each household on his St Vincent estate had access to about half an acre; and John Bowen Colthurst suggested that a slave family in St Vincent may have had access to a maximum of two acres during the 1830s.[39]

Throughout the slave period, the time allowed for slaves to cultivate provision grounds was both minimal and seasonal. Before the 1820s it amounted to between 14 and 19 working days which could be utilized only 'out of crop' when the sugar canes had been reaped. After April or May the designated time, usually Saturday, was then doled out on the basis of a half day weekly or a full day fortnightly. Planters expected, as various witnesses explained to the parliamentary committees in 1790, that slaves would supplement the allowance by their 'spare hours' – the afternoon rest period, after sunset out of crop, on Sundays and in the three-day holiday at Christmas.[40] This allocation and schedule reflected planters' prejudices and priorities. According to Alexander Campbell, 'very little labour' was required for planting and weeding the provision ground; therefore 'the Negroes need not work half of the time allowed them in their gardens'. Further, because provisions could not be planted before the rains in May and June slaves had 'no occasion to work in their gardens, but out of crop-time'.[41] In brief, planters did not intend for their production schedule to be affected by any inconvenient dispersal of the labour force. Mrs Carmichael declared that 'no sugar could be made on Friday, Saturday or Monday', if labour time was granted during the grinding season: 'the sugar made on Friday must be potted on the following morning, and canes cut on Friday would be sour by Monday morning'.[42]

Abolitionist pressure forced a roughly 50 per cent increase in the allowance during the 1820s – from 14 and 19 days to between 26 and 35 days. But, while 'full working days' were substituted for the optional weekly half-day, the seasonal stipulation was retained.[43] Little alteration occurred during the apprenticeship period, the final phase of slavery. The seasonal stipulation was dropped in Grenada, St Vincent, and St Lucia, but in Tobago the allowance was reduced from 35 to 14 full working days and the seasonal restriction on the use of the allowance was extended to six months – July to December.[44]

Slaveowners did not supervise or assist slaves in the cultivation of provision grounds. Planters, as individuals or as official 'guardians', had responsibility for providing land enough for the slaves' maintenance.[45] But that responsibility was discharged in perfunctory fashion. Planters did lay out ground and distribute lots to individuals and families, but they paid little or no attention to the precise location of lots and seldom bothered to demarcate their boundaries clearly.[46] Although some planters probably sent their gangs to assist in the heavy work of clearing forests for the establishment of provision grounds, the main business of clearing and preparation of the ground was left to the slaves themselves.[47] Planters needed to be satisfied that provision grounds were productive if only to ensure that their gangs would be fit for labour and that plantation stores and fields would not be raided for food. Their interest in the slaves' practices of husbandry was excited only to the extent that slaves broke the prohibition against cultivation of staple crops or created fire hazards for central plantation property by 'slash and burn' methods of cultivation.[48] As a result, planters seldom inspected the grounds to check on the state of cultivation or the fertility of the soil and slaves were left to indicate when soil was depleted and new ground required.[49] Plantation supervisory staff probably mustered slaves for provision-ground duty on Saturday afternoons and on Sundays, but that action was probably more a police exercise against the threats of desertion and malingering than a deliberate effort to ensure the adequacy of slave maintenance. Planters, in spite of Dr Collins' advice to the contrary, apparently offered little or no assistance to slaves in regard to supplies of plants and seeds, information about crop selection, rotation and preservation, or protection of crops against theft.[50] Therefore, slaves were generally forced to rely on their own scanty resources. How they coped with institutionalized neglect was illustrated by John Jeremie, president of the Royal Court in St Lucia in 1825. Jeremie found that the slaves on St Lucia were 'extremely careful of their provision grounds', cultivating them 'with assiduity' and guarding them 'night and day', that they 'never forgive a theft on them', and that 'nothing is more likely to keep them at home than the cultivating of their gardens'.[51]

Slaves' choice of crops reflected the pressure and circumstances which created and sustained the provision-ground system. The main staples of the slave diet were dominated by root crops and starches (yams, eddoes, cassava, sweet potatoes), tree crops (plantain, banana and breadfruit), and grains and legumes (Indian and Guinea corn, many varieties of peas and beans).[52] In addition, slaves produced some vegetables and fruit. Dietary preference was one element in the slaves' choice, as the yam and plantain, traditional staples of the West African diet, were 'a favorite and good food', or 'what the potato is to the lower classes in Britain'.[53] Quality of soil was another determinant. Cassava, arrowroot, peas and vines could subsist in poor soil, therefore occupied land that was perceived as unfit for staple crop cultivation. Restricted labour time both determined the amount of land that could be cultivated and constrained the choice of crop. Slaves preferred crops that did not require close and constant attention, such as high-yield crops like plantains and bananas that quickly propagated themselves. Not surprisingly, the yam and sweet potato, whose growth inhibited weeds, were featured in the slaves' crop regime. Moreover, most slaves raised a variety of small stock in their gardens and backyards and exploited the fishing resources of the islands' rivers.[54]

* * *

The produce of the provision ground and yard or garden formed the basis for an expanding local market. In the Windward islands eighteenth-century slave laws show that those markets, as in Jamaica, made their appearance early in the life of the plantations. Legislation, which had as its rationale the discouragement of theft, also sought to outlaw door-to-door peddling by slaves, to reduce marketing by slaves through enforcement of the pass laws and to prohibit the trading of cattle, plantation staples, precious metals and jewellery by slaves entirely. But these prohibitions themselves confirm the existence of unsupervised marketing by slaves. Moreover, the marketing of 'logs of wood, firewood, fresh fish and dunghill fowls, goats, hogs, and vegetables of any sort' by slaves was not interdicted.[55] This division in the productive function provided unintended incentives for slaves to produce and trade surpluses. By 1790 planters pointed to the slaves' virtual monopoly of the internal markets for locally produced food, firewood and charcoal, and fodder. Urban dwellers purchased much of their food from slaves and the planters themselves depended on slaves for the greater part of their supply of poultry and fresh meat.[56] 'A few poultry and crops', Alexander Campbell observed, 'were raised by the proprietors, about their homes, but their chief consumption is bought of the slaves'.[57] By the end of slavery this 'breach' in the slave system was virtually complete: while the restriction on the trade in plantation produce was retained, slave participation in the internal markets was officially recognized by the formal concession of the slaves' right to attend market on a designated day, and slaves were openly protesting the choice of market day and the organization of markets. Customary arrangements had overturned legal restrictions, and what had grown outside the law had become recognized in law.[58]

Scattered evidence suggests that produce grown by plantation slaves animated elaborate urban markets in the Windward Islands.[59] Slave supply and urban demand stimulated commodity exchange and increased slaves' purchasing power. This in turn sustained an expanding distributive network linking slave producers to free and slave consumers, plantation to town, and slave to market. Plantation slaves, mainly women, marketed produce, either utilizing hucksters as intermediaries or selling in the markets on their own account. Itinerant traders, usually coloured slaves and freed persons, based in town or on the plantations, hawked dry goods around the countryside, tapping the savings of slaves or bartering their 'finery' for the slaves' produce. Urban slave hucksters, operating either as slave hirelings or as agents for their owners, sometimes functioned as retailers of the plantation slaves' produce and were a steady source of the small items needed by plantation slaves. Merchants and shopkeepers furnished imported goods which increasing purchasing power brought within the reach of plantation slaves. Towns were central to this network – as sites of the main markets, as the main source of demand for slaves' produce and as mercantile and financial centres. Slaves thus heightened the scale of urban activity in commodity exchange and increased employment and accumulation in internal markets.

Competition for market shares between small and large urban operators and between urban retailers and rural producers was a natural consequence of this expanding market. Barry Higman demonstrates that *free* merchants and shopkeepers sought to confine *slave* hucksters to the sale of locally produced goods. For example, in 1815 hucksters selling bread about the streets of St George's, the capital of Grenada, had to be licensed.[60] For similar reasons, urban traders strongly supported the closure of Sunday markets, since they too perceived that their abolition would increase their own market share. Slave producers often did their retailing in the Sunday market, selling in the central market or in the street, effectively eliminating the urban middlemen. After 1823, when the British government, in response to abolitionist pressure, ended or curtailed Sunday markets as a means of ameliorating the slaves' moral and material condition, it received strong support from urban traders. These traders reasoned that the abolition of Sunday markets would reduce competition offered by rural retailers on that day. Moreover, the substitution of a weekday as the new market day would strengthen their position in the exchange of slave produce, because the change of market day would disrupt the slaves' traditional commercial routine and deprive them of access to the large volume of business that was transacted on a weekend. Events on Grenada illustrate how this advantage was exploited. After 1828 hucksters in St George's engrossed the produce brought into town by the rural slaves on Thursday, the new official market day, and then retailed it at inflated prices.[61]

The slaves' reaction to the formal abolition of the Sunday markets reveals the extent to which they competed with free traders and perceived the effect on their own interests of a disturbance of traditional arrangements. By 1825 market day had been switched in Grenada and Tobago to Thursday and to Saturday in St Lucia, while in St Vincent the main market in the capital, Kingstown, was closed from ten on Sunday mornings. But four years later the governor of St Vincent ruefully reported that he was issuing 'the most peremptory orders' to the Clerk of Market and to the Chief Constable 'to carry the law into complete effect'.[62] In St Lucia, in 1831, marketing on Sunday was still outlawed, but the governor was being directed by the Colonial Office to 'appoint' a market day, even though the Legislative Council had recently switched the market from Saturday to Monday.[63] Slave resistance in the form of complaint and open defiance to such changes explains the gap between legislative enactment and implementation. In Grenada slaves greeted the change in the market day with 'much dissatisfaction'.[64] In St Vincent the governor admitted that 'nothing but absolute force' would shift slaves 'from a long customary enjoyment (as it is estimated by them) of marketing on Sunday'. Slaves had indicated that they thought 'the abolition of this privilege' constituted 'one of the greatest hardships imposed on them'. The governor was fully alive to the economic implications of the switch in the market day, in that prices of provisions also were increased 'to the great injury of domestics and other slaves in Kingstown, who rely upon the market for subsistence'. Therefore he concluded that the moral issue was likely to lose out to the economic: 'until the Negroes shall have acquired a sufficient degree of religion to induce them to observe the Sabbath from a principle of morality, they will not give up their habits of trafficking on Sundays'.[65]

The imprecision of available evidence makes it difficult to assess the slaves' material gains from provision grounds. Most contemporary observers, planter and official alike, suggested that the annual returns were substantial enough to provide 'comparative wealth', 'an approach to real comfort' and that accumulation did take place.[66] Witnesses before the parliamentary committees of 1789–91 estimated the slaves' annual earnings at £6 to £20, with 'industrious' slaves on fertile soil earning as much as £30 to £40.[67] James Baillie, a Grenada planter, claimed that some slaves on his estate possessed property 'worth forty, fifty, one hundred and even as far as two hundred pounds sterling' and that such property was 'regularly conveyed from one generation to another, without any interference whatever'.[68] Alexander Campbell, impressed with the slaves' 'fine clothes' and lavish 'entertainments', concluded that '*one half of the current specie*' in the ceded islands (Dominica, Grenada, St Vincent, and Tobago) '*is the property of the Negroes*'.[69] Later commentators, like Mrs Carmichael and John Bowen Colthurst, echoed these sentiments. For Mrs Carmichael, any St Vincent slave could earn £30 annually, 'and very many may save much more'.[70] For Colthurst, the returns were less ample – £2.10 for any family and £7.10 for the 'industrious' family.[71] For both of them, however, each element of the slaves' domestic economy brought material benefit and possibilities for accumulation. Provision-ground and garden produce fed slaves and stock; surplus produce was exchanged for dietary supplements, for 'finery' and for the 'little articles' like candles, soap and tobacco; small stock and poultry were marketed for cash which was saved or employed in the purchase of small luxuries. Therefore, according to Mrs Carmichael and Colthurst, some slaves saved 'large sums', as much as £100 or £150.[72]

The accuracy of these estimates and the conclusions they underpin must be queried for at least three reasons. First, these observers were partisans of one stripe or another. Witnesses before the parliamentary committees of 1789–1791 were, like Sir William Young and Mrs Carmichael, apologists for slavery. Colthurst, a self-proclaimed abolitionist, was perhaps eager to inflate the significance of evidence that slaves had adopted capitalistic values and had therefore vindicated all that their supporters hoped of them.[73] Second, the claims took little account of the disparities in quality and size of provision grounds and of the capacity (or industry) of the slaves to exploit them. Most observers did qualify their more liberal estimates by linking them to the performance of 'industrious' slaves. But, as Dr Collins and James Stephen suggested, the terms 'industrious slave' and 'bad' and 'lazy' slave carried special connotations.[74] The apparently ample returns of the industrious slave might relate as much to the quality of the land and to the availability of labour for its cultivation as to the drive and determination of the slave. Similarly, the poor returns achieved by lazy slaves who, by the estimate of the Chief Justice of St Vincent, constituted the bulk of the slave population, might have been a consequence of depleted soils, debility induced by malnutrition, hunger and overwork, or a simple lack of interest. Third, the planter's evidence was internally inconsistent, if not contradictory. On the one hand they pointed to an 'abundance' of provisions, to well-stocked internal markets, 'dimity jackets' and 'muslins', furniture and substantial savings; on the other hand they asserted that slaves 'in general are subject to thieving' and accepted that there was a correlation between the incidence of theft and the adequacy of slaves' nutrition.[75] 'All the estates', Alexander Campbell claimed, 'are obliged to keep guards on the Negro provision gardens and to guard the cattle pens, storehouses, and rum cellars'.[76] Finally, these sanguine conclusions overlooked the extreme vulnerability of the provision-ground sector of the economy. Provision grounds had no defence against drought or flood: crops burned in drought and floods washed away the mountain ground. In Grenada, after the 1831 hurricane, hunger drove slaves on the Lataste estate to eat unripe provisions, which made them ill, forcing them to rely on their masters for rations of expensive imported grain. Eventually the slaves had to re-establish provision grounds on new land.[77] Provision grounds thus may have provided slaves with a more secure source of nutrition and some, but not all, slaves were hardy enough to cope with the competing labour demands of plantations and provision ground and could therefore create opportunities for the improvement of their standard of living.[78]

*   *   *

The participation of slaves in provision-ground cultivation and marketing exposed, as Mintz has often pointed out, the contradiction and inconsistencies of the slave regime.[79] Slaves cultivated land and disposed of its produce without supervision from their owners. Slaves worked their provision grounds in family groups. Slaves selected crops and determined the methods of cultivation, the extent of provision saving and cash accumulation. They did so, moreover, with an energy and enthusiasm that sharply contrasted with their work habits and low productivity in gang labour plantation export staples.

Slave families in 'the constant occupation' of provision ground forced their owners to recognize rights of occupancy to portions of plantation ground.[80] Slaves would not move from their ground without notice or without replacement grounds being provided, and they could bequeath rights of occupancy as well as property.[81] The increasing ability of slaves to produce marketable food surpluses and to consume imported goods created and sustained markets, and their involvement in those markets eventually secured a legal right of participation.

These achievements were particularly remarkable because they were secured mainly by the slaves themselves. Their owners contributed land and grudgingly donated small portions of the slaves' labour time, but they did not intend or expect more from the provision-ground system than a reduction in the cost of slave maintenance. In extending proto-peasant activity, slaves often had to cope with planter hostility; the best that they could hope for was the unintended complicity of indifference. Therefore, while it may be possible to accept Bryan Edwards' 'coalition of interests' in the elaboration of the plantation complex, it is difficult to see how it was a 'happy' arrangement. Rather, its existence involved a barely disguised persistent and unequal competition for resources.

The competition was predicated upon, on the one hand, the slaves' perception that provision-ground cultivation and marketing offered a partial escape from the hard and long routine of supervised plantation labour, and, on the other hand, their recognition of the ever-present limitations on their ability to exploit this means of escape fully. The demand for regular plantation labour naturally deprived them of the time and energy to optimize the material and psychological returns from provision cultivation and marketing. The prime limiting factor was, of course, slavery itself. But, if most slaves were seldom disposed towards suicidal confrontation with their owners and overseers, then resistance took the form of continuous efforts to explore and exploit what little the social system offered – to cope with slavery, not by direct confrontation, but by attempts to make lives of their own.[82] Resistance therefore may have been subsumed under a competition and scramble for land and labour resources.

Competition for land did not usually involve claims to larger portions of plantation ground. Rather competition revolved around the quality of land allotted to slaves, the distance of that land from slaves' residences, and rights of occupancy to that land. In 1831 a confrontation between slaves and the manager-attorney on the Lataste estate in Grenada – which may be regarded as a form of industrial action – provides an excellent view of that competition. On that estate the slaves' provision ground was mountain land, but its occupancy had been rendered insecure by the dismissed attorney, William Houston, 'who made no scruple at saying he would turn them away from those grounds at ten days' warning'. In June 1831 the provision grounds were badly damaged by floods spawned by a hurricane. By September the slaves faced starvation, and they indicated that they were 'quite dissatisfied' with the quality and location of their provision grounds, that they were 'anxious to get a new piece of land' and were cultivating the damaged grounds with 'reluctance'. In response, the manager-attorney admitted the validity of the complaints – 'the land is poor and is now run out' – and, though he chided the slaves for murmuring at 'the will of the Almighty', he quickly sought replacement ground. By late September he had succeeded in leasing 'a piece of excellent new land for the Negroes', which was two miles nearer the estate than the old ground and with which the slaves seemed 'well pleased'.[83] Slaves had invoked their customary rights, and the manager-attorney had recognized the policy of satisfying them.

Essentially, slaves wanted what they did not control but what was within their masters' power to concede: adequate maintenance to be provided by provision grounds with good soil in a convenient location, and full rights to crops through secure occupancy of grounds. Laws designed to guarantee them minimal levels of maintenance – the periodic inspection of provision grounds – were a dead letter. Slaves thus took it upon themselves to remind their masters that inadequate maintenance would be met with theft, desertion and even insurrection. Their tactics included persistent complaint, 'reluctance' (the go-slow), and desertion, perhaps in that order. The most commonly used tactic, however, was self-help. Some slaves took advantage of the negligible restrictions on the appropriation of land for provision ground by scouring the mountains and high valleys for suitable provision ground.

Therefore, what John Bowen Colthurst saw as the indulging of a 'wandering propensity' was often the exercise of initiative, the far-ranging search for the adequate maintenance that masters failed to provide.[84]

Available evidence does not indicate the effectiveness of any of these tactics. However, inferences may be drawn from two developments. First, slaves consolidated the provision grounds and marketing complex, and this required rising production and, perhaps, productivity of provision grounds. Therefore the slaves' success may have forced planters to respond to their statements of grievance. Second, legislation near the end of slavery (usually in the local abolition acts) promised improvement in levels of maintenance. This was mainly the achievement of the abolitionists, and of James Stephen in particular. In 1824 his monumental work, *The Slavery of the British West India Colonies Delineated*, dissected as never before the practices of the slave system. But the story Stephen told was the story of the plight and struggle of West Indian slaves; so, to the extent that Stephen's work stimulated reform, the slaves' actions must be held partly responsible for the amelioration of their own condition.

Scramble for labour services was probably more intense than the competition for land, because labour was the slaves' scarcest resource. Supervised plantation labour normally occupied 55 hours in a six-day week. It left little for slaves themselves; the portion they controlled was small and intermittent and might be reduced without notice by demands from their masters for extra duty or other chores on a Sunday.[85] Yet slaves were faced with competing claims on their time – recuperation from the plantation routine, provision-ground cultivation, marketing, and leisure time activities. If slaves gave priority to one claim, the effect on maintenance or health could be disastrous. Sickness or distance from provision grounds or markets could aggravate the situation. Therefore the slaves' existence must have been hectic and full of frustrations; it required some ingenuity to juggle competing claims and conserve energy for the tasks that awaited the small amount of time they controlled. Their problem, as rural producers, was how to maximize the use of available labour time in own-account activities and how, in the face of supervised plantation labour, to gain extra time for those activities.

Slaves tried to solve this double problem in at least three ways. The first tactic involved co-operation with masters and other slaves. Slaves in supervisory positions were permitted by masters either to *hire* or freely avail themselves of the labour services of other slaves.[86] Non-elite creole slaves sought their masters' patronage and may have competed with each other for the temporary labour services of newly arrived slaves during their seasoning period. Masters apprenticed new slaves to creole slaves and, according to Sir William Young, the creoles' scramble for an allocation 'was violent, and troublesome in the extreme'.[87] The second tactic stressed co-operation among slaves. Observers remarked on the higher average earnings which 'Negroes and slaves having children' achieved compared to those of 'single slaves'.[88] Obviously the pooling of land and labour resources in family groups created possibilities for a more efficient deployment of labour and for more intensive exploitation of provision ground and internal market. Children may have been mainly employed around the yards and gardens, tending the stock; women were the main market-people preparing, transporting and selling produce; and men presumably bore the major responsibility for clearing and preparing the grounds.

The third tactic was 'theft' of masters' labour time. Slaves stole constantly because independent economic activities expanded even though the allowance of labour time did not increase before the 1820s. This theft could not often be obvious – absence from gang or late return from meal breaks – though these actions may have played a part. Supervision and the certainty of punishment for malingering and temporary desertion most likely checked the incidence of overt malingering. Theft had to be subtle – theft through energy conservation and the deliberate reduction of performance levels. If one takes account of the length and intensity of the plantation work schedule, slaves' success in energy conservation must be a main explanation for the contrast between their 'sodden, stupid and dull' demeanour in the plantation fields and their 'lively, intelligent and even happy' behaviour in their provision grounds and in the markets.[89] No doubt, as Mintz argues, unsupervised provision-ground cultivation did give slaves opportunities to express fully their humanity, but both that expression and provision-ground cultivation required reasonably high energy levels to sustain them.[90]

* * *

Proto-peasant activity, the competition this generated, and the limited gains which slaves made in that competition nurtured and confirmed their attitudes about those activities and their relationship to plantation labour. These own-account activities and coerced labour, in an uneven mix, dominated the slaves' experience; and slaves employed proto-peasant activity continuously during slavery to reduce the extent and impact of coerced labour. Therefore, from the slaves' perspective, their own-account activities were probably as important as coerced labour in defining their status, their humanity and their notions of freedom. Perhaps it is not too fanciful to suggest that humanity and freedom may have been equated by them with their independent activities. Further, slaves doubtless perceived that their forced involvement in plantation labour was the factor which constrained their exploitation of the potential in proto-peasant activity and was the critical limiting factor on their acquisition of freedom and full expression of humanity. Therefore, they may have concluded that when they had a choice in the matter they should rearrange the allocation of labour time to give priority to the transforming element of own-account activities.

Post-slavery labour relations reveal the influence of such attitudes. Both apprentices and ex-slaves utilized the greater control of the labour time which slavery abolition conferred to de-emphasize regular plantation labour and to emphasize own-account activities.[91] However, they tried to do all this *within the confines of the plantation* which was still dependent on regular gang labour. This suggests that the scope of that competition was to some extent culturally determined.

NOTES

1. See Sidney W. Mintz and Douglas G. Hall, *The Origins of the Jamaican Internal Marketing System*, Yale University Publications in Anthropology, No.57 (New Haven, 1960), 3–26; Mintz, *Caribbean Transformations* (Chicago, 1974); 'Caribbean Marketplaces and Caribbean History', *Nova Americana*, 1 (1978), 333–44; 'Was the Plantation Slave a Proletarian?' *Review*, 2 (1978), 81–98; Robert Dirks, *The Black Saturnalia: Conflict and Its Ritual Expression on British West Indian Slave Plantations* (Gainesville, 1987); 'Regional Fluctuations and Competitive Transformations in West Indian Societies' in C.D. Laughlin and I.A. Brady (eds.), *Extinction and Survival in Human Populations* (New York, 1978); B.W. Higman, *Slave Populations of the British Caribbean, 1807–1834* (Baltimore, 1984); Kenneth F. Kiple, *The Caribbean Slave: A Biological History* (New York, 1984); Richard B. Sheridan, *Doctors and Slaves: A Medical and Demographic History of Slavery in the British West Indies, 1680–1834* (New York, 1985).
2. See, in particular, Sidney W. Mintz, 'Slavery and the Rise of Peasantries', *Historical Reflections*, 6 (1979), 213–42.
3. What is meant by 'competition' is not much different from what Dirks outlines in *Black Saturnalia*, 98–102. But I am not sure how the ecological formulation clarifies the political issues that were present.
4. The primary sources for a description and analysis of the provision ground system in the Windward Islands are limited. The earliest description can be found in absentee proprietor, Sir William Young, 'A Tour through the several Islands of Barbados, St. Vincent, Antigua, Tobago and Grenada in the years 1791 and 1792' in Bryan Edwards, *History, Civil and Commercial of the British Colonies in the West Indies* (London, 1801), 3: 249–84. A second was produced by David Collins, a successful doctor-planter, resident in St Vincent for over 20 years, who published *Practical Rules for the Management and Medical Treatment of Negro Slaves in the Sugar Colonies* (Freeport, NY, 1971 [1803]). The fullest account is provided by Mrs A.C. Carmichael in her *Domestic Manners and Social Condition of the White, Colored, and Negro Population of the West Indies*, 2 vols. (London, 1833). She lived in St Vincent for over two years between 1820 and 1823, and was a keen observer and

assiduous collector of information, although favouring the planters' side of the abolition question. The final description can be found in the journal of a Special Magistrate in St Vincent, John Bowen Colthurst, who served during the last seven months of the Apprenticeship: W.K. Marshall (ed.), *The Colthurst Journal* (Millwood, NY, 1977).

Two supplementary sources can amplify this information: the slave laws, particularly those enacted under abolitionist pressure for slavery amelioration, and the testimony provided by witnesses before the parliamentary committees of (1789–91) on the slave trade and slavery. See Sheila Lambert (ed.), *House of Commons Sessional Papers of the 18th Century* [*HCSP*], Vols. 69, 70, 71, 77, 82. Nine witnesses gave evidence on conditions in Grenada, St Vincent, and Tobago, and these included leading proprietors and officials, nearly all of whom qualified for expert status because of their professional experience and long residence in the islands.

5. James Stephen, *The Slavery of the British West India Colonies Delineated*, 2 vols. (London, 1824), 2: 261.
6. Higman, *Slave Populations*, 204.
7. *HCSP*, Vol. 71, 114, 147, evidence of Alexander Campbell. See also evidence of Gilbert Francklyn (Tobago), 85, and of James Seton, Governor of St Vincent (Vol. 69, 427).
8. See Grendada Act No. 2 of 1766, quoted in B.A. Marshall, 'Society and Economy in the British Windward Islands, 1763–1823', Ph.D. Diss. (University of the West Indies, 1972), 302.
9. *HCSP*, Vol. 69, 427, evidence of Governor Seton.
10. *British Parliamentary Papers* [*BPP*] (Dublin, 1969, 1971), Vol. 71, 155, Vol. 77, 435; B. Marshall, 'Society and Economy', 303. In Tobago, the stipulation was one acre 'well planted with provisions' for every five slaves. In St Lucia, it was 500 plants of manioc or other vegetable for each slave.
11. Mintz, 'Caribbean Marketplaces', 335.
12. See evidence of Gilbert Franklyn and Ashton Warner Byam (*HCSP* Vol. 71, 85, 105).
13. Richard B. Sheridan, 'The Crisis of Slave Subsistence in the British West Indies during and after the American Revolution', *William and Mary Quarterly*, 3rd series, 33 (1976), 615–41.
14. Mintz and Hall, *Origins*, 3.
15. *HCSP*, Vol. 71, 105. Emphasis added.
16. Ibid., Vol. 71, 144. See Edward Kamau Brathwaite, 'Controlling Slaves in Jamaica', unpublished paper, Conference of Caribbean Historians, Georgetown, 1971.
17. J.D. Momsen, 'The Geography of Land Use and Population in the Caribbean with special reference to Barbados and the Windward Islands', Ph. Diss. (University of London, 1969), 132–3; D.L. Niddrie, *Land Use and Population in Tobago* (Bude, Cornwall, 1961), 17, 43; W.M. Davis, *The Lesser Antilles* (New York, 1926), 8.
18. See evidence of Alexander Campbell and James Bailie (*HCSP*, Vol. 71, 144, 199).
19. Collins, *Practical Rules*, 76.
20. *Parliamentary Papers* (*PP*), 1842, Vol. 13. Evidence of Henry Barkly before the Select Committee on West India Colonies (Q. 2661).
21. *HCSP*, Vol. 69, 428, evidence of Governor Seton. See *PP*, Vol. 13, evidence of H.M. Grant before the Select Committee on West India Colonies (Questions 31–72).
22. *Colthurst Journal*, 171. See John Anderson, 'Journal and Recollections', 26, Aberdeen University Library, Scotland.
23. For example, Sir William Young in Edwards, *History*, 3: 248; John Jeremie, First President of the Royal Court in St Lucia, in *BPP*, Vol. 71, 223; and W.C. Mitchell, Attorney of Lataste estate in Grenada in Mitchell to Baumer, 3 Sept. 1831, *Lataste Estate Papers*, Moccas Court Collection, National Library of Wales.
24. *HCSP*, Vol. 70, 132, Grenada Act of 3 Nov. 1788; B. Marshall, 'Society and Economy', 319.

25. *Colthurst Journal*, 170; Carmichael, *Domestic Manners*, 1: 135–7.
26. Anderson, 'Journal', 26.
27. Stephen, *Slavery*, 2: 262.
28. The Grenada Abolition Act referred to provision grounds located 'a considerable distance from their place of abode'. See Higman, *Slave Populations*, 204.
29. *Colthurst Journal*, 171.
30. *HCSP*, Vol. 71, 199; Edwards, *History*, 3: 271.
31. *HCSP*, Vol. 71, 132, evidence of Gilbert Francklyn; *Lataste Estate Papers*, Moccas Court Collection, Mitchell to Baumer, 3 and 25 Sept. 1831.
32. *HCSP*, Vol. 70, 131, Grenada Acts of 10 Dec. 1766 and 3 Nov. 1788. Inspectors, later called Guardians, were given the responsibility of inspecting provision grounds, of determining their adequacy for maintenance, and of fining planters for infractions of the law.
33. *BPP*, Vol. 77, 140, Tobago Slave Act, 1829.
34. Ibid., Vol. 77, 369, St Lucia Second Supplementary Ordinance, 1830; ibid., Vol. 79, 126, Order in Council, 1831. The local ordinance in 1830 had stipulated 'at least one *carré* [3 ⅓ acres] for every two full grown slaves', but the Order in Council of 1831 reduced the size to half an acre for each slave 15 years and over.
35. Section 10 of Tobago Slavery Abolition Act.
36. Section 10 of St Vincent Slavery Abolition Act. Emphasis added.
37. *HCSP*, Vol. 71, 85, 199, evidence of James Baillie and Gilbert Francklyn; Edwards, *History*, 3: 274.
38. Dirks, *Black Saturnalia*, 75.
39. *HCSP*, Vol. 71, 172, 182; Edwards, *History*, 3: 271; *Colthurst Journal*, 170.
40. *HCSP*, Vol. 71, 105–6, 145, 148, 199–200, evidence of James Baillie, Alexander Campbell and Ashton Warner Byam; ibid., Vol. 69, 428, evidence of Governor Seton; ibid., Vol. 82, 164, evidence of Drewery Ottley.
41. Ibid., Vol. 71, 146, evidence of Alexander Campbell; also evidence of Ashton Warner Byam (104–7); Carmichael, *Domestic Manners*, 1: 174–5.
42. Carmichael, *Domestic Manners*, 1: 174.
43. *BPP*, Vol. 71, 57, 95, Grenada Consolidated Slave Law, 1825; ibid., Vol. 77, 140, 369, Tobago Slave Act, 1829 and St Lucia 2nd Supplementary Ordinance, 1830.
44. Section 11 of Tobago Abolition Act.
45. B. Marshall, 'Society and Economy', 301–3, 318–22.
46. *HCSP*, Vol. 71, 146, 199–200, evidence of James Baillie and Alexander Campbell; Collins, *Practical Rules*, 87–99.
47. *HCSP*, Vol. 71, 132, 199–20, evidence of Gilbert Francklyn and James Baillie.
48. *BPP*, Vol. 71, 106, 228, St Vincent Consolidated Slave Act, 1825 and St. Lucia Ordinance, 1825.
49. *HCSP*, Vol. 71, 132, evidence of Gilbert Francklyn; *Lataste Estate Papers*, Mitchell to Baumer, 3 and 25 Sept. 1831.
50. *HCSP*, Vol. 71, 145, 200, evidence of Alexander Campbell and James Baillie; Collins, *Practical Rules*, 91–9.
51. *BPP*, Vol. 71, 223, enclosed in Acting Governor to Bathurst, 30 Aug. 1825.
52. *HCSP*, Vol. 71, 146, evidence of Alexander Campbell; Carmichael, *Domestic Manners*, 1: 162–78.
53. *HCSP*, Vol. 71, 146, evidence of Alexander Campbell; Carmichael, *Domestic Manners*, 1: 152.
54. Carmichael, *Domestic Manners*, 1: 51–3, 179.
55. *HCSP*, Vol. 70, 149, St Vincent Act for the Better Government of Slaves, 11 July 1767, Section X; B. Marshall, 'Society and Economy', 292–6.
56. *HCSP*, Vol. 71, 86, 107–8, 191, evidence of Gilbert Francklyn, Ashton Warner Byam, James Baillie.
57. Ibid., Vol. 71, 173, evidence of Alexander Campbell.
58. Mintz, 'Caribbean Marketplaces', 336; Mintz and Hall, *Origins*, 12–13.
59. This paragraph is based mainly on the analysis of Higman.
60. *St George's Chronicle*, 13 May 1815, quoted in Higman, *Slave Populations*, 238.

61. *Grenada Free Press*, 19 Aug. 1829, quoted in Higman, *Slave Populations*, 241.
62. *BPP*, Vol. 77, 136, Brisbane to Murray, 22 May 1829. Emphasis added.
63. Ibid., 366, Ist Subsidiary Ordinance, 1830 to HM's Order in Council; Vol. 79, 101–3, Order in Council, 1831.
64. Ibid., Vol. 71, 78, Patterson to Bathurst, 23 Nov. 1825.
65. Ibid., Vol. 77, 136, Brisbane to Murray, 22 May 1829. For comparable response in Antigua, see D.B. Gaspar, 'Slavery, Amelioration, and Sunday Markets in Antigua, 1823–1831', *Slavery and Abolition*, 9 (1988), 11–21.
66. Edwards, *History*, 3: 271; Carmichael, *Domestic Manners*, 1:5.
67. *HCSP*, Vol. 71, 107–8, evidence of Alexander Campbell, Ashton Warner Byam; Vol. 82, 163–4, evidence of Drewery Ottley.
68. Ibid., Vol. 71.
69. Ibid., Vol. 71. Emphasis added.
70. Carmichael, *Domestic Manners*, 1: 176–9.
71. *Colthurst Journal*, 163, 171.
72. Ibid., 171; Carmichael, *Domestic Manners*, 1: 194–7.
73. For example, Drewery Ottley, (*HCSP*, Vol. 82, 163–4), suggested that, on a 200-slave estate, only about 12 to 18 slaves would earn annually the £6 to £8 which was within the reach of 'an industrious but ordinary Field Slave'.
74. Collins, *Practical Rules*, 77–9; Stephen, *Slavery*, 2: 264–71.
75. *HCSP*, Vol. 71, 145, 148, evidence of Alexander Campbell. See also evidence of John Giles (ibid., Vol. 82, 75).
76. Ibid., Vol. 71, 151. See also evidence of Gilbert Francklyn (Vol. 71, 87) and of Drewery Ottley and John Giles (ibid., Vol. 82, 75, 176).
77. *Lataste Estate Papers*, Mitchell to Baumer, 3 and 25 Sept. 1831.
78. Stephen, *Slavery*, 2: 270–71; Higman, *Slave Populations*, 212–18.
79. See Mintz, 'Was the Plantation Slave a Proletarian?' and 'Caribbean History'.
80. *Colthurst Journal*, 10.
81. *Lataste Estate Papers*, Mitchell to Baumer, 3 and 25 Sept. 1831; Carmichael, *Domestic Manners*, 1: 197; *HCSP*, Vol. 71, 95, 191, evidence of James Baillie and Gilbert Francklyn.
82. Mintz, *Caribbean Transformations*, 212.
83. *Lataste Estate Papers*, Mitchell to Baumer, 3 and 25 Sept. 1831.
84. *Colthurst Journal*, 171.
85. *HCSP*, Vol. 82, 75, 109, evidence of John Giles and John Terry. Both observed that the plantation chore of 'picking of grass' on Sundays and in the afternoon break was 'a great hardship on slaves'. Giles also complained that slaves received no compensation in time for the loss of their Sundays to guard duty.
86. Ibid., Vol. 71, 107, evidence of Ashton Warner Byam; Higman, *Slave Populations*, 212.
87. Edwards, *History*, 3: 272; *HCSP*, Vol. 71, 147–8, evidence of Alexander Campbell.
88. *HCSP*, Vol. 71, 148. See also Gilbert Francklyn's evidence (87, 95–6), and *Colthurst Journal*, 171.
89. Mintz, 'Was the Plantation Slave a Proletarian?', 94.
90. Mintz, 'Caribbean Marketplaces', 340; *Caribbean Transformations*, 151–2.
91. See W.K. Marshall, 'Commentary One' on 'Slavery and the Rise of Peasantries' in *Historical Reflections*, 6 (1979), 243–8; and 'Apprenticeship and Labor Relations in Four Windward Islands' in David Richardson (ed.), *Abolition and Its Aftermath* (London, 1985), 202–24.

Une Petite Guinée: *Provision Ground and Plantation in Martinique, 1830–1848*

Dale Tomich

During the nineteenth century the working activity of slaves in the French West Indian colony of Martinique extended beyond the production of export commodities. The planters of Martinique, under constant pressure to reduce costs, obliged their slaves to produce goods for their own subsistence in their 'free' time, that is outside the time devoted to the plantation's commercial crop. Instead of receiving the legally required amounts of food and clothing, slaves were commonly given plots of marginal land and a free day on Saturday in order to produce at least a portion of their own consumption needs on their own account.[1] By encouraging slaves to work for themselves the masters could avoid the effort and expense of the large-scale cultivation of provisions. Instead, they had only to furnish some clothing, a fixed weekly ration of salt meat or fish and perhaps rum, and occasional medical care.[2]

This arrangement directly benefited the master. The expense of maintaining the slave population placed a heavy economic burden on the planter. Imported consumption goods were always expensive and their supply was often irregular, while the availability of both land and time for provision-ground cultivation emerged from the conditions of sugar production in Martinique. Planters perceived it as in their interest to spend as little money, time, or energy as possible on slave maintenance. This perception did not change appreciably at least as long as the slave trade lasted, and for many it went beyond the end of the slave trade and even of slavery itself. Allowing slaves to produce for their own subsistence from resources already at hand instead of purchasing the necessary items on the market reduced the slave-holder's cash expenses. The burden of reproduction costs was shifted directly to the slaves themselves, and they were kept usefully employed even during periods when there was no work to be done on the sugar crop. Although such practices meant that after long hours of toil in the canefields the slaves had to work still more just to secure the basic necessities of life, many planters hoped that it would give the slaves a stake in the plantation and instill in them regular habits and the virtues of work and property.[3]

While provision-ground cultivation arose from the planter's attempts to reduce costs and create an interest for the slave in the well-being of the estate, it resulted in the formation of a sphere of slave-organized activity that became necessary for the operation of the plantation system. This sphere of activity neither was simply integrated into the organization of the sugar estate, nor, as some contend, did it form an independent 'peasant breach' with a logic of its own.[4] Instead, provision-ground production and the commercial production of sugar were intimately bound to one another in ways that were simultaneously dependent and antagonistic. Although slave provision-ground cultivation was spatially and temporally separate from export commodity production, it developed within the constraints of estate agriculture: not only did final authority over the use of the land and the disposition of labour reside with the master, but the time and space for provision ground cultivation also arose from the rhythm and organization of sugar production. None the less, such activity offered an opportunity for slave initiative and self-assertion that cannot simply be deduced from its economic form. The slave provision ground became, in the expression of Maléuvrier, the Intendant of Saint Domingue, 'une petite Guinée', where slaves could organize their own activity for their own purposes.[5] These practices both shaped and were shaped by Afro-Caribbean cultural forms through which the definitions of social reality of slavery and the plantation were at once mediated and contested. Through this activity, slaves themselves created and controlled a secondary economic network which originated within the social and spatial boundaries of the plantation, but which allowed for the construction of an alternative way of life that went beyond it.[6]

Provision-ground production and the activities associated with it developed within and through the antagonistic relation between master and slave. If, for the master, the provision ground was the means to guarantee cheap labour, for the slave, it was the means to elaborate an autonomous style of life. From these conflicting perspectives evolved a continuing struggle – at times hidden, at times overt – over the division of the available labour time of the estate into export-crop production and provision-crop production. At issue was not only the amount and kind of work to be performed but also its social meaning and purpose. In this process, as much cultural as economic in both its causes and its consequences, the slaves contested the definition and meaning of time and space, labour and power.

The condition for the autonomous development of provision-ground cultivation and marketing was the slaves' appropriation of a portion of the labour time of the estate and its redefinition around their individual and collective interests, needs and values within and against the predominant slave relation. This struggle for 'free' time entailed and was conditioned by struggles to appropriate physical space and the right to property and to the disposition over their own activity. In turn, the consolidation of slave autonomy in provision-ground cultivation provided leverage to contest the conditions of staple crop production. These interrelated practices transformed and subverted the organization of labour within slavery even as they reinforced it. In this process the bonds of dependence of the slave upon the master began slowly to dissolve and the slaves' activities gradually transformed the foundations of slave society itself. The changing role and meaning of these independent activities were both cause of and response to the increased pressure for profitability on the plantation system during the first half of the nineteenth century. While these practices had existed virtually since the beginning of slavery in the colony, they assumed new importance with changing economic and political conditions and the imminent prospect of emancipation.[7]

EVOLUTION

Masters had provided slaves with small gardens to supplement their rations since the beginning of slavery in the French colonies, but the practice of giving the slaves provision-grounds and a free day each week to grow their own food dated to the introduction of sugar cane into the French Antilles by Dutch refugees from Pernambuco during the first half of the seventeenth century. The origins of this latter practice can be traced back further still to São Tomé in the sixteenth century.[8] Thus the diffusion of sugar cane entailed not merely the movement of a commodity but the spread of a whole way of life. With the appearance of sugar cultivation in the French Caribbean subsistence crops for the slaves were neglected in favour of planting cane and the 'Brazilian custom' was rapidly adopted by planters eager to reduce their expenses. Masters no longer distributed rations to their slaves. Instead, they expected slaves to provide their own food, shelter, clothing, and other material needs from the labour of their 'free' day.

But this practice failed to ensure a regular and sufficient supply of food. Slaves were often poorly nourished. Indeed, frequent food shortages prevented masters from dispensing with the distribution of rations altogether. Provisions for these rations were produced as an estate crop by compulsory gang labour under the supervision of drivers and overseers. Further, critics of the custom of free Saturdays claimed that it gave the slaves too much freedom and encouraged theft and disorder. Too many slaves neglected their gardens, preferring to hire themselves out rather than grow food during their free time. They were said to squander their earnings and rob their masters and neighbouring plantations for food. Nevertheless, despite these problems, the custom continued to spread slowly but steadily throughout the French colonies.[9]

The metropolitan authorities agreed with the critics and sought both to stop what they perceived to be the excesses resulting from the free Saturday and to ensure adequate nourishment for the slave population. The proclamation of the Royal Edict of 1685 or *Code Noir* by the metropolitan government was the first attempt to establish a uniform dietary standard for slaves in all the French colonies and to end the prevailing disorder. It sought to make masters totally responsible for the maintenance of their slaves and to prescribe standards for food, shelter and clothing to be provided to the slaves. Under the regulations the practice of individual slave gardens and free Saturdays in lieu of rations was to be suppressed in favour of regular weekly food allowances of determined composition and quantity.[10]

This edict remained the fundamental legislation governing slavery in the French colonies throughout the *ancien régime*. The distribution of slave rations seems to have been more widely practiced in Martinique than elsewhere in the French Antilles, and slaves there had the reputation of being better fed than elsewhere in the French colonies. Even so, throughout the course of the eighteenth century administrators in Martinique complained continually that the slaveowners were concerned only with sugar and, although they provided a part of the slaves' nourishment, the slaves were obliged to secure the rest on their own account. The persistent failure to regulate the slaves' diet and treatment and especially to prohibit the practice of slave provision-grounds was evidenced by the succession of declarations, edicts, ordinances, regulations and decrees, too numerous to recount, promulgated by both metropolitan and colonial authorities during the seventeenth and eighteenth centuries. Colonial officials lacked the means to enforce the regulations in a society dominated by slaveholders who jealously guarded their 'property rights', particularly when it cost them time or money. Planters expressed their preference for slave self-subsistence and their reluctance to spend money on slave maintenance, especially food, persisted throughout the *ancien régime* and into the nineteenth century. Far from dying out, the practice of free Saturdays and slave provision-grounds expanded and increasingly became an established part of colonial life.[11]

The revisions of the *Code Noir* enacted in 1784 and 1786 attempted to ameliorate the lot of slaves and reconcile the law with the growing importance of provision-grounds in the colonies. The practice of the free Saturday was still forbidden, but instead of prohibiting slave provision-grounds the new legislation recognized their existence and attempted to regulate them. It decreed that each adult slave was to receive a small plot of land to cultivate on his or her own account. The law still, however, required the distribution of rations. The produce of these plots was to supplement the *ordinaire*, not replace it. The prohibition against the substitution of the free Saturday for the legal ration was restated by the Royal Ordinance of 29 October 1828 which reformed the colonial penal code. But custom was stronger than law and ministerial instructions advised colonial authorities to tolerate the replacement of the ration by the free Saturday when it was voluntary on the part of the slave.[12]

These modifications of the earlier legislation were a step toward recognizing the realities of colonial life, but the law still regarded provision-ground cultivation only as a supplemental activity and continued to insist on the distribution of the *ordinaire* as the primary means of providing for slave maintenance. However, depressed economic conditions after 1815 made complete dependence on the ration impractical and scarcities caused planters to increase their reliance on provision-ground cultivation. In 1829 a parliamentary commission reported that before the sugar boom of 1823 most plantations in the French West Indies could only rarely provide their slaves with the *ordinaire*. Planters had to require their slaves to provide for their own subsistence and were thus deprived of a portion of their labour. Yet the commission concluded that '[a]lmost all the Negroes now received the quantity of codfish and other food prescribed by the regulations, and their masters could employ them full-time in the cultivation of sugar cane'. In his testimony before the commission, Jabrun, a planter from Guadeloupe, observed that slaves in that colony were better fed, better dressed and better housed than they had been some years previously. Nevertheless, he also noted that, although the provision-grounds normally supplemented the ration, poverty, shortage of credit and consequently difficulty in obtaining provisions still caused some planters to substitute the free Saturday for the ration. De Lavigne, a planter from Martinique, testified that in general the substitution of the free Saturday had ceased there. While this latter claim was certainly exaggerated, the evidence presented by both Jabrun and De Lavigne suggest a cyclical aspect to provision-ground cultivation. In contrast to periods of low sugar prices when land and labour could be given over to provision-grounds, with the high prices of the sugar boom of the 1820s many planters may have devoted their attention entirely to sugar cultivation and purchased necessary

provisions. Undoubtedly a variety of individual strategies were possible and, while continuous cultivation of provision-grounds may be
demonstrated for the colony as a whole, it may not necessarily be the
case for individual estates.[13]

Despite the shortcomings and abuses of free Saturdays and slave
provision-grounds and the repeated attempts to suppress them, the
scale of these activities grew steadily. By the nineteenth century they
had become increasingly central to the functioning of the colonial
economy. During the 1830s masters, with few exceptions, encouraged
their slaves to grow their own foodstuffs, and the substitution of free
Saturdays for the legally prescribed rations had become widespread.
Slaves were given as much land as they could cultivate. They both
produced and marketed crops without supervision and were so successful that the colony became dependent upon their produce for a
substantial portion of its food. As one observer stated in the 1840s, 'the
plantations which produce foodstuffs [*habitations vivrières*] and the
slaves who cultivate gardens more than guarantee that the colony is
supplied with local produce'. Measures prohibiting these activities
were disregarded with the common consent of both masters and slaves.
Enforcement would not only have inhibited the efforts of the slave
cultivators, but could also have reduced the island's food supply.[14]

By the 1840s authorities both in France and the colony no longer
regarded these practices as threats to order but rather felt that they
contributed to social harmony. The reports of local officials stressed
the social benefits of independent cultivation by slaves. One of them
expressed the opinion that the free Saturday was an 'effective means of
giving [the slave] the taste for property and well-being, and consequently, to make them useful craftsmen and agriculturalists desirous of
family ties'. For another, writing in 1842, it meant nothing less than
bringing slaves up to the standards of the civilized world:

> But the slaves, for whom the custom of free Saturdays is estab-
> lished, prefer it to the ration because they work on their own
> account and find some profit from that state of affairs. It is clear
> evidence that man, even though a slave, has an interest in money
> and likes to enjoy the fruits of his labours while freely disposing of
> that which belongs to him. The black is forced to enter into types
> of social transactions that can only serve as a means of civilizing
> him.

This 'civilizing' aspect was seen to be especially important because of
the imminent prospect of emancipation. The report continued: 'In this
regard, the custom of the free Saturday must be preferred to the legally

sanctioned ration because, beyond everything else, it is a road toward free labour'.[15]

The reforms of the July Monarchy were a decisive step in the recognition of existing practices in the colonies and prepared the way for emancipation. The law of 18 and 19 July 1845, known as the Mackau law, allowed the substitution of provision-grounds for the *ordinaire*. While the land itself remained the property of the master, its produce belonged to the slave, and the state recognized the latter's legal personality and right to chattel property. The Mackau law confirmed and regularized what was already a customary practice and gave it legal sanction. In the words of its authors, '[t]he law only recognizes a state that has long existed in practice and makes it a right to the great advantage of the black and without detriment to the master'. These legally enforcable rights were less precarious and dependent upon the whim of the proprietor than the previous custom. Slaves could now assert their purposes with the support of the colonial state. The authorities saw in these practices not the source of disorder but the means to regulate slavery and provide a transition to free labour. The purpose of the Mackau law was to ease the transition to freedom by giving slaves skills, property and therefore a stake in society. In the words of one local official,

> [o]n the eve of complete emancipation, it is the interest of the masters to see the taste for labour and the spirit of economy develop in the slaves. Now, without property there is no industrious activity. It is only for oneself that one has the heart to work. Without property there is no economy. One does not economize for another.[16]

INTEGRATION AND ADAPTATION

According to French abolitionist Victor Schoelcher, the provision-ground was the principal source of well-being for slaves in Martinique under the July Monarchy. Indeed, its importance grew as the crisis of the sugar industry and mounting indebtedness limited the planters' resources. Customarily, slaves who were given half a day free a week were allotted only half a ration, while those who received a full day were to provide food for themselves. In addition, Sundays, rest periods and evenings during the week belonged to the slaves and could be devoted to subsistence activities. Schoelcher recorded that on a great number of plantations in Martinique such arrangements had become a sort of exchange between the master and his slaves. 'This transaction', he wrote, 'is very favorable for the master who no longer has capital to lay out to ensure the supply of provisions. And it is accepted with good will by the black who in working Saturday and Sunday in his garden derives great benefits'.[17]

With few exceptions, masters encouraged their slaves to grow their own foodstuffs wherever possible. The practice of giving Saturdays to the slaves appears to have been far more common than the distribution of the *ordinaire* as the means of providing subsistence for slaves. Although some of the most prosperous planters preferred to give rations to their slaves, provision-grounds were almost universal and appear to have existed even where the *ordinaire* was distributed. For example, according to one report, in Lamentin, one of the major sugar-growing regions of the colony, free Saturdays were denied on almost all the plantations and slaves received the legal allotments. Nevertheless, the slaves kept gardens and drew considerable revenues from sales to local markets. Not surprisingly, the distribution of clothing allowances was more widely practiced than that of food rations, although the public prosecutors [*procureurs*] reported that many planters expected their slaves to provide their own clothing as well as their food from the income of their gardens. This practice was especially widespread among the less prosperous planters, particularly in the poorer southern *arrondissement* of Fort Royal. Only wealthy planters could afford to clothe their slaves. Others could do so only when the harvest was good, if at all. Several public prosecutors objected to planters making the slaves provide their own clothing and admonished the slaveholders to stop the practice. Thus, while there were diverse combinations and possibilities of conditions of subsistence, provision-grounds and free Saturdays had become a common experience for the majority of slaves in Martinique during the nineteenth century. These slaves provided for their own maintenance, in whole or in part, through independent labour beyond their toil in the canefields.[18]

The successful development of autonomous provision-ground culti-vation and marketing in Martinique depended upon the initiative of the enslaved. It was the result of slaves adapting to New World conditions and acquiring the skills and habits necessary to produce and market these crops. At least one contemporary observer stressed the import-ance of cultural adaptation by the slaves in developing subsistence agriculture and also suggested that slave provision-grounds became more prevalent after the slave trade ended in the early 1830s. 'Thus, previously, the progress of the population did not take place in accordance with the laws of nature', he noted.

Each year, the irregular introduction of considerable numbers of blacks increased the possibility of a scarce food supply in the country. These new arrivals in the colonies, knowing neither the soil, the climate, nor the special agriculture of the Antilles, could not count on themselves for their support. It was necessary to provide sufficient and regular nourishment for them, but they had no skills to contribute. Thus, the proprietors were quite properly compelled to plant a certain amount of provisions since their slaves did not know how or were unable to plant enough ...

He continued,

The slaves of today have less need of constant tutelage than previously. They are able to supply themselves without depending upon the generosity of their masters. The latter hardly plant provisions at all any more because the slaves plant well beyond the amount that is necessary for consumption ...'

Indeed, nineteenth-century accounts indicate that the slaves by and large preferred to have an extra day to themselves and raise their own provisions rather than receive an allowance of food from the master. 'This practice', observed one government official,

is completely to the advantage of the slave who wants to work. A day spent by him cultivating his garden, or in some other manner, will bring him more than the value of the nourishment the law prescribes for him. I will add that there is no *atelier* which does not prefer this arrangement to the execution of the edict [*Code Noir*]. Once it has been set, it would be dangerous for the master to renounce it.[19]

The slaves who wanted to plant provisions were given as much land as they could work. These plots were usually on the uncultivated lands on the margins of the estate, often scattered in the hills above the cane-fields. However, both De Cassagnac, a local planter, and Schoelcher write that some planters in the 1840s allowed caneland to be used for provisions as a form of crop rotation. When the sugar cane had exhausted the soil in a field, the slaves were permitted to plant provisions there until the land was again fit for cane. The provision grounds were then shifted to other fields. (According to historian Gabriel Debien, larger grounds which were located away from the slave quarters only appeared after 1770, but these were still intended to supplement the rations provided by the master rather than furnish the main items of the slave diet. The staples of the slave diet – manioc, potatoes, and yams – were grown by the master in the fields belonging to the plantation.) The plots allotted to slaves were frequently quite extensive, as much as one or two acres according to Schoelcher. All available sources agree that the slave provision grounds were well kept. Produce was abundant, and the land was not allowed to stand idle. Manioc, the principal source of nourishment of the slave population, was harvested as often as four times a year. Besides manioc, the slaves raised bananas, potatoes, yams, and other vegetables on these plots.[20]

In addition to the provision grounds, there were also small gardens in the yards surrounding the slave cabins. They were intended to supplement the weekly ration, not replace it, and all the slaves, including those who received the *ordinaire*, had them. In these gardens slaves grew sorrel, squash, cucumbers from France and Guinea, green peppers, hot peppers, calabash vines, okra and perhaps some tobacco. They also planted fruit trees and, if the master permitted, kept a few chickens there as well.[21]

Of course, not all slaves were willing or able to endure the burden of extra work in the provision grounds. Infants, the aged, the infirm, expectant mothers or those nursing children – all of whom could not provide for themselves – received a food allowance from the master, even on the plantations where the slaves grew their own foodstuffs. Also included among the non-participants were those slaves who refused to raise a garden. In Fort Royal, a public prosecutor wrote, '[o]nly the lazy receive a ration and they are almost ashamed of it'. Of these 'lazy' slaves, Schoelcher commented:

> We do not want to deny, however, that there are many Negroes who show a great indifference to the benefit of free Saturdays. It is necessary to force them to work for themselves on that day. It does not surprise us that beings, saturated with disgust and struck by malediction, are little concerned to improve their lot during the moments of respite that are given to them. Instead, they prefer to surrender to idleness or become intoxicated to the point of delirium from the melancholy agitation of their African dances.

The free Saturday, while generally received enthusiastically by the slaves, was not universally accepted. For many slaves it simply meant more work, and they refused. They withdrew their voluntary co-operation and threw the burden of maintenance back on the master. De Cassagnac expressed surprise that on many plantations, if the slaves were given the free Saturday, they would not work. They had, in his view, to be treated like children and be forced to work for themselves. It was necessary to have a driver lead them to the gardens and watch them as carefully as when they were working for the estate.[22]

But compulsion was not usually necessary, and often individual planters went to great lengths to support the efforts of their slaves.

Sieur Telliam-Maillet, who managed the 'Ceron' plantation in Diamant ploughed his slaves' provision-grounds. Even though he supplied the *ordinaire*, M. de Delite-Loture, who owned nearly 300 slaves in the *quartier* of Sainte Anne, bought or rented land in the highlands of Rivière Pilote which he cleared so that his slaves could work it for themselves. Each week he had them taken nearly two leagues from the plantation to these gardens and he paid for the transport of their produce as well. Schoelcher reports that in some *quartiers* the masters provided the slaves who worked such gardens with tools, carts, mules and a *corvée* of workers, and the masters and the slave cultivators divided the harvest in half. Other masters considered such an arrangement beneath their dignity and simply abandoned the land to the slaves.[23]

For even the most industrious slave dependence on the planter was inescapable. As Schoelcher remarked, 'the greater or lesser wealth of the slaves depends a great deal on the benevolence of the master'. Whichever mode of providing for the the slaves was adopted, one inspection report noted, 'their nourishment is assured everywhere, and the master is always ready ... to come to the aid of the slave when the latter has need of him'. Indeed, seasonal fluctuations could require the master to come to the assistance of his slaves. 'In years of great drought', De Cassagnac wrote, 'subsistence crops do not grow. Then planters who previously gave the free Saturday once again give the *ordinaire*. Those are disastrous years ..'.[24]

Even at best, the slaves who produced their own provisions were exposed to risk and uncertainty. They were generally given land of inferior quality that was incapable of supporting sugar or coffee. At times the planters deprived them of their free day under various pretexts. If for some reason they fell ill and could not work their food supply was jeopardized. Drought or bad weather might make cultivation impossible. The prospect of theft and disorder was then increased and, at the extreme, the physical well-being of the labour force was threatened.[25]

Nevertheless, provision-ground cultivation could be advantageous for the slave. Access to this property meant that the slaves' consumption was no longer entirely dependent on the economic condition of the master. Rather, slaves could use their free time and the produce of their gardens to improve their standard of living. They demonstrated exceptional initiative and skill and used the opportunities presented to them to secure at least relative control over their subsistence and a degree of independence from the master. According to one contemporary estimate, the incentive provided by the gardens doubled slave output. With the free day and the other free time that could be husbanded during rest periods and after tasks were finished on work days, slaves could produce beyond their immediate subsistence needs. The sale of this produce in the towns and cities allowed slaves to improve both the quantity and quality of goods available to them and to satisfy tastes and desires that the master could not supply. Thus improvement in the slaves' well-being was due to their own effort, not any amelioration of the regime.[26]

The slaves developed market networks that were an important feature of the economic and social life in Martinique, and the colony came to rely on the produce of the slave gardens for a substantial portion of its food. Sunday was the major market day in the towns; however, smaller markets were held on other days. Important market towns such as the ones at Lamentin, François, Trinité and Robert attracted slaves from all parts of the island and brought them into contact with the world beyond the plantation. Soleau, a visitor to the island in 1835, describes the Lamentin market:

> This town is one of the most frequently visited by the slaves of the colony. It has a fairly large market where they come to sell their produce on Sunday. I have been told that the number of slaves that gather there is often as high as five or six thousand. I passed through there that day while going to the quartier of Robert, and encountered many blacks on the road who were going to the town. All were carrying something that they were doubtlessly going to sell – manioc flour, potatoes, yams, poultry, etc.

An astonishing variety of goods were exchanged at the town markets. In addition to manioc, fruits, vegetables, yams, fresh or salted fish, animals and slave handicrafts, these included manufactured goods such as shoes, dry goods, porcelain, crystal, perfume, jewellery and furniture. Barter undoubtedly played a large part in these exchanges, especially in local markets, but the money economy was significant and prices were set in major towns for the main articles of trade. The scale of exchange at these town markets was so great that they caused the urban merchants to complain. But their protests had little effect, for, as one planter noted, the town markets were a great resource for the interior of the island.[27]

The Sunday market was as much a social event as an occasion for exchanging goods. Slaves went to town to attend mass, to meet friends from other parts of the island, drink tafia, smoke, eat roast corn, exchange news and gossip, and perhaps to dance, sing or gamble. It was an opportunity for display, and the slaves wore their best. An observer painted a striking picture of the appearance of the slaves at the Lamentin market:

These slaves are almost always very well dressed and present the exterior signs of material well-being. The men have trousers, shirts, vests, and hats of oilskin or straw. The women have skirts of Indian cotton, white blouses, and scarves, some of which are luxurious, as well as earrings, pins and even some chains of gold.

According to Soleau the signs of prosperity presented by slaves of Martinique on market day were unusual in the Caribbean and even in rural France:

> One thing struck me that I have never seen in Cayenne, Surinam, or Demerara. It is the cleanliness and the luxury of the clothing of the slaves that I encountered. The lazy, having nothing to sell, remained on the plantations. In France, generally, the peasants, except for their shoes, were not better dressed on Sunday and did not wear such fine material.

The colourful and bustling markets punctuated the drudgery and isolation of plantation life. Slaves from town and country, young and old, male and female, as well as freedmen, sailors, merchants, planters, anyone who wanted to buy or sell, mingled in the crowds. These markets offered incentives to slaves and enabled them to improve the material conditions of life as well as to acquire skills, knowledge and social contacts that allowed them to increase their independence, assert their individuality and vary the texture of their lives. Their initiatives developed new economic and social patterns and mobilized productive forces that otherwise would have remained dormant.[28]

APPROPRIATION

While provision grounds and free Saturdays never ceased to serve the interests of the slaveowner, they were not simply a functional adaptation to the requirements of the plantation economy. Rather, they form what Roger Bastide describes as a 'niche' within slavery which allowed collective self-expression by the slaves – a niche where Afro-Caribbean culture could develop. The slaves had complete responsibility for the provision grounds and were able to organize their own activity there without supervision. The use of these parcels and their product was not simply a narrow economic activity, but was integrated into broader cultural patterns. The work of preparing the soil, planting, cultivating, harvesting and the disposition of the product were organized through ritual, kinship and mutual obligation. The provision grounds were important for aspects of slave life as diverse as kinship, religious belief, cuisine and healing practices. There kin were buried, and singing, dancing and story-telling took place. These activities provided an avenue for the slaves to exercise decision making and demonstrate self-worth that would have been otherwise closed off by slavery. But, except for Schoelcher's vague comment that the slaves cultivated their gardens 'communally', there is little detailed information as to how they organized their activities. This lack of documentation is perhaps mute testimony to the genuine autonomy that the slaves enjoyed in the conduct of these activities.[29]

The provision grounds formed a nodal point within the social relations of slavery which allowed slave practices, values and interests to emerge and develop and to assume autonomous forms of organization and expression. Long before the promulgation of the Mackau law, slaves established rights and prerogatives with regard not only to the produce of the land but also to the provision grounds and gardens themselves. Masters were compelled to recognize these claims. 'The masters no longer acknowledge any rights over the gardens of the *atelier*. The slave is the sovereign master over the terrain that is conceded to him', admitted the Colonial Council of Martinique. 'This practice has become a custom for the slaves who regard it as a right which cannot be taken from them without the possibility of disrupting the discipline and good order of the *ateliers*', confirmed one official. Slaves regarded the provision grounds as their own. When they died, the garden and its produce was passed on to their relatives. 'They pass them on from father to son, from mother to daughter, and, if they do not have any children, they bequeath them to their nearest kin or even their friends', wrote Schoelcher. Often, if no relatives remained on the estate, kinsmen came from other plantations to receive their inheritance with the consent of the master. Here, as elsewhere, the autonomous kinship organization of the slave community served as a counterpoint to the economic rationality of the plantation, and the master was obliged to respect its claims.[30]

Slaves defended their rights even at the masters' expense, and there was often a subtle game of give and take between the two. While travelling through the *quartier* of Robert, Schoelcher was surprised to find two small patches of manioc in the midst of a large, well-tended canefield. The proprietor explained that the slaves planted the manioc when the field had been abandoned. When he wanted to cultivate the field he offered to buy the crop, but they demanded an exorbitant price. The master then called upon the other slaves of the estate to set a fair price, but this too was rejected by the slaves who had planted the manioc. 'I'll have to wait six or seven months until that damned manioc is ripe', the proprietor complained. Another planter, M. Latuillerie of Lamentin, upon returning from a long trip, found that his slaves had abandoned the plots allotted to them in favour of his canefields. He could not simply reclaim his land. Instead, he first had to agree to give the occupants another field. Schoelcher also observed large mango trees in the middle of canefields which stunted the cane plants in their shadow. The masters would have cut them down, but they remained standing because they were bequeathed to some yet unborn slave. He noted,

> [t]here are some planters who do not have fruit trees on their plantations because tradition establishes that such and such a tree belongs to such and such a Negro, and they [the planters] have little hope of ever enjoying them because the slave bequeaths his tree just like the rest of his property.[31]

The elaboration of autonomous provision-ground cultivation remained intertwined with and dependent upon the larger organization of plantation labour not only spatially, but temporally. The practice of the free Saturday transformed the character of the working day in the French Caribbean. An examination of this custom calls attention to the historical processes through which the cultural definitions of work and its relation to the larger matrix of plantation life were contested. As the slaves became socialized into the routine of plantation labour they were able to lay claim to the free Saturday and use it for their own ends. They felt that they had a right to such 'free' time and resisted any encroachment upon it. According to the report of one public prosecutor published in 1844:

> It would be almost impossible for a planter to take even a little bit of time belonging to his slave, even if the authorities ignored the situation. There is a spirit of resistance among the slaves that prevents anyone from threatening what they consider to be their rights.

Another official emphasized:

> There would be discontent if the proprietors took away the free Saturday to give the provisions prescribed by the edict ... The Negroes prefer this method which assures them of an extra day each week. Everywhere that it has not been adopted the blacks desire it and beg for it. To try to abolish it where it was once been established would be to provoke disorder and revolt.[32]

The slaves effectively appropriated a part of the disposable labour time as their own. In practice, time on the plantation became divided between time belonging to the master and time belonging to the slaves. The time available for export commodity production was restricted and the master had to bargain with the slaves. Time became a kind of currency, and a complex system of accounting emerged. If masters found that they needed slaves on a Saturday or at another time when the slaves had been exempted from labour, such work was voluntary and slaves were generally compensated for their services. Often masters indemnified slaves with an equivalent amount of time rather than money. It was reported that the slaves on one plantation were made to work on Sunday during the harvest but were given the following Monday off. (This report added that the planter would be warned that this change was not in accord with religious rites and the regular habits of the slaves.) On the infrequent occasions when the master of another plantation needed the labour of his slaves on a free Saturday or a Sunday for some pressing work, they were given an equivalent amount of time on a weekday. A public prosecutor reported that this planter kept a precise account of the extra time that the slaves put in and indemnified them scrupulously.[33]

Thus time belonging to the slaves was not only distinguished from that belonging to the masters but also opposed to it. At the extreme, the former encroached upon the latter. For slaves the time separate from work was a sphere of autonomous activity; it was 'free' time where they could dispose of their energies as they saw fit and within which they created a community organized around their beliefs, values and collective action. Their use of this free time could become subversive of plantation discipline. (According to Monk Lewis, a Jamaican planter, the slaves on his plantation referred to their free Saturday as 'playday'.) This was especially apparent in the case of the slaves' nocturnal activities. Although prohibited by law (in earlier times the *Code Noir* prescribed whipping and branding and, for repeated offenses, even death), slaves enjoyed considerable freedom of movement at night. 'During the week, when work is finished', noted one observer

> the slaves leave the plantation and run to those where they have women ... The liberty of the night, that is, the right to use their nights as they wish, is a veritable plague. With this type of liberty, the Negroes have every means to indulge in their debauchery, to commit thefts, to smuggle, to repair to their secret meetings, and to prepare and take their revenge. And what good work can be expected during the day from people who stay out and revel the whole night? When the masters are asked why the slaves are allowed such a fatal liberty, they reply that they cannot take it away from them.

De Cassagnac wrote that '[f]or the blacks the night is a moment of supreme and incomparable sweetness that the whites will never understand'. Night provided an opportunity for the exercise of individual freedom and collective self-expression away from the watchful eye of the authorities. It became the occasion for dancing, music and religious rites – activities that expressed values antithetical to the subordination of life to work and the rejection of the role of sober, industrious and self-regulated labour desired by the planters. If the slaves had learned to adapt to the exigencies of plantation labour, they none the less refused to reduce themselves to mere instruments of production.[34]

Thus the free Saturday was important as the appropriation of a quantity of time and as the qualitative transformation of the meaning of that time. Through their activity slaves were able, in some limited way, to define the nature of freedom for themselves. 'Free' time became free for the slave and not merely a period when sugar was not being produced. Its appropriation provided a base for the assertion of the slaves' purposes, needs and cultural forms in other aspects of plantation life including the organization of work and the composition of the working day. Thus the appropriated time became significant both because of its consequences for the material reproduction of the enslaved population and as an arena in which slaves were able to contest the conditions of domination and exploitation and the conceptions of social life imposed by the plantation regime. While slaves regarded 'free' time as a resource to be protected and if possible expanded, masters had to contain the slaves' demands within the limits of economic efficiency and social order. In the development of this process the historical trajectory and limits of slave production and the master–slave relation can be traced.

Instead of separating the direct producers from the means of subsistence, slavery provided them with the means of producing a livelihood. While slaves gained access to the use of property and had the opportunity to improve their material conditions of life, the price of subsistence was work beyond that required for sugar production. With these developments, the time devoted to the slaves' maintenance became separate from commodity production and a de facto distinction between time belonging to the master and time belonging to the slave was created.

The planters' response to the slaves' appropriation of the free Saturday was to transform their initiative into an instrument of labour discipline and social control. During the 1830s planters in Martinique implemented a system of task work to create an inducement for slaves to work and guarantee the performance of a given amount of labour during the day. Through experience, planters were able to calculate for each of the different types of work to be done on the plantation how much the average slave could do in a day without being overworked.

Every morning each slave in the gang was assigned their daily task based on this customary amount of labour. The slaves could do their daily quota of work as they liked and were free to dispose of the time remaining after its completion as they wished. Under the task system slaves might gain several hours each day which could be spent in the cultivation of their own gardens or in some other employment. The slaves thus had the opportunity to improve their condition, while slaveowners obtained the required amount of labour. On the other hand, slaves who did not use the time well had to spend the whole day working in the masters' fields in order to complete the required task. The punishment was proportional to the effort, or lack thereof, and if the slaves' failure to meet their assignment was too great their free day could be jeopardized.[35]

Task work could only function when the slave population had sufficiently assimilated the routine of plantation labour to respond to its incentives. For self-regulation to replace external domination slaves had to understand and accept the rhythm of work, organization of time and system of rewards and punishments that characterized the plantation regime. Only then could the notion of free time appear as a reward to the slave. Only if the slaves formed a concept of their self-interest and appropriated time for themselves within this framework could the task system operate and the larger appropriation of the slaves' activity by the master take place. Such slave initiative and planter response contributed to the mutation of the relations of work. Once slaves had a recognized interest, their relation to the master could no longer rest upon absolute domination and authority, but instead had to admit bargaining and negotiation between interested parties – however unequal and antagonistic their relationship. Thus implementation of task work marked a further transformation of the master–slave relation; it bears witness to the adaptation of the African slave to the American environment which was both cause and effect of this change.[36]

Provision-ground cultivation and task work suggest the limits of pure coercion as a means of enforcing labour discipline. Their success was dependent upon the integration of the enslaved population into the productive and social processes of the slave plantation. For these measures to work, both master and slave had to recognize the existence of certain privileges and at least a limited degree of independence for the slave. Paradoxically, however, both master and slave became more closely tied to the maintenance of these privileges. The possible range of action of each was restricted, and the character, if not the content, of labour relations was altered decisively.

Task work was thus an expression of the social limit of the slave relation. While planters might influence individual behaviour and set the parameters of the action of the group through the systematic manipulation of rewards and punishments, such measures merely adapted the slaves to the existing organization of production with a greater or lesser degree of enthusiasm. The task system guaranteed the completion of a minimum amount of work and perhaps reduced the costs of supervision but it did not alter the composition of the working day or increase surplus production. The self-interest created by this system was not a reward earned through commodity-producing activity but was formed outside of this work and through a release from it. After slaves completed their predetermined task they were free to look after their own affairs; literally, they were free to tend their own gardens. Such a system might provide slaves with an incentive to give a bit more of themselves but it demonstrates the incapacity of slavery to create individual self-interest in production itself. Rather, individual self-interest and identification with the job and the plantation were created not in commodity production but in social reproduction. The economy of time and labour was dissolved into the maintenance of a given body of labourers on the one hand and the regular performance of a predetermined quantity of labour on the other: it thus resolved itself into a social–political question as the master–slave relation was challenged from within.

The slaves' appropriation of the free Saturday and their autonomous elaboration of the activities associated with it had far-reaching consequences for the development of slavery in the French West Indies and helped to shape the historical limits of the slave system in Martinique. It was an initiative by a population that, over the course of its historical experience, had learned to adapt to the labour routine, discipline and organization of time of the slave plantation and confronted slavery *within* its own relations and processes. The result was simultaneously to strengthen and weaken the slave system. On the one hand the labouring population became more effectively integrated into the relations and processes of slave production and more responsive to its rewards and punishments. The operating expenses of the plantation were reduced and a greater surplus was available to the planter. On the other hand slaves were able to appropriate aspects of these processes and establish a degree of control over their own subsistence and reproduction. They claimed rights to property and disposition over time and labor that masters were forced to recognize, and they were able to resist infringements upon those rights. While it meant more work for the slaves, they were able substantially to improve their material well-being and increase their independence from the master. They restricted the master's capacity to exploit labor and presented a fixed obstacle to surplus production. The amount of labour time at the disposition of the planter was limited and the slaves acquired a means of resisting the intensification of work at the very moment that the transformation of the world sugar market demanded higher levels of productivity and greater exploitation of labour from French West Indian plantations.

The very ability of masters to compel the participation of slaves in the new conditions of life and labour and the complexity and originality of the slaves' response altered the character of the master–slave relation. Within the context of continuing domination, exploitation and material scarcity, new forms, meanings and goals of social action emerged alongside older ones and became the focal points of a new constellation of conditions, needs and capacities on both sides. The slaves' assertion of rights to provision-grounds and free time and the autonomous use of these resources reduced their dependence on the master and undermined his authority. Custom, consent and accommodation assumed greater weight in the conduct of daily life where coercion had prevailed. The acquisition of skills and property and the establishment of economic and social networks enabled the enslaved to realize important material and psychological gains. The slaves thus began to fashion an alternative way of life that played an important role both in eroding the slave regime and in creating the conditions for a transition to a new form of social and economic organization. Slave struggles for autonomy and planter efforts to maintain their domination developed the slave relation to its fullest extent and created within slavery both the embryo of post-emancipation class structure and the conditions for the transition to 'free labour'.[37]

Significantly, the autonomous provision-ground cultivation and marketing elaborated within slavery provided freedpeople with an alternative to plantation labour after emancipation. These activities played an important role in helping the former slaves to resist the new encroachments of plantation agriculture and shape a new relation between labour and capital. The very practices that planters had encouraged during slavery now incurred their wrath. Carlyle scorned Quashee and his pumpkin, but far from representing the 'lazy Negro' it was a testimony to the capacity of the Afro-Caribbean population to learn, adapt, create and articulate an alternative conception of their needs despite the harshness of slavery. Probably few could escape the plantation entirely after emancipation but for the great majority of freed slaves the existence of provision-ground cultivation and marketing networks enabled them to struggle effectively over the conditions of their labour. The skills, resources and associations formed through these activities during slavery were decisive in enabling freed people to secure control over their own conditions of reproduction and to establish an independent bargaining position *vis-á-vis* the planters after slavery.[38]

The immediate consequence of emancipation in Martinique, as throughout the French and British Caribbean, was the withdrawal of labour – particularly the labour of women and children – from the plantation sector, and struggles with the planters over time, wages and conditions of work in which the labouring population asserted its independence and initiative. The success of these efforts forced a new relation of production on the plantation system itself as the planters attempted to recapture the labour of the emancipated population or find a substitute for it under conditions that guaranteed profitability. This resulted in the formation of new coercive forms of labour extraction in which the laboring population maintained control over subsistence activities and petty commodity production to one degree or another. Seen from this perspective the reconstruction of the post-emancipation plantation system and the transition from one form of coerced labour to another were not the inevitable results of unfolding capitalist rationality. Rather, it was a process whose outcome was problematic, requiring violence and compulsion to reassert control over labour in the face of material and social resources acquired by the labouring population while still enslaved. It is best understood as the product of the contradictory relation between production and social reproduction within the relations of slavery and of the struggle between masters and slaves over alternative purposes, conceptions of needs and modes of organization of social and material life.

NOTES

1. Some planters gave only half a day on Saturday and continued to supply a part of the slaves' rations themselves. In addition, slaves in Martinique commonly had Sundays free.
2. A. Soleau, *Notes sur les Guyanes françaises (Cayenne, Surinam, Demerary, la Martinique, la Guadeloupe)* (Paris, 1835), 9–10; France, Ministère de la Marine et des Colonies, *Commission instituée par décision royale du 26 mai 1840, pour l'examen des questions relatives à l'esclavage et à la constitution politique des colonies* (Paris, 1840, 1841, 1842, 1843), 205.
3. Félix Renouard, Marquis de Sainte Croix, *Statistique de la Martinique* (Paris, 1822), 2: 105.
4. Ciro Flammarion S. Cardoso, *Agricultura, Escravidão e Capitalismo* (Petrópolis, 1979); Tadeusz Lepkowski, *Haiti* (Havana, 1968), 2 vols.
5. Cardoso, *Agricultura, Escravidão e Capitalismo*, 145.
6. These simultaneously complementary and antagonistic processes crystallized in the practices and embryonic property relations that Sidney Mintz has described as the formation of a 'proto-peasantry'. He uses this term to characterize those activities that allowed the subsequent adaptation to a peasant way of life by people while they

were still enslaved. As Mintz emphasizes, the formation of this proto-peasantry is both a mode of response and a mode of resistance by the enslaved to the conditions imposed upon them by the plantation system. Thus, it is not a traditional peasantry attacked from the outside by commodity production, the market economy, and the colonial state, but rather it is formed from within the processes of historical development of slavery and the plantation system. See Sidney W. Mintz, *Caribbean Transformations* (Chicago, 1974); 'Slavery and the Rise of Peasantries', *Historical Reflections* 6 (1979), 213–42; 'Currency Problems in Eighteenth Century Jamaica and Gresham's Law', in Robert A. Manners (ed.), *Process and Pattern in Culture* (Chicago, 1964), 248–65; Sidney W. Mintz and Douglas Hall, *The Origins of the Jamaican Internal Marketing System*, Yale University Publications in Anthropology No. 57 (New Haven, Conn., 1960), 3–26.

7. Walter Rodney, 'Plantation Society in Guyana', *Review*, 4 (1981), 643–66; Sidney W. Mintz, 'Descrying the Peasantry', ibid., 6 (1982), 209–25.

8. Gabriel Debien, *Les esclaves aux Antilles françaises (XVIIe-XVIIIe siècles)* (Basse-Terre; Fort-de-France, 1974), 178–9; Marian Malowist, 'Les débuts du système de plantations dans la période des grandes découvertes', *Africana Bulletin*, 10 (1969), 9–30.

9. Debien, *Les esclaves aux Antilles françaises*, 178–86; Lucien Peytraud, *L'Esclavage aux Antilles françaises avant 1789 d'après des documents inédits des Archives Coloniales* (Pointe-à-Pitre, Guadeloupe, 1973), 217.

10. The *Code Noir* legally prescribed the weekly food ration for an adult at two and a half pots of manioc flour (1 pot = 2.75 livres) or seven and a half livres of cassava and three livres of fish or two livres of salt beef. This allotment was known as the *ordinaire*. The master was also obligated to provide the slave with two changes of clothes per year, one change to be distributed every six months. The men were to receive a shirt, trousers and a hat, while the women were given a shirt, skirt, scarf and hat. Children received only a shirt. In addition, each individual was given one cloth jacket each year. France, Ministère de la Marine et des Colonies, *Exposé général des résultats du patronage des esclaves dans les colonies françaises* (Paris, 1844), 177, 219–25; Debien, *Les esclaves aux Antilles françaises*, 176–7, 181, 183–5; Antoine Gisler, *L'Esclavage aux Antilles françaises (XVIIe - XIXe siècle). Contribution au problème de l'esclavage* (Fribourg, 1965), 23–5, 35–8; Peytraud, *L'Esclavage aux Antilles françaises*, 216–24.

11. Debien, *Les esclaves aux Antilles françaises*, 176–7, 181, 183–6, 215; Gisler, *Les Esclaves aux Antilles françaises*, 23–5, 35–8; Peytraud, *Les Esclaves aux Antilles françaises*, 216–24; Ministère de la Marine, *Commission du 26 mai 1840*, 205.

12. Victor Schoelcher, *Des Colonies françaises. Abolition immédiate de l'esclavage* (Paris, 1842), 8–9; Ministère de la Marine, *Exposé général des résultats due patronage*, 177, 267; Louis-Philippe May, *Le Mercier de la Rivière (1719–1801)* (Aix-Marseille, 1975), 1; 119–21.

13. France, Ministère du Commerce et des Manufactures, *Commission formée avec l'approbation du Roi... pour l'examen de certaines questions de législation commerciale. Enquête sur les sucres* (Paris, 1829), 23, 52, 67, 156, 248.

14. Sainte Croix, *Statistique*, 2: 105; P. Lavollée, *Notes sur les cultures et la production de la Martinique et de la Guadeloupe* (Paris, 1841), 10; Ministère de la Marine, *Exposé général des résultats du patronage*, 182–7; *Commission du 26 mai 1840*, 205.

15. Ministère de la Marine, *Exposé général des résultats du patronage*, 183–4, 290.

16. Ibid., 177–88, 288–91, 332–3; Ministère de la Marine, *Commission du 26 mai 1840*, 205–6, 208–9.

17. Schoelcher, *Abolition immédiate*, 11; Lavollée, *Notes sur les cultures*, 123.

18. Ministère de la Marine, *Exposé général des résultats du patronage*, 89–90, 182–5, 177, 219–25, 288–91, 332–3; France. Archives Nationales – Section Outre Mer [herafter ANSOM], *Généralités*, Carton, 9, Dossier 99, De Moges, 'Mémoire'.

19. Ministère de la Marine, *Exposé général des résultats du patronage*, 104–5, 180–88, 290; ANSOM, *Généralités*, Carton 144, Dossier 1221, 'Éxécution de l'ordonnance royale', 2: 40, 51.

20. Debien, *Les Esclaves aux Antilles françaises*, 178–91, 205–7; Ministère de la Marine, *Exposé général des résultats du patronage*, 182–7, 290; *Commission du 26 mai 1840*, 206; Adolphe Granier de Cassagnac, *Voyage aux Antilles* (Paris, 1842), 174–5; Schoelcher, *Abolition immédiate*, 9–12; Lavollée, *Notes sur les cultures*, 10; Sainte Croix, *Statistique*, 2: 105.

21. Ministère de la Marine, *Exposé général des résultats du patronage*, 180–88, 290; Schoelcher, *Abolition immédiate*, 9–13; ANSOM, *Généralitiés*, Carton 144, Dossier 1221, 'Éxécution de l'ordonnance royale', 2: 40, 51; Debien, *Les esclaves aux Antilles françaises*, 178–91; Mintz, *Caribbean Transformations*, 225–50.

22. De Cassagnac, *Voyage aux Antilles* 176; Schoelcher, *Abolition immédiate*, 12; Anon. [Collins], *Practical Rules for the Management and Medical Treatment of Negro Slaves in the Sugar Colonies* (London, 1811), 87–94.

23. De Cassagnac, *Voyage aux Antilles*, 174–5; Schoelcher, *Abolition immédiate*, 12; Ministère de la Marine, *Exposé général des résultats du patronage*, 182–5, 288–91; 332–3; ANSOM, *Généralitiés*, Carton 9, Dossier 99, De Moges, 'Mémoire'.

24. Ministère de la Marine, *Exposé général des résultats du patronage*, 180–88, 290; Schoelcher, *Abolition immédiate*, 12–13, De Cassagnac, *Voyage aux Antilles*, 174–5; ANSOM, *Martinique*, Carton 7, Dossier 83, Dupotêt à Ministre de la Marine et des Colonies, Fort Royal, 5 avril 1832.

25. Soleau, *Notes sur les Guyanes*, 9–10; Lavollée, *Notes sur les cultures*, 123; Debien, *Les esclaves aux Antilles françaises*, 178–80; Peytraud, *Les esclaves aux Antilles françaises*, 217; Gisler, *Les esclaves aux Antilles françaises*, 48.

26. Mintz, *Caribbean Transformations*; Ministère de la Marine, *Exposé général des résultats du patronage*, 110, 188, 303–5; B.W. Higman, *Slave Population and Economy in Jamaica, 1807–1834* (Cambridge, 1976), 129; Soleau, *Notes sur les Guyanes*, 9–10; ANSOM, *Martinique*, Carton 7, Dossier 83, Dupotêt à Ministre de la Marine et des Colonies, Fort Royal, 5 avril 1832.

27. Soleau, *Notes sur les Guyanes*, 59; ANSOM, *Généralitiés*, Carton 144, Dossier 1221, 'Éxécution de l'ordonnance royale', 51; *Martinique*, Carton 7, Dossier 83, Mathieu à Ministre de la Marine et des Colonies, 10 mars 1847, No. 1508; Sainte Croix, *Statistique*, 2: 13–15; M. Le Compte E. de la Cornillère, *La Martinique en 1842: Interets coloniaux, souvenirs du voyage* (Paris, 1843), 123–4.

28. De la Cornillère, *La Martinique en 1842*, 123–4; Soleau, *Notes sur les Guyanes*, 59; Ministère de la Marine, *Exposé général des résultats du patronage*, 102.

29. Jean Besson has demonstrated the importance of family land for distinctively Afro-Caribbean conceptions of kinship and property in the free villages of post-emancipation Jamaica. 'Family Land and Caribbean Society: Toward an Ethnography of Afro-Caribbean Peasantries' in Elizabeth M. Thomas-Hope (ed.), *Perspectives on Caribbean Regional Identity*, Centre for Latin American Studies, University of Liverpool, Monograph Series No. 11 (Liverpool, 1984), 57–83 and 'Land Tenure in the Free villages of Trelawny, Jamaica: A Case Study in the Caribbean Peasant Response to Emancipation', *Slavery & Abolition*, 5 (1984), 3–23; Melville J. Herskovits, *Life in a Haitian Valley* (New York, 1937), 67–8, 76–81; Schoelcher, *Abolition immédiate*, 9; M.G. Lewis, *Journal of a West India Proprietor, 1815–1817* (Boston, 1929), 88; Roger Bastide, *The African Religions of Brazil: Toward a Sociology of the Interpenetration of Civilizations*, trans. by Helen Sebba (Baltimore, 1978), 58.

30. Schoelcher, *Abolition immédiate*, 9–13; Ministère de la Marine, *Exposé général des résultats du patronage*, 180–88, 290; *Commission du 26 mai 1840*, 208–9; ANSOM, *Généralitiés*, Carton 144, Dossier 1221, 'Éxécution de l'ordonnance royale', 2: 40, 51.

31. Ministère de la Marine, *Exposé général des résultats du patronage*, 180–88, 290; Schoelcher, *Abolition immédiate*, 9–13; ANSOM, *Généralitiés*, Carton 144, Dossier 1221, 'Éxécution de l'ordonnance royale', 2: 40, 51.

32. Mintz, *Caribbean Transformations*; Ministère de la Marine, *Exposé général des résultats du patronage*, 180–88, 290, 303–5.

33. Ibid.; ibid., 303–5.

34. Debien, *Les esclaves aux Antilles françaises*, 209; Lavollée, *Notes sur les cultures*, 123–4; Lewis, *Journal of a West India Proprietor*, 81; *Les esclaves aux Antilles françaises*, 156; De Cassagnac, *Voyage aux Antilles*, 168, 211; Cf. Schoelcher, *Abolition immédiate*, 53n.; Yvan Debbasch, 'Le marronage. Essai sur la désertion de l'esclave antillais', *Année Sociologique*, 3e Series (1962), 131–8.
35. Soleau, *Notes sur les Guyanes*, 8–10.
36. Ibid., 8–9; Edward Brathwaite, *The Development of Creole Society in Jamaica, 1770–1820* (Oxford, 1971);, 298–9.
37. Mintz, *Caribbean Transformations*.
38. Ibid., Douglas Hall, 'The Flight From the Plantations Reconsidered: The British West Indies, 1838–1842', *Journal of Caribbean History*, 10–11 (1978), 7–23.

Slave Workers, Subsistence and Labour Bargaining: Amity Hall, Jamaica, 1805–1832

Mary Turner

The slave rebellion that swept the sugar growing parishes of western Jamaica in December 1831 utilized three strategies, arson, armed resistance and strike action, and made two demands, free status and wage work. The rebellion, though it advanced slave emancipation, was defeated. Its strategy and goals, however, provide a new perspective on the conduct of class struggle within the slave system.[1]

The attempted general strike in 1831 suggests that sugar estate workers had prior small-scale experience of strike action and other forms of group and collective bargaining practices. The gang and team work required in field and factory for agro-industrial sugar production provided a ready made framework for such activity. The rebels' claim to wages also implies that their bargaining aimed to improve their uncertain and limited command of subsistence. Both the aims and strategies of the rebel slave workers, in short, indicated similarities between the methods of struggle used by slave and wage workers.

Slaves faced fundamentally the same problems as serf, contract or wage labour: they were forced to spend their lives expending labour over and above what was necessary for their own subsistence. Improvement in work conditions for all categories of workers meant increasing rewards for labour expended and modifying the coercive powers of the owners of the means of production.

My earlier study of sugar workers in the parish of St Thomas in the East established that the rebels' attempted general strike did indeed reflect their prior experience.[2] Verbal protests by groups, or by the entire body of field workers, and appeals for mediation of disputes supported by strike action – forms of class struggle characteristically associated with contract and wage workers – were clearly adumbrated by sugar estate slaves. They attempted to exert some control over work conditions to improve their subsistence. The impetus for these developments derived from the integration of the slaves in the commercial economy in which the coerced labour estates were embedded. The greater part of the Jamaican slave population, as in St Thomas in the East parish, largely subsisted themselves from provision grounds and sold any surplus at market. The juxtaposition of cash valued labour on their provision grounds and coerced labour on the estates fuelled efforts to improve the terms for coerced labour. The 1807 abolition of the slave trade assisted this development, since thereafter the planters were forced to rely on their existing workforce and its reproduction to keep the estates in operation.

A further study of these developments focuses on Vere, a sugar producing parish in southern Jamaica, where slaves characteristically did not have provision grounds, but subsisted on rations – imported and estate grown – distributed by estate owners and managers and supplemented by produce from small parcels of land, significantly smaller than the provision grounds.

Slave subsistence by estate grown, rationed staples supplemented by slave allotment produce, termed here the ration-allotment system, also characterized the Leeward Islands (St Kitts, Nevis, and Antigua), the Bahamas, Barbados, Demerara-Essequibo and Berbice and affected some 30 per cent of the British Caribbean slave population. It developed when the American Revolution disrupted trade patterns and made complete dependence on imported food too costly in terms both of food prices and slave deaths for most planters to sustain. By the early nineteenth century the system, with local variations, was well established throughout the Caribbean. It reflected, in varying degrees, conflicting claims of export and subsistence crops to limited land resources.[3] In Vere parish it maximized the land available for sugar on an outstandingly fertile alluvial plain, 15 miles wide, drained by the Rio Minho and its tributaries, which extended south from the Clarendon mountains to the sea.[4]

The main features of the ration-allotment system suggest that this method of slave subsistence may have influenced the incidence, the form and the dynamics of labour bargaining. The distribution of a staple food (Guinea corn, plantains or yams) clearly indicated that the fundamental contractual term for the extraction of slave labour was the supply of subsistence. In some circumstances the rations also demonstrated a vast discrepancy between the scale of the staple food crop the slaves planted and the share distributed at the discretion of owners and managers. Slaves so inclined could calculate, by pint or quart of corn or pounds of plantain, the extent to which they were deprived of the results of their labour. The struggle for subsistence consequently was directed to claiming a regular or increased supply of staple food rather than, as in the provision ground parishes, to claiming time for household cultivation.

The slaves' restricted rations and access to land limited the surplus they could market and consequently their access to cash rewards. At the same time the variables that affected slaves in the provision ground system, such as the quality of land, distance from the estate and from the market, the size and age structure of the household units engaged in cultivation, also affected slaves in the ration-allotment system.

One further factor that may have influenced the development of labour bargaining practices was the location of provision grounds and allotments. The former were on the fringes or in the backlands of the estates and provided the slave work force with an unsupervised meeting place for all forms of political activities, from the articulation of grievances to planning rebellion. The slaves' allotments, by contrast, were usually attached to the cane land and were exposed to white oversight. In short, the ration-allotment system appeared to sharpen and focus conflict between slaves and managers over the distribution of estate produce, but seemed to reduce the tension between coerced estate labour and cash rewarded labour by curtailing access to market while simultaneously limiting opportunities for political organization.

These considerations informed the investigation of labour bargaining at Amity Hall estate in the 'Grand Square' of Vere parish, some of the best cane producing land in Jamaica. Located just seven miles inland from Carlisle Bay and to the east of the Rio Minho, Amity Hall in 1816 had a work-force of 229, which tended 300 acres in cane. The absentee owner, Henry Goulburn, who had inherited the property in 1805, devoted himself to a political career and paid the estate no consistent attention. Estate revenues were a significant element in his income, however, and he tried to improve its efficiency. From 1805 to 1818 he employed an experienced Scotsman, Thomas Samson, as resident attorney.

Samson was a good manager in terms of sugar produced. The estate averaged 336 hogsheads per year under his management as compared with an average of 205 hogsheads subsequently.[5] But Sampson economized on slave subsistence, which was kept to eight pints of Guinea corn a week for seven months of the year; the allotments comprised a strip of between one and one and a half acres, half of which was used for vegetables for the overseer's house. This provided some 16 square yards per head. The allotments, like the provision grounds, were of course supplemented by gardens in the slave village, which at Amity Hall occupied 18 acres.[6]

The miniscule scale of Amity Hall allotments establish conclusively the distinction to be drawn between the ration-allotment and the provision ground subsistence systems; some grounds in the post slave trade period were as much as one or one and a half acres and the suggested average was nearly three quarters of an acre per slave.[7] Comparison with the ration-allotment system elsewhere in the Caribbean is difficult. The 1798 legal minimum in the Leeward Islands was a mere 40 square feet; post 1807 practice in Demerara-Essequibo, however, indicates one tenth of an acre per head was standard.[8] But compared with rations elsewhere Amity Hall's Guinea corn allowance was also meagre. The 1798 Leeward Islands law prescribed nine pints per week and random data for Demerara-Essequibo, where the rationed staple was plantain rather than corn, indicate that 45 pounds of plantain, equivalent to nine pints of corn, were supplied weekly. The small corn ration indicated a minimum acreage in subsistence crops at Amity Hall. The eight pint ration required approximately 800 bushels and Amity Hall attorneys, perennially optimistic, estimated about 30 bushels to the acre in a good year. On this optimum estimate a home grown corn ration required about 30 acres. By comparison, the legal requirement in Demerara-Essequibo was one acre in subsistence crops for every five slaves, the equivalent of 46 acres at Amity Hall.[9]

The Amity Hall slaves suffered chronic underfeeding which could assume crisis proportions as a result of hurricane or drought. In 1816, when a hurricane reduced sugar production to a mere 90 hogsheads, they attacked the remains of the estate crop, chopping down canes to eat, raided neighbouring estates for food and, one observer commented, 'lay down often in the fields from sheer debility'. Some ran away in desperation, only to be severely disciplined by Samson when they were forced to return.[10]

The conditions at Amity Hall were by no means unprecedented for slaves in either the ration-allotment or the provision ground system. For much of the eighteenth century slave owners and managers in Jamaica presided over a seasonal hunger cycle, at its most acute in provision ground parishes between June and September, between crop which fuelled labour on cane juice and the September provision harvest. These circumstances turned each estate into an armed camp which repelled invaders searching for food and disciplined its own workers for eating the canes they were sent to weed – functions fulfilled by slaves bought as trustees by special rewards, including cash, for arrests. Severe floggings followed any infraction of estate discipline. While masters aimed to leave their own slaves capable of work, intruders could get 150 or even 250 lashes. Once the provision ground system was thoroughly established, however, it could secure the slaves' subsistence outside crisis years; but in the ration-allotment system, as conditions at Amity Hall demonstrate, despite the supposedly 'rationalizing' effects of increased slave prices and the abolition of the slave trade on management practices, slaves remained underfed.[11]

Subsistence standards at Amity Hall improved when Samson went on home leave 1816–17; his replacement, George Richards, almost doubled the corn ration, from eight to 14 pints per head and extended it from seven to eight months. On paper this brought Amity Hall rations in line with rations elswhere. In Antigua, for example, Parham estate distributed 28 pounds of estate grown yams and eddoes, the equivalent of 14 pints of corn per head, and in Barbados the FitzHerbert estates distributed ten to 14 pints of corn or between 28 and 35 pounds of yam or potatoes.[12]

The increase at Amity Hall appears substantial and slaves at Parham and on the Fitzherbert estates were reputedly properly fed. George Richards, however, considered 14 pints weekly was 'little enough'; it was no more than a horse was fed after a ten mile ride – a measure only too well known to the slaves who fed the overseer's horse. To supply even this ration required an increase in the corn acreage at Amity Hall from its customary 30 to about 60 acres; and Samson, on his return, claimed only 27 acres were in corn. But Richards certainly did expand the allotments; a 13 acre disused cane piece adjacent to the existing allotment strip was ploughed for the slaves' use. This substantially increased the allotment land available and brought it to approximately one-sixteenth of an acre per head.[14]

The slaves, nevertheless, remained underfed and in the early months of 1818 had an opportunity to manifest their discontent to their owner's brother, Major Archibald Goulburn, when he visited the estate to supervise the installation of a steam engine to replace the windmill. Every aspect of the estate betrayed, in Major Goulburn's view, bad management: the fences were in bad order, weeds rampant, the canes thin, stunted and plundered to an incredible extent, and the slaves' village comprised miserable huts crowded together. Despite the allotments which he saw 'crowded with produce', he found the slaves very badly fed and showing 'every outward sign of being much discontented with their present attorney'.[15]

Slave hunger and discontent jeopardized the utility of the new steam technology. Steam powered grinding required fewer workers but imposed new work routines and more intense labour; it underlined both the need for worker co-operation and an adequate diet. As an investment in fixed capital the steam engine also highlighted the problem of maintaining the estate's labour supply. Samson, with Henry Goulburn's agreement, made replacements in the traditional way by purchase. Since slaves were rarely available in small lots, except in work house sales, this also involved heavy capital outlay. In 1818, for example, Samson purchased 42 (eight adults, plus youths and children) and the expense – more than £3,000 – was sustained only by selling estate land in Manchester parish.[16]

The hunger, discontent and declining numbers of the slave work force at Amity Hall contrasted sharply, moreover, with the conditions Major Goulburn observed at neighbouring Bog Estate where George Richards resided. He found it 'delightful to travel over and look at the happiness of every black face on that estate'. Richards claimed he had cut down his slaves' work load by reducing the acreage in cane from 500 to 250 acres and produced more sugar as a result. At the same time proper subsistence – its quantity and nature were not specified secured a steadily expanding work force; the population at Bog had increased from 300 to 430.[17] While Richards' figures may be inflated, population growth at Bog Estate reflected the fact that, in contrast to every other parish in the island, Vere sugar estate slaves moved from a position of negative natural increase to one of consistent positive gains between 1817 and 1832.[18]

Richards' management methods and Richards himself, who Major Goulburn considered 'a very superior man from every point of view', combined with the manifest hunger and discontent at Amity Hall, resulted in Samson's dismissal; George Richards took over over at Amity Hall in August 1818.[19]

In the meantime the slaves, who expected some immediate benefit from Major Goulburn's visit – Samson ignored instructions to feed them well – turned to the Major's friend and their old benefactor. Several visited Richards to state their grievances and appeal for mediation. Richards, perhaps anticipating Goulburn's decision, tried to restrain them by 'salutary advice', but some, impatient of redress, ran away and did not return until Samson left. The new attorney was therefore under pressure to meet the slaves' expectations and immediately took over 26 acres of marginal cane land on the edge of the estate for Guinea corn. This land made Amity Hall capable of supplying a 14 pint corn ration for seven months of the year – a ration sufficient to allow some allotment produce, including exportable articles, arrowroot, ginger and honey, to be marketed.[20]

Yet the slaves' hold on the corn ration and its quantity remained uncertain. Richards, nearing the end of his career, did not attend the estate regularly and left ration distribution to the overseers who were prone to appropriate it. Corn stealing was, in Richards' eyes, 'the greatest sin, for it is the greatest cruelty in an overseer in Vere'. He dismissed one overseer in 1820 partly on this account, although the sin only came to his attention after the overseer's arrest for smuggling flour from Carlisle Bay. The overseer left the corn stores empty.[21]

While Richard's irregular supervision of estate business put the slaves' rations at risk, it also added to their responsibilities. To compensate for his absences and keep a check on the overseers Richards made it a habit to consult with some of the slaves. He sent occasionally 'for Negroes of all diversities, head-driver, attendant, or sick – speak to them and give them directions'. Delegated responsibilities extended the slaves' control of their work routine and, subsequent events suggest, augmented the authority of the driver, John Gale.[22]

Richard's attorneyship proved unsatisfactory from Goulburn's point of view; his accounts of estate business were infrequent and incomplete, and he failed to stem the decline of the estate's population, which decreased from 267 to 251 between 1818 and 1825. His successor, Alexander Bayley, took over in February 1825, briefed to improve production and reproduction rates. Consequently, Amity Hall slaves faced new demands which involved destruction of customary rights, work loads and work routines.

Each slave was re-classified as a worker and gang responsibilities were re-defined. Women and children had their work loads increased; children under ten were allotted tasks Bayley rated 'trifling exercise', possibly weeding. Since women, in the characteristic Jamaican fashion, outnumbered men in the first field gang and had done so since 1812, young mothers who previously had nursed their babies were forced to relinquish them to nursing women and return to work. Three women had babies no more than nine months old and another nine had children under eighteen months; these nursing mothers comprised almost a third of the first gang women who numbered 39 in all.

Bayley's re-organisation sought to cope with the shortage of prime field hands which began to develop as soon as the slave trade ended and was manifest island-wide by 1817. By that date young workers between 15 and 24 were in particularly short supply in Vere and the full impact of this was felt a decade later in reduced numbers of prime 25- to 35-year-olds.[23]

Bayley's innovations inevitably generated grievances expressed in slow, sullen and careless work. But the slaves' dependence on estate distributed rations provided management with a mechanism for inducing co-operation; Bayley compensated for the new demands by providing regular rations. First, a limited quantity (480 bushels) of corn was purchased to secure, minimally, a ten pint ration. At the same time corn production was extended to an unprecedented degree: no less than 100 acres were planted capable of producing 3,000 bushels in a good year, two years' supply of a 14 pint ration to insure against drought. The time allowed for allotment cultivation (26 Saturdays) was also scrupulously maintained.[24]

The proportion of subsistence to export crop production land at Amity Hall now compared favourably with the pattern found elsewhere in the ration-allotment system. Common practice tended to keep 25 per cent of cultivated land in food crops although in Antigua, as at Amity Hall, the proportion was in the region of 30 per cent. Amity Hall's corn stocks proved necessary in 1828 when drought reduced the corn crop by half. The estate accounts indicate no corn purchases or sales after 1826. But, compared with the standards laid down by the British government in 1832 (21 pints of Guinea corn or 56 pounds of yams a week, together with half an acre of land per adult slave and 40 days a year for cultivation) Amity Hall standards remained low.[25]

Although secure rations and allotment production permitted the 1825 crop to be completed without any notable disruption, the following crop season culminated in a strike. The slaves' work-load over the year proved heavier as increased corn planting paralleled increased cane holing. Vere was a dry weather parish which allowed for successful ratooning, reaping successive crops from the same root. Nevertheless, a proportion of ratoons had to be replaced every year, at a labour cost of 25 man days per acre, to maintain production levels. Bayley required 45 acres holed for planting in 1826, the balance of the crop to come from ratoons and new canes. The slaves were also exposed to the steam powered grinding system that Richards had neglected to keep in good order. Cane cutting was delayed by rain and then by recurrent break-downs of the steam engine (the boiler was due for replacement) and the failure of wind. Customarily strenuous regular work was intensified by irregularity and slaves took to absconding to the woods for a few days at a time. Offenders were flogged 'to curb the habit'. Routine appeared to be restored when the new boiler arrived from Liverpool at the beginning of March, but in late April about 50 of the 'most efficient people' – presumably the mill workers and the first gang – stopped work *en masse* and took to the woods.[26]

The strikers demanded the removal of the overseer, Mr Petrie, who tackled production problems by flogging the workers for any breach of discipline. The implementation of this policy fell on the driver, John Gale, who had reputedly enjoyed in Richards' regime 'more authority than any of the white people'. Petrie's conduct made it impossible for Gale to mediate management demands and retain the respect of the work force. Verbal confrontations, intended to impress Petrie with the need to recognize the driver's authority, ensued. When this failed the strike followed.[27]

In this crisis Bayley invited two neighbouring magistrates, one of them George Richards the ex-attorney, to conduct an investigation on the estate. The slaves who remained in the village were 'called up' and presented their grievances. Bayley, who 'did not think it right to concede without hesitation and might have a bad tendency', tried to temporize. He promised the slaves that in future offences should be

written down and attended to only on his monthly visits and offered the
slaves in the woods free pardon. But the strikers stayed away and
workers still on the estate worked slowly.

At the beginning of crop season, when the slaves quit work in small
groups, Bayley told Goulburn there was no reason he could fathom
for their conduct. Collective action persuaded him that Mr Petrie's
'anxiety for the well being of the Estate has been too great and he has
been more exact in the execution of his duty than I wished him to be'.
Nevertheless, management exacted a price for the total disruption of
production: Petrie was dismissed, but Gale was sent to trial at the Slave
Court for insolence to the overseer and sentenced to four months in
Clarendon workhouse.[28]

Deprived of their leader the strikers slowly drifted back to work; by
the beginning of June only a hard core of two or three remained in the
woods. But pressure on management continued. Some of the standing
cane was destroyed by fire shortly after the strike and the slaves
proceeded to harvest the rest at their own pace. As a result, to maximize
sugar production, Bayley was forced to employ a jobbing gang (the
equivalent of 20 workers for two weeks) to assist taking off the crop,
which at 276 hogsheads proved the best for his administration. Cane
holing that year, moreover, was reduced to 18 acres, one good sized
cane piece.[29]

Goulburn's response to Bayley's account of these events provides
an excellent example of the way in which slave assaults on planter
authority were translated into its opposite, the successful exercise of
managerial authority. It also shows how documents generated by the
slave owners assisted them to preserve confidence in the hegemony
they claimed, as well as convince history that they did indeed exercise
it.

Goulburn first welcomed Bayley's explanation for the slaves 'leaving
the estate': he failed to acknowledge that they abandoned the sugar
works and disrupted production. It was as if they left 'home'. Bayley
was praised for his 'attentive examination' of the workers' complaints,
as if the initiative for the investigation lay with management rather than
the workers. The real cause of the complaints was then located not in
the conduct of Petrie but in that of Gale; the complaints themselves had
no substance. The dismissal of Petrie could then be conceptualized as
'deferring to the *prejudices* of the negroes'. The overseer, representing
the slave owner's interests, was a blameless sacrifice to the irrational
workers.[30]

The most significant feature of the Amity Hall strike, compared with
equivalent manifestations in St Thomas in the East, was management's
determination to exact a price for the strike by the removal of its leader.

Managers in the provision ground system regarded book-keepers and overseers as eminently dispensable, but took care not to lose the co-operation of skilled and confidential slaves and were chary of exerting their authority over head men. Their attitude reflected experience in dealing with self-subsisting petty traders who had accustomed them to labour bargaining. There were St Thomas in the East managers who took strikes in their stride by the 1770s. This is not to claim that slaves who attempted to bargain always did so with impunity; nevertheless, grievance procedures were acknowledged to exist, were frequently followed and demonstrated respect for slave leaders. Bayley's action reflected the comparative underdevelopment of these procedures at Amity Hall.

The punishment inflicted on the driver appears to have curbed recourse to strike action or formal verbal expressions of grievance. But in August 1827 a new wave of hostility to the estate managers gripped the estate which made it impossible to 'carry on the capabilities of the Estate to their fullest extent'; apparently the slaves sat down rather than took to the woods. No leaders were identified and Bayley was reduced to hoping that 'time, perseverence and patience' would bring the estate back into production. The slaves were again disputing their work load; the jobbing gang introduced after the strike had not re-appeared and the slaves were expected, as in 1825, to take off the crop and dig cane holes. In the up-shot, 27 acres – compared with 18 acres after the strike – were eventually ploughed before planting.[31]

The following season, in the absence of acknowledged procedures for labour bargaining, the slaves found another method of exerting pressure to achieve their ends. Drought had reduced allotment yields and affected the corn crop. To protest their work load and the absence of jobbers they used arson. Fire destroyed acres of cane (Bayley reported officially 16) and nearly destroyed the mill but left the slaves' allotments intact. It was a dry season in a dry parish – equipment at Amity Hall included a fire engine – but Bayley assumed arson. He postulated for his own peace of mind and his employers' that responsibility lay with one 'idle, skulking', vengeance-seeking indi-vidual rather than, for example, the women in the first gang or any other group of workers.[32]

A fire that did no damage to the slaves' food supply, but reduced sugar production could serve as a bargaining tool. It posited a threat to white authority as well as profit margins and forced management to recognize its dependence on worker co-operation to fight the fire and salvage the crop. Cuban slaves used it effectively when they were forced from their *conucos* in the mid-nineteenth century sugar boom; planters restored the *conucos* specifically to protect their crops from arson. The number of fires at Amity Hall and its vicinity between 1828 and 1832, which all took place after the corn harvest and before crop-over, evidently made an impact on Vere planters. In 1830, writing from fire-scarred Chesterfield estate, one of Bayley's colleagues told Henry Goulburn, 'You dare not at your peril make a bad use of your authority'.[33]

At Amity Hall the 1828 fire marked a watershed in worker–management relations. The slaves forced Bayley to acknowledge that they remained determined to limit the exploitation of their surplus labour. He took immediate steps to reduce the area kept in cane: first by limiting the area to be cane holed (seven acres) and subsequently, with Goulburn's permission, reducing the area to be kept in cane production to 260 acres. He took this decision despite the slack capacity of the steam grinding mill which could process a greater cane acreage than the slaves customarily cultivated.

Estate labour from this time forward was regularly supplemented by jobbers, used to clean pastures in 1829, but to harvest the crop in 1830, while the estate slaves undertook the lighter work of cleaning pastures. When no jobbers were used no cane holing was done and if gaps appeared in the rows of ratoons they were 'supplied', patched in with new canes. Most importantly, perhaps, Bayley decided to 'let go as strayed' several cows and calves which disappeared after the slaves had cheerfully assisted in a fire fighting exercise at neighbouring Hillside estate in 1831. Bayley's decision, taken before the December rebellion sent its repercussions throughout the island, signified his acknowledgment that bargaining was essential to slave labour extraction. Subsequently, the slaves ended night work during crop and a strike free decade ensued, brought to an end on Emancipation Day 1838 by a wage slave strike for higher wages.[34]

One aspect of the Amity Hall experience highlights the importance of a cash labour breach in the coerced labour system which was significant in both the provision ground and ration-allotment systems: the jobbing gang. These gangs introduced a work force for which the estate paid hire, often to the estate attorney or overseer himself. In a straightforward commercial way jobbing put a price tag on the work estate slaves did. Though the labour of both the slave estate worker and the slave jobber was coerced, the price paid for the jobber's labour established a price for tasks on the estate. Slaves knew what labour on their own grounds or allotments earned; the jobbers established the cash value of estate work and provided a useful yardstick for slaves who were able to bargain for cash rewards.

The existence of this alternative work-force in conditions of labour scarcity also enhanced the value of estate-based labour. Jobbers employed by management to increase the amount of work opened the way for estate slaves to decrease the amount of work they did, to redistribute their work-load to hired workers, to make it customary for jobbers to do the cane holing, or to take off crop. This aspect of the slaves' struggle to improve their conditions was facilitated by the efforts of whites below the rank of planter to better their own lot by acquiring or expanding land holdings, a struggle in which jobbing gangs were instrumental.

Jobbing gangs originated in the planters' debt crisis which followed the 1763 peace. At that time, slaves were purchased by people with surplus cash and hired out at rates so exorbitant that, it was argued, the planters would have been better off to borrow at 15 per cent to buy outright.[35] But by 1773, in St James Parish alone, of the 63 families listed as next in degree to planters no less than 39 were jobbers, two thirds of whom owned no land, and of the balance who claimed to be penkeepers a third had only two to five head of stock. When jobbers became penkeepers, moreover, jobbing remained for some 40 per cent a lucrative line of business.[36]

Experienced planters warned against the use of jobbers but the abolition of the slave trade made them the only reserve army of labour available and the practice increased. Jobbers formed a new strata of permanent migrants in the slave population, and their status and living standards were on the whole lower than those of the estate slaves. Hiring jobbers opened the way for the slaves to pressure, as they did at Amity Hall, for lower work-loads. In some instances their success was spectacular: by 1825 militant workers and complaisant managers put sugar production at Grange Hill estate, St Thomas in the East, almost entirely into the hands of jobbers. The jobbing gangs constituted a force to assist the transformation of estate slaves' work conditions, and slaves in both the ration-allotment system and the provision ground system found means to utilize it.[37]

The ration-allotment system in other respects provided a weak base for the slaves' struggles with management. The slaves' basic subsistence was directly in the hands of estate owners and managers and the size and regularity of this subsistence largely determined the slaves' form of struggle. Shortfalls in subsistence drove the slaves to desperate, often individual or small group action – attack on the estate crops, running away, banditry and theft. Under frontier conditions, food shortages could lead to mass flight by the whole work-force, as happened at Providence plantation, for example, in seventeenth-century Surinam.[38] Nineteenth-century Vere presented no such opportunity, and slaves foraged as best they could. The pursuit of food put a premium on individual or household survival; it did not spark collective action. This contrasts sharply with the struggle for subsistence in the provision ground system which required the slaves to secure time to work their grounds. This concession could only be won by collective rather than individual action.

Adequate rations steadily supplied by management conversely had a reverse effect; a reasonably fed work-force could pay attention to other necessities of life and strike action rapidly followed on increased workloads exacted by increased flogging. The problem which then faced the slaves was management's determination to intimidate them by punishing their leader to reassert their subordination as ration fed workers. The next phase of struggle, consequently, consisted in forcing management to recognize the need for negotiation by counter-intimidation. A diffuse, apparently leaderless and somewhat turbulent work stoppage was followed by outright sabotage – a form of low-intensity guerrilla warfare – which served to secure an immediate redress of grievance and legitimate the bargaining process.

The ration-allotment system as practised at Amity Hall hampered the development of bargaining procedures and delayed until the 1820s processes well established 50 years earlier in St Thomas in the East. The subsistence system, ration-allotment or provision ground, shaped the slaves' political trajectory in the coerced labour system and influenced owners and managers. The fact that slaves with provision grounds were also self-subsisting petty traders was an aspect of reality which was bound to influence owners and managers when demands were made for informal contract terms, task work, cash and material rewards for estate work over and above established routines. Conversely, managements' command of the slave workers' food supply in the ration-allotment system enhanced their sense of control and the difficulty slaves had in establishing the bargaining process.

The definitive judgement on the ration-allotment system was made by slaves themselves. Managers in Vere found it difficult to import slaves from surrounding parishes because, as one Amity Hall attorney expressed it, 'mountain' negroes 'will not take to Guiney corn'. The same form of complaint was commonly made throughout the Caribbean, and evidence from Brazil suggests slaves preferred the provision ground system even when the labour was beyond their capacity. Their expressed distaste for the sheer monotony of the diet and for a food distributed only to slaves and stock also implies their political distaste for a subsistence system which curtailed their capacity to transform their condition.[39]

NOTES

1. Mary Turner, *Slaves and Missionaries: the Disintegration of Jamaican Slave Society, 1787–1834* (Urbana, 1982), 153–9.
2. Mary Turner, 'Chattel Slaves into Wage Slaves: a Jamaican Case Study', in Malcolm Cross and Gad Heuman (eds.), *Labour in the Caribbean: From Emancipation to Independence* (London, 1988), 14–31.
3. B.W. Higman, *Slave Populations of the British Caribbean, 1807–1834* (Baltimore, 1984), 41, 204.
4. G.S. Ramlackhansingh, 'Amity Hall, 1760–1860: the Geography of a Jamaican Plantation', M.Sc. Econ. (London University, 1966), 16.
5. Ibid., 86.
6. T. Samson to H. Goulburn, 28 March 1816, Box 51, Goulburn Papers, Surrey Record Office, Kingston on Thames (all subsequent references will be by box numbers); A. Goulburn to H. Goulborn, 22 Feb. 1818. The size of the allotment strip had probably been stable for some time. An area of 13 acres, half of which was designated 'negro grounds' in the 1814 Crop Account, was simultaneously credited with producing ten hogs heads of sugar, a quantity yielded by 10–14 acres elsewhere on the estate. Box 59, Crop Account July 1814–Aug. 1815. One acre is 4,840 square yards.
7. Turner, *Slaves and Missionaries*, 43; J.R. Ward, *British West Indian Slavery, 1750–1834: The Process of Amelioration* (Oxford, 1988), 113.
8. The 1816 Jamaica Slave Code specified that slaves should have sufficient time to cultivate their provision grounds but made no regulation as to scale of either allotments or provision grounds. A standard three shillings and four pence per head expenditure was recommended where no land for food cultivation was available. Higman, *Slave Populations*, 207, 209, 210.
9. Ibid., 208; Box 51, T. Samson to H. Goulborn, 7 Nov. 1817; A. Goulborn to H. Goulborn, 22 Feb. 1818.
10. Box 51, G. Richards to H. Goulborn, 5 Sept. 1818. The classic account of rebellion prompted by short rations is embedded in the oral history of the Abaisis clan of the Surinam Saramaccas; cf. Richard Price, *First-Time: The Historical Vision of an Afro-American People* (Baltimore, 1983), 71.
11. Ward, *British West Indian Slavery*, 23–4, 27–8, n. 40; Turner, 'Chattel Slaves', 16.
12. Box 51, A. Goulborn to H. Goulborn, 22 Feb. 1818; Ward, *British West Indian Slavery*, 115, 117–18.
13. Box 51, A. Goulborn to H. Goulborn 22 Feb. 1818.
14. Box 51, T. Samson to H. Goulborn, 16 Oct. 1817: G. Richards to H. Goulborn, 16 Jan. 1819.
15. Box 51, A. Goulborn to H. Goulborn, 22 Feb. 1818.
16. Box 51, T. Samson to H. Goulborn, 21 July 1814, 4 Oct. 1816, 12 April, 9 July 1818: G. Richards to H. Goulborn, 5 Sept. 1818.
17. Box 51, A. Goulborn to H. Goulborn, 22 Feb. 1818.
18. B.W. Higman, *Slave Population and Economy in Jamaica 1807–34* (Cambridge, 1976), 102, Table 15, 105.
19. Box 51, G. Richards to H. Goulborn, 5 Sept. 1818.
20. Box 51, G. Richards to H. Goulborn, 16 Jan. 1819. Attorney William Taylor's much-quoted evidence to the House of Commons Committee 1831–2 claimed that in Vere the corn ration itself secured the slaves' market connection since in good years they could live from their allotments and use the corn to feed chickens for the Kingston market. His evidence was contested by the more experienced attorney James Simpson on the cogent ground that Taylor was not aquainted with Vere; in any case, the suggestion was that slaves made a market connection only in good seasons. *Parliamentary Papers*, House of Commons, Vol. 20, 1831–32 (721), Q.152, 5448.
21. Box 51, G. Richards to H. Goulborn, 16 Jan. 1819, 9 Jan. 1821; Box 54, A. Bayley to H. Goulborn, 15 Oct. 1825, 29 Sept. 1827, enclosure.

22. Box 51, G. Richards to H. Goulborn, 9 Jan. 1821.
23. Box 51, Increase and Decrease of Slaves, 1813–25; Box 54, A. Bayley to H. Goulburn, 12 March 1825, 22 Nov. 1828; Higman, *Slave Population and Economy*, 81–3, Fig. 15.
24. Box 54, A. Bayley to H. Goulburn, 12 March., 14 April, 1825, 6 May 1826, 12 Feb. 1829; Box 59, 1826 Account.
25. Higman, *Slave Populations*, 208–9; Box 54, A. Bayley to H. Goulburn, 12 Jan. 1828. No corn sales or purchases are recorded in estate accounts after 1826; *Anti-Slavery Reporter*, Jan. 1832, 18–19.
26. Box 54, A. Bayley to H. Goulburn, 6 Aug. 1825, 3 March 1826, Statement enclosed with A. Bayley to H. Goulburn, 5 Oct. 1831; Ramlackhansingh, 'Amity Hall', 29.
27. Box 54, A. Bayley to H. Goulburn, 6 May 1826. There is no evidence as to John Gale's colour; slaves of his status were customarily mulatto.
28. Ibid.
29. Box 54, A. Bayley to H. Goulburn, 10 June, 8 July 1826; Statement enclosed 5 Oct. 1831; Box 59, Accounts 1826.
30. Box 54, H. Goulburn to A. Bayley, 24 Aug. 1826 (italics added).
31. Box 54, A. Bayley to H. Goulburn, 3 Aug. 1827, Statement enclosed 5 Oct. 1831.
32. Box 54, A. Bayley to H. Goulburn, 7 May 1828.
33. Rebecca Scott, *Slave Emancipation in Cuba: Transition to Free Labor, 1860–1899* (Princeton, 1985), 15. Neighbourhood fires occurred as follows: 1828 Chesterfield, mill destroyed; 1830 fire spreads from the border of Amity Hall to Monymusk, Harmony Hall and Greenwich; 1831 Hillside, mill destroyed and Salt Savannah, trash house and trash heaps destroyed, for which see Box 54, Bayley to Goulburn, 8 May, 11 Sept. 1830, 13 March, 10 April 1831. Box 54, Malcolm MacLeod to H. Goulburn, 23 Sept. 1830, enclosed A. Bayley to H. Goulburn, 6 Feb. 1831.
34. Box 59, Accounts 1831, 1832; Box 54, Bayley to Goulburn, 13 March, 4 July 1829, 16 March 1831, Statement enclosed 5 Oct. 1831; Ramlackhansingh, 'Amity Hall', 72, 183.
35. Long Add. Ms. 12404, 317–8 ff., British Library.
36. Long Add. Ms. 12435, 3–4 ff.; Verene A. Shepherd, 'Pens and Pen-keepers ina Plantation Society: Aspects of Jamaican Social and Economic History, 1740–1845', Ph.D. Diss. (Cambridge University, 1988), Table 13, 48–9.
37. Turner, 'Chattel Slaves', 24–5.
38. Price, *First-Time*, 71.
39. Box 51, T. Sansom to H. Goulburn, 21 July 1814; Stuart B. Schwartz, *Sugar Plantations in the Formation of Brazilian Society: Bahia, 1550–1835* (Cambridge, 1985), 138.

Subsistence on the Plantation Periphery: Crops, Cooking, and Labour among Eighteenth-Century Suriname Maroons[1]

Richard Price

Throughout Afro-America cooking and eating were core areas of cultural resistance and persistence, as well as foci of ongoing creativity and dynamism. Wherever slaves and, especially, maroons had the physical and psychological space to cultivate their own gardens without external interference, subsistence activities (and the beliefs and values associated with them) became central not only to the physical well-being of these Afro-Americans but to their spiritual and moral life as well. Knowledge of the subsistence (and, in some cases, marketing) activities of slaves, in those parts of Plantation America where they were permitted or encouraged to spend their 'free time' in this fashion, remains relatively scanty, despite Sidney Mintz and Douglas Hall's pioneering identification of this area of research in the 1950s.[2] Considerably more details are now available, however, concerning the subsistence activities of certain *former* slaves and their descendants – the eighteenth-century Saramaka Maroons of Suriname, who concluded a peace treaty (granting them freedom and autonomy) with the Dutch crown in 1762. These materials are presented here in the hope that, because of their relative ethnographic richness, they may suggest analogues, contrasts, and above all new questions for research among historians whose window on that part of slave life beyond the view of the great house, the fields, and the factory has been narrower than they might wish.

My own knowledge of what these eighteenth-century Maroons grew in their gardens and around their houses, how and what they hunted, how they cooked and ate, and what they thought about all these activities is pieced together from diverse sources – German missionary diaries and dictionaries, Dutch military and administrative reports, and the oral testimonies of modern Saramakas. In this paper I more often present the results of these investigations than the evidence, since the latter is often embedded in discursive texts that do not lend themselves to article presentation.[3]

HORTICULTURE AND GATHERING

By the mid-eighteenth century Saramakas had already developed a
unique calendar with which they conceptualized and regulated horticultural tasks. Strikingly African or non-European (for example, in its
focus on named seasons rather than months and in its lunar basis), it was
at the same time clearly influenced by the experience of plantation
slavery (for example, in the Portuguese-Jewish timing of New Year and
the several Portuguese-Jewish names for days of the week). It stands as
a signal example of the ways that Saramakas appropriated bits of
plantation culture and moulded and integrated them into their own
nascent African-derived system, transforming their original function
and meaning (in this case, regulating work and worship) to make them
fully their own.[4] Recently I attempted to capture something of the work
rhythm regulated by this calendar in describing the activities of an
eighteenth-century Saramaka chief, Alabi, during the second half of
1772 (based on missionary documents and administrative reports):

> Alabi and his kinsmen devoted the month of August to felling
> trees in the new gardens, the most dangerous and difficult of
> horticultural tasks. Groups of three or four men worked together,
> first carefully 'examining the site' (S. *luku goon basu*), walking for
> several hours through the area scouting ecological hazards and
> potentials: Was the soil moist? sandy? heavy? Were there large
> boulders or silk-cotton trees that might house *apukus* [forest
> spirits], termite nests that housed fierce *akataasi* spirits, or the
> tell-tale holes of snake-gods, all of which had to be given a wide
> berth? When they had settled on a potential site for a garden, one
> of the older men balanced a palmfrond device on two quickly cut
> short poles, and prayed to the god-who-has-the-place to permit
> them to make their gardens there. Then, retiring for the night,
> they ate cassava cakes and fishbroth, served by the women who
> had accompanied them, before slinging their hammocks in the
> open sheds they had constructed near the river. The next morning
> they returned to see if the palmfrond was still in place, signaling
> that the god was at ease with their plans.[5] During the next several
> days they cleared the underbrush with machetes, before settling
> down to the heavy axe-work.
>   Working in pairs, often balancing on precarious platforms built
> around a thick trunk high above the folded buttresses of a forest
> giant, Alabi's brothers swung in alternating rhythm at the hard
> trunks, singing melodically complex call-and-response axe-songs

that at once boasted of their own strength and prowess (giving them the courage to continue) and spoke directly, by name, to the forest spirits, begging their assistance in the dangerous task at hand.[6]

After several weeks of labor, Alabi and his companions paddled upstream, returning again in October to set fire to the then-dry fields ... Once the rains came, during the final two moons of the year, planting – carried out for the most part by the women – took place in earnest, and before New Year's most crops were in the ground: rice, cassava, plantains and bananas, peanuts, sugar cane, maize, sweet potatoes and a variety of other root crops, capsicum, okra, watermelon, pineapple, and various others.[7]

The missionaries nowhere provide a comprehensive list of eighteenth-century Saramaka cultigens, but they mention in passing a startling number of species. Taken together, the Moravian records make clear that Saramakas, while escaping from slavery and living on the plantation periphery before the long southward migrations of the early eighteenth century, brought with them and elaborated in their temporary villages – during wartime – the full array of crops that their descendants plant today. Indeed, except for several quite unimportant twentieth-century crop introductions, the eighteenth-century repertoire was identical to that of two centuries later (see Table 1). The major crops were rice, cassava, plantains and bananas, and (mainly as a cash crop) peanuts; each of the first three was grown in a garden devoted primarily to that crop, with other cultigens interspersed in the same field – what Saramakas referred to as a 'rice ground', a 'cassava ground', or a 'banana ground'.[8] Rice, which today comprises some 70 per cent of the Saramaka diet by bulk, already held a central place in Saramaka farming by the mid-eighteenth century, but there are indications that it may have been more evenly balanced with cassava and plantains than today.[9] A particular meal centred on one or another of these three staples (the cassava in the form of round 'bread'), with meats or fish or green vegetables (okra, wild greens and so forth) as sauces. Other crops – sweet potatoes, maize, bananas, sugar cane and so on – had their specialized uses and were served outside of the main-meal framework.[10]

Table 1 represents a considerable oversimplification in that Saramakas distinguish (and distinguished in the eighteenth century) a large number of *subvarieties* of most of the crops mentioned. In the 1960s Sally Price and I elicited more than 70 named rice varieties then being planted; we found 15 varieties of okra, four of maize, a dozen of sweet potato, four of sugar cane, 15 of tania, six of watermelon, ten of hot

TABLE 1

A COMPARISON OF GARDEN-GROWN FOOD CROPS ACCORDING TO
18TH-CENTURY MISSIONARY RECORDS & OUR OWN OBSERVATIONS

	1770s	1970s
rice	x	x
wild rice	x^1	x
cassava	x	x
plantains	x	x
bananas	x	x
yams (*Diascorea alata* & other spp.)	x	x
sweet potato	x	x
napi (*Diascorea trifida*)	x	x
tania (*Xanthosoma sagittifolium*)	x	x
peanuts	x	x
gobogobo (*Voandzeia subterranea* Thouars – an African groundnut)	x	x
sugar cane	x	x
maize	x	x
okra	x	x
pineapple	x	x
maracudja (passion fruit)	x	x
bean (*Phaseolus* spp.)	x	x
pigeon pea	x^2	x
hot pepper	x	x
cashew	x	x
papaya	x	x
pumpkin	x	x
cucumber	x^3	x
coffee	x	x^4
bokolele ('wild' spinach)	$-^5$	x
watermelon	–	x
dasheen (*Colocasia esculenta*) and suu [F.G. Creole '*chou caraibe*']	–	x^6
gherkin, *waindja*, *kesipe*, eggplant, tomato, stringbeans, ginger	–	x^7
sesame	–	x^8

1. Wild rice (*matu alisi*) is grown today only for use in ritual food-offerings to the eighteenth-century ancestors. It is unclear from the missionary documents whether eighteenth-century Saramakas cultivated this type of rice or simply gathered it where it grew near swampy places in the forest.
2. I am equating modern Saramaccan *pesi* (etymologically from English 'peas') with Schumann's *pua* (from French 'pois') on the basis of descriptions (and the fact that the terms are in complementary distribution).
3. Saramakas insisted to me that cucumbers – now considered a *bakaa* ('western' or 'whitefolks'') food – were introduced to Saramaka only during the twentieth century (along with tomatoes, eggplant, and suchlike). Perhaps it was the missionaries themselves who originally introduced the crop, which disappeared with their early-nineteenth-century departure, only to be reintroduced a hundred years later.
4. Coffee is grown by Saramakas today only for use in ritual. During the eighteenth century, not only Saramakas but also the missionaries grew it – the latter on a fairly large scale, with mixed success, both to supply their own needs and as a cash crop for export.

5. Modern Saramakas collect this wild green in the forest and, occasionally, plant it in their gardens. A characteristically 'women's' food, this is one the missionaries would have been likely to miss, even if Saramakas planted it.
6. These two root crops were introduced from French Guiana at the turn of the present century.
7. These crops, and several others planted only rarely today, were introduced from coastal Suriname during the present century.
8. This is a relatively recent introduction, considered to be essentially a coastal or Djuka Maroon crop. Some Saramakas now grow it in their gardens but only for use in medicines, not for food.

pepper, 15 of bananas-plantains, 20 of cassava, seven of yams, nine of *napi* (another root crop) and so on. Despite Brother Schumann's mention of five subvarieties of 'yam', there is insufficient information in the eighteenth-century records to do a comparison at this level of detail.[11]

Saramaka villages, like Afro-American slave settlements in many parts of the hemisphere, were dotted with cultivated trees and plants, and other useful plants were encouraged to grow in the environs as well. The missionaries mention as cultivated village plants, coffee, cacao, oranges, limes, shaddocks, bananas, sugar cane and cashew, as well as cotton, tobacco, gourds, calabashes and various medicinal plants.

By the mid-eighteenth century Saramakas had also developed deep knowledge of the vegetation that grew wild in the Suriname forest. They made cooking oil from at least five different species of palm, in the most labour-intensive of all food preparation procedures.[12] They felled at least two species of palm to extract their 'hearts' or 'cabbages' and ate the fruits of five others. The missionaries noted at least eight additional wild trees from which Saramakas gathered fruit as well as mentioning two kinds of wild spinach. The repertoire of wild medicinal plants was also extensive: despite the missionaries' horror at the 'heathen' practices connected with curing, they mention a number of trees and bushes exploited by Saramakas as medicine – the '*jongro*' tree for a laxative, the annatto for various ritual uses, and others. And Saramakas drew on forest resources for a variety of other needs as well – from the crabwood tree that provided the fruit that was placed in a basketry holder as bait for bow-fishing, to the '*ingri sopu*' plant that provided soap, to the '*kandea*' tree whose resin provided natural candles, to the '*kwattri*' tree whose bast was formed into shoulder straps for muskets, to the various basketry and arrow-making reeds (especially *Ischnosiphon gracilis*), the several fish-drugging vines and bushes, and the many special woods used to fashion furniture, utensils and canoes – to mention only a few. All building materials also came from the forest.[13] And Saramakas exploited other aspects of forest life through 'gathering' as well: for example, female leaf-carrying ants

(*Atta cephalotes*) were 'considered a delicacy' at certain stages of their development;[14] grilled or fried palmnut grubs (the larvae of *Rhynchophorus palmarum*) were much appreciated;[15] and wild honey was extracted from trees whenever available.

Despite the rich crop repertoire that Saramakas had developed by the mid-eighteenth century, periods of near famine were not rare. Lean years might result from early rains (which prevented fields from being properly fired), not enough rain after planting or depredations from leaf-cutting ants and other horticultural pests. The crunch, when it came, usually occurred in the early months of the year, just before the new crops were ready to harvest but when those of the previous year had already been consumed. In early April 1780, for example, one of the Moravian diarists wrote, 'The starvation among the local negroes

TABLE 2

A COMPARISON OF WILD FOREST PLANTS USED FOR FOOD ACCORDING TO
18TH-CENTURY MISSIONARY RECORDS & OUR OWN OBSERVATIONS

	1770s	1970s
awara palm [*Astrocaryum segregatum*] (oil, fruit)	x	x
amana palm [*Guilielma gasipaes* Bailey] (oil)	x	x
maripa palm [*Maximiliana maripa* Drude] (oil, fruit, and 'cabbage' or 'heart')	x	x
maka palm [*Astrocaryum sciophilum* Pulle] (oil, fruit)	x	x
pina palm [*Euterpe oleracea* Mart.] ('cabbage' or 'heart')	–[1]	x
kokoabra palm [?] (fruit)	x	x
morosi palm [*Mauritia flexuosa* L. fil.] (fruit)	x	x
kumu palm [*Oenocarpus bacaba* Mart.] (oil, fruit)	x	x
watji [*Inga* spp.] (fruit)	x	x
kimboto [any of several Sapotaceae] (fruit)	x	x
mamadosu [*Duroia eriopila* L. fil] (fruit)	x	x
mboa (*Amaranthus* spp. – wild spinach)	x	x
tonka [*Dipteryx odorata* Willd.] (beans)	x	x
cashew (fruit)	x	x
bullitiri [balata, *Manilkara bedentata* Chev.] (fruit)	x	x
maracudja (fruit)	x	x
apanta, lokisi [*Hymenaea courbaril*], *afonafion*, *kwatibobi* [*Chrysophyllum cuneifolium* A. DC.], *ate*	–[2]	x
bokolele (wild spinach)	–	x
malobi [*Ecclinusa guianensis* Eyma] (fruit)	–	x

1. Since eighteenth-century Saramakas exploited maripa trees for their 'cabbages', and since pina palms were used for roofing and other non-food purposes, it seems likely that pina 'cabbages' would have been used as well, though the missionaries do not mention them.
2. I learned about these five edible fruits or seeds only by asking, hypothetically, about 'survival' food for a man lost in the forest. It seems quite likely that such survival knowledge would have been greater, not less, in the eighteenth century, and that the missionaries were simply unaware of these and similar potential forest foods.

has reached enormous proportions. Yesterday evening a baptized man came to us and asked for a meal. We could not help him as we ourselves have nothing in the house'.[16] And the following year a missionary on a river trip noted that he and his companions 'came to a small village where they had nothing to eat, so we had to retire to our hammocks hungry'.[17] During such periods non-cultivated forest foods must have been particularly important dietary supplements – palm cabbages and various palm fruits, different kinds of wild vegetables and so on.

HUNTING, FISHING, AND DOMESTIC ANIMALS

Once active concern about the war against the whites had receded, hunting and fishing became a primary activity for men. And though the Moravians were not particularly interested in Saramaka forest activities, a close reading of the missionary records makes clear that the Maroons had already developed an extensive repertoire of hunting and fishing techniques, derived from Suriname Indians as well as their diverse African homelands.[18]

Saramakas captured fish by shooting with bow and a variety of arrow-types, with various kinds of ingenious traps, with several different drugging techniques and (though it seems to have been relatively unimportant) with hook-and-homemade (*singaasi*) line. Schumann mentions three kinds of arrow wood, with the main reed shaft (as tall as a man) harbouring a thinner, harder, much shorter piece of wood, which itself housed the tip; pitch from the *mani* tree bound shaft and tip under a tightly-wound layer of homespun cotton thread, and there were at least five kinds of tips (hooked, triple-pointed, detachable-tipped, and so on). Today each such arrow-type has a specific use, for example the *pina* (Schumann's *pinna*) – a harpoon with a line made from the *singaasi* plant – is used only in torchlight fishing for a species of large striped fish that, at a certain period of the year, ascend the rapids at night, and *taanze* (Schumann's *transeh*) – which have an extra-long hardwood section, whittled to a point – are used solely for the fish called *kakaaku*. And there were special techniques for bow fishing involving other props as well: Schumann describes how a basketry *musini* was filled with *kaapa* fruit and hung by a line near the riverbank, where the *mbooko* fish were attracted and shot with a bow (a technique I witnessed 200 years later). The former place of bow-and-arrow fishing as a measure of manhood is today preserved, at a time when the less skill-requiring handline fishing has become more popular, in the way old people heap compliments on a youth who has brought back a fish he has shot. And little boys still learn to hunt with small bows, using village-dwelling lizards as targets, as an important marker of masculinity.

The missionaries describe two kinds of fish-traps, the first of which (*bakisi*) is still used today to catch *nyumaa* and *pataka*.[19] The second, which Schumann called *dika* (modern Saramaka *nika*) is little used by Saramakas today though it is still found in the plantation area from which many of the ancestors of Saramakas escaped.[20] Saramakas know several other weirs and traps, though all are considered old-fashioned and nearly obsolete. This knowledge, and the frequency of references to such items in Saramaka folktales, suggests that they were even more important in the eighteenth century than the missionaries knew.[21]

The Moravians mention three kinds of fish-drugging – all familiar to me from the 1960s. The first is today a women's technique in which small balls containing the leaves of *Tephrosia toxicaria* (S. *wanapu*) are thrown in a stream and individually consumed, with the drugged fish scooped out with a basketry net. The second used *uwii ndeku* (*Lonchocarpus* spp.), the leaves from a bush, to drug streams. But by far most important, in the eighteenth century as today, were the roots of the forest vine *Lonchocarpus nicou* D.C., beaten on river rocks to release their active ingredient, rotenone, after which large quantities of 'drunk' fish could be speared, shot with bows and arrows, scooped up in baskets, or caught with bare hands, for a distance of several rapids downstream from the release of the drug.[22]

Hunting was not a missionary preoccupation and they say little about it. But they make clear that bows and arrows (which are no longer used except for fish) played a major role during the whole second half of the eighteenth century, when guns and powder were often scarce. And arrow poison, no longer known to Saramakas, was apparently in frequent use.[23] In addition, Saramakas used several kinds of traps (still known today): a 'fall' for armadillos, a trap used for opossum and agouti and another for wood rats, both modelled directly on West African precedents, and others.[24] And animals and fish were not only used for eating: drumheads were made from deerskin, as were hunting sacks; the tails of stingrays were used in medicine, certain monkey's tails were used as whiskbrooms, opossum bones served as repellents against cockroaches, the feathers of a certain inedible bird were used to clean out earwax and so on.

Table 3 lists those game, fish and bird species mentioned by the missionaries; all of these, as well as a number I did not find in the written records, are still eaten by Saramakas today. Note that the list is by far most complete for game – which, especially in the case of certain large mammals (rather than monkeys, lizards and so on) formed the missionaries' preferred food – and that none of the major species hunted today was omitted. In contrast, only a small proportion of the fish and birds hunted today appear by name in the missionaries' documents; in these cases, the Moravians usually wrote generically of eating 'fish' or 'birds', but there is no reason to think that Saramaka knowledge was any less developed in these areas.

TABLE 3

GAME, FISH, AND BIRDS HUNTED IN THE EIGHTEENTH CENTURY
ACCORDING TO MISSIONARY RECORDS

18-century name	GAME
adjinja	tree porcupine, modern *adjindja*
akkuschuweh	'small, four-footed animal, kind of rabbit (sometimes this animal is called *sranda*)' (Schumann), modern *akusuwe*
alattu	wood rat (hunted especially by youths), modern *alatu*
awali	opossum, modern *awali*
babun	howler monkey, modern *babunu*
bambi	'a very pretty kind of lizard the negroes like to eat' (Schumann), modern *bambi*
batta	small deer, modern *mbata*
boffre	tapir, modern *bofo*
djrenjeh	squirrel, modern *djendje*
kamba	the medium-sized armadillo, modern *kamba*
kappasi	the smallest armadillo, modern *kapasi*
kapwiwa	the capybara, modern *kapiwa*
keeskees	'a small monkey' (Schumann), modern *kesikesi*
konikoni	agouti, modern *kokoni*
kossari	deer, modern *kusai*
kussiri	a small monkey, modern *kusii*
kwatriwoijo	a small marsupial, modern *kpati-woyo*
kwatta	'a long-haired black monkey' (Schumann), the spider monkey, modern *kwata*
loggosso	turtle, modern *logoso*
makaku	'a small brown or grey monkey' (Schumann), modern *makaku*
malloleh	the largest armadillo, modern *malole*
pakkira	the collared peccary, modern *pakia*
pingo	'the best kind of wild pig' (Schumann), the white-lipped peccary, modern *pingo*
siku	'an African monkey' (Schumann), modern *saki*
silo	sloth, modern *silo*
sranda	a rodent, modern saanda (see s.v. *akkuschuweh*)
tamanua	the giant anteater, modern *tamanoa*
waijamakka	'for the negroes a delicacy' (Schumann), the iguana, modern *wayamaka*
walleli	the lesser anteater, modern *walili*
waniku	'kind of monkey' (Schumann), modern *waniku*
warapuja	the otter, modern *awaapuya*
warrana	'West Indian hare' (Schumann), the paca, modern *waana*

FISH

akomu	kind of eel, modern *akomu*
jakki	modern *djaki*
jumarra, haimar	'the best fish in the country' (Schumann), modern *nyumaa*, or the related *pataka*
kullelu	modern *kululu*
kakraku	'awful tasting but much loved by the negroes' (Schumann), modern *kakaaku*
lobolobo	modern *logbologbo*
moroko	modern *mbooko*
plenja	the piranha, modern *peenya*

BIRDS

akami	the trumpeter, modern *akami*
alalla	'a pretty blue and red parrot' (Schumann), modern *alala* the dove, modern *pumba*
bomba	
gabiam	hawk, modern *gabian*
gwanini	eagle, modern *gbanini*
kinollo	'the prettiest kind of parrot' (Schumann), modern *kindoo-alala* (?)
kiwallala	'an ugly kind of parrot' (Schumann), modern (?)
makkapuija	modern *amakapunya*
malai	'bush turkey' (Schumann), modern *maai*
mauwi	'a smaller bush hen' (Schumann), modern *mawi*
namu	'bush hen' (Schumann), modern *anamu*
pattupattu	wild duck, modern *patupatu*
prakiki	'a small parakeet' (Schumann), modern *paatjitjı*
prikittu	'a small parakeet' (Schumann), modern *piikutu*
sorrosorro	'the largest parakeet' (Schumann), modern *soosoo*
suwi	'kind of bush hen, smaller than most others' (Schumann), modern *sui*
tokkro	'a smaller bush hen' (Schumann), modern *tokoo*
waijonne	'a small parrot' (Schumann), modern *wayona*
woko	a bush turkey, also called Powies, modern *oko*

Saramakas, in the eighteenth century as today, had relatively few domestic animals compared with their Amerindian neighbours in the South American rain forest. Chickens, kept as much for their crucial role in divination and offerings to gods and ancestors as for food, were the only edible animals present in every village – though only a few people in each settlement kept them. Men often had hunting dogs, trained, as today, by Amerindians who traded them to Saramakas for 'whitefolks' goods' obtained on the coast or at the biennial tribute-distributions. Other than these, domestic animals were rare: the missionaries mention an occasional duck, a few pigs and sheep, and even a couple of cows, but I believe these were largely confined to the tiny band of Christian Saramakas. In any case, today – and within the memory of the oldest Saramakas I know – pigs, sheep and cows are prototypical 'whitefolks" or 'foreign' animals, associated only with visits to the coast.

FOOD PROCESSING, COOKING, AND MEALS

By the mid-eighteenth century Saramakas had already developed the techniques for processing rice and cassava, their two most important staples, that their descendants use today – the first composed largely of African utensils and knowledge, the second of those learned from the Amerindians who once inhabited Saramaka territory. Rice preparation involved threshing (Schumann, s.v. *sakkuli*) – separating the heads from the stalks – by beating with sticks; winnowing (s.v. *blo*) – separating the grain from the chaff – on a circular wooden tray (s.v. *plattupau*); pounding with large wooden mortar and pestle (s.v. *fumm, matta, tatti*) to remove outer husk and inner cuticle from the rice grains; and then a final whitening (s.v. *weti*) by winnowing once more.[25] Cassava processing followed the standard Amerindian steps and equipment: washing, peeling, and grating the roots (on a board with inlaid sharp stones (s.v. *lala*)); expelling the poisonous juice with a basketry squeezer (s.v. *matappi*); mashing the pulp in a mortar and pestle (s.v. *kassaba*); sifting the flour in a basketry sieve (s.v. *manari*); and, eventually, cooking the flour in large round cakes (s.v. (*kassaba-*)*kuka*) on a griddle (s.v. *kibenge, alinatu*) made of earthenware or, by the late-eighteenth century, iron.[26]

Meat and fish were preserved primarily through smoking, as salt remained a scarce commodity until the twentieth century (s.v. *memeh, maemae, sula*), but the missionary records make clear that large kills were distributed, as today, through broad kinship networks, diminishing the need for preservation. Cooking pots – mainly earthenware but with some iron, especially after the Peace – were set on three earthenware hearthstones (*makuku* – a KiKoongo word) and fuelled by wood, lit by flintstones and a tree fungus (Schumann 1778, s.v. *fungu*). Gourds and calabashes provided most containers and eating utensils (s.v. *gollu, kuja, tappadorro, kallabas*). Moravian Brother Riemer, describing his very first meal in Saramaka in 1779, left a graphic picture, coloured by his Middle European lenses, of how his hosts ate:

> Then they led me into another hut where many of them were preparing food according to their custom. All of the negroes sat down on very low stools in order to eat the food, which stood in calabashes on the ground, and my negro [slave] brought a little stool from our canoe for me, so that I could sit and eat.
>
> After the women and children had, as a group, stepped back

from the men's hut, we could partake of our meal, which consisted
of banana pudding – which is rather like mashed potatoes – and
peanut broth. (According to the old custom which the negroes
have brought from their fatherland, Guinea, the male and female
sex eat separately, so that a husband never takes a meal in the
presence of his wife. The Europeans believe that the reason is
this: those negresses who live in freedom generally rule over
their husbands, work very little, and pay little attention to their
husband's business. But even among them, there are some
reasonable women who work hard and maintain a clean and
orderly household.) The negroes eat with their fingers, taking the
food, dipping it in broth, and then placing it into their mouths.
True, this does not look appetizing, but I must confess that the
negroes carefully wash their mouth and hands before eating. And
often they repeat this each time a new dish is served. I asked them
why their womenfolk do not eat with them, as we Europeans
believe it is more pleasant to take our meals together. They were
very surprised and one of them answered, in a rather apathetic
manner, 'Well, they prefer to eat by themselves, as well'.[27]

This initial description is supplemented by many others that make clear
the importance of male–female separation, group eating, sitting on low
stools, taking food from calabashes with the fingers, washing before
and after courses and other African-derived patterns.

As for food preparation, meat and fish seem normally to have been
boiled, sometimes after having been browned in oil, and then eaten
either with rice or by dipping cassava cakes into the broth (Schumann,
s.v. *blaffo*). Small fish were also sometimes grilled directly on the
fire or fried in oil. But more complex recipes abounded[28] and can be
glimpsed through the missionaries' brief allusions: *tummtumm*, which
Schumann described as 'a thick vegetable mixture, usually made with
bananas';[29] *fadda*, 'a fine dish made by pounding bananas, boiling
them, and mixing them with [ground] peanuts, so that it forms a thick
puree'; *apitipiti*, 'dumplings of green bananas' (today made with
cassava flour); *dokkunu*, 'peanut butter';[30] *angu*, 'a dish made with rice
or banana flour, cooked into a thick puree and eaten with okra or
peanut sauce' (today solely a ritual dish); *assogidi*, 'a thick pap of
bananas and corn, made from roasted, ground up corn mixed with
mashed bananas' (today made from roasted corn and sugar, and used in
rituals for the eighteenth-century ancestors); *akra*, a kind of pancake
cooked in the oil of the *kumu* palm; *akumaba*, 'a dumpling made from
rice flour'; and *dumbru*, a kind of 'dumpling'. There were at least four
locally-made alcoholic drinks, all of Amerindian origin: *tapana*, 'a

drink made from cassava and sweet potatoes that is, when well-fermented, strong and agreeable' (today used in rituals); *tumma*, boiled cassava juice; *woko*, a fermented banana drink, with a complex preparation; and fermented sugar cane juice.

It is probably worth making a brief anthropological pitch – even if the supporting details are not always easily available for the past – for the examination of the cultural meanings of different kinds of crops and foods. Just as, for example, our Martiniquan neighbours get special pleasure from thinking about ripening *ignames* (as opposed to other rootcrops) – because of their association with Christmas, their (hidden) relationship to Africa, and probably much else – eighteenth-century Saramakas, as already mentioned, saw rice as prototypical 'food', *pingo* (peccary) as 'meat' par excellence, and (to cite a more interesting example) in contrast to slave preferences in the American south ('there is nothing in all butcherdom so delicious as a roasted possum'),[31] opossum as a relatively undesirable meat, to be eaten only when nothing else was available to accompany rice. And foods appropriate for eighteenth-century meals were divided conceptually from those considered *piki nyanya* ('snack foods') – sweet potatoes, maize, bananas, palm fruits, and so forth.[32]

LABOUR AND IDEOLOGY

Following the Peace of 1762 Saramakas lived in a most uneasy relation with their former colonial masters, dependent on them for biennial tribute specified in the treaty, bound by that same agreement to return post-treaty maroons and ever-aware of living on the periphery of a world in which slavery remained in full force.[33] Labour for whitefolks was not, for the time being, directly in question – except in so far as a small number of Saramakas grudgingly provided the German missionaries resident in their villages with services in exchange for goods or cash. However, limited trading with the coastal slave society was permitted by the treaty and some Saramakas occasionally grew rice and peanuts or made canoes for export (either trading them for molasses and rum on the Suriname River plantations or shopping with the proceeds in Paramaribo for salt, tools, cloth and so forth – both highly dangerous ventures during the period). And, yet more important, Saramaka men were almost constantly engaged in political interactions with colonial officials within Saramaka territory that kept very much alive the adversarial relations that had characterized slavery and would mark their entry into wage labour following general emancipation in Suriname in 1863.[34]

There is a folktale that captures much of the tone of Saramaka ideology regarding what they call 'labour for whitefolks' (*bakaa wooko*).[35] In the tale, plantation slavery and wage slavery are poetically merged, and the Saramaka secret to slaves' or Maroons' survival in these contexts is clearly spelled out: never accept the white man's definition of the situation. Eighteenth-century Saramakas who had lived through both slavery and war learned to survive and even triumph in situations of gross inequality. This folktale, though recorded in the twentieth century from their descendants, joins such Saramaka historical accounts as 'Kwasimukamba's Gambit' or such folktales as *Nouna*, as central expressions of Saramaka identity, as it had already been developed by the time of the treaty.[36] And it is a telling comment, from a Saramaka perspective, about the alienation of labour that occurred (and continues to occur) in coastal situations, beyond Saramaka territory.

It used to be there was plenty of wage-labour work. You'd go off to look for work, and there would always be some job available. There was one guy and you'd just go ask him for work, a white man. He was the one in charge of it. Now when you went to ask him for work, You'd say, 'Well, Brother, I've come to ask you for a job'. Then he'd say to you, 'Well, look. I've got some.' He has a big tremendous rice field. He's got a cacao field. He's got all kinds of fields spread out all around. He's got pigs. He's got cows. He's got chickens. He's got ducks. So you just appear out of nowhere, and ask him for a job, and he says to you, 'Well, Brother, I've got some cacao over there. You could go gather the beans and bring them back to me. I'll give you a bag'. So off you'd go. But when you went to touch it, one of the cacao plants would break off, and all the beans would fall down and run all over the place. The plant would be absolutely stripped. So you walk back to the king. (That's the white man who has the jobs. He's just like a king.) You'd talk to him and say, 'Well, king. Here I am. I went and touched one of the cacao plants to get the beans, and they all fell on the ground'. So you told him about how everything fell down to the ground. The man says, 'Really? Well, my boy, when the cacao fell like that, did it hurt you?' He said, 'Yes, my king, it hurt me'. King says, 'OK, bring your butt over here'. [laughter] He'd slice off a kilo of butt. One kilo of flesh that he just cut right off and took. When the time came, you'd just go to your house and die.

Then the next person would come along asking for work. He'd say, 'My king, I've come to ask you for a job'. He'd say, 'Well, no problem. In the morning, just go let out the cows I've got over there, let them out of the pen and bring them outside'. In the morning, the man went and opened the pen right up. The cows fell down, *gulululu*, fell down, all over the ground, dead. He went back and said, 'My king, I went like you said and opened the cows' pen over there. All of them fell down on the ground, dead'. He said, 'My boy, did it hurt you?' He said, 'Yes, my king'. The king said, 'Bring your butt over here'. He turned his butt toward the king and went over. The king sliced off one kilo and took it. The guy went off and died.

So that's the way it went. He just kept killing people. But the name of the king – I forgot to mention that. The king was 'King Nothing-hurts-him' (or 'King Nothing-angers-him').

But there was a young guy who decided to go ask for work. His mother didn't want him to. She said, 'Child, don't go. The place where you're going to go ask for work – Well, not a single person has gone to ask for work there and returned. If you go ask for work there, you're as good as dead and gone. Don't go'. He said he was determined to go. He arrived. He said, 'My king, I've come to ask you for a job'. 'All right', he said. He said, 'My boy, do you know who I am?' The boy said, 'No'. He said, 'I am King Nothing-hurts-him'. He said, 'OK, no problem'. And he went off to the work he had. He went off to pick the cacao. As he reached up to touch it, all the beans fell down and ran all over the ground. He went back to the king. He said, 'King, I went to touch the cacao over there to harvest it, and it all fell down onto the ground before I even touched it'. He said, 'My boy, did it hurt?' The boy said, 'No. My king, it didn't hurt me'. King said, 'OK. No problem. It's all right'. He said, 'Let's go to sleep for the night'.

In the morning he said, 'Well, my boy? I'd like you to go harvest a field of rice I've got over there. Just go on and cut the rice'. He went off, reached out to cut a stalk of rice, and they all fell and covered the whole area, *gulululu*. He went back, and he said, 'My king, I went to cut the rice over there and all the stalks fell over to the ground'. He said, 'My boy, didn't it hurt?' He said, 'No. How could it have hurt me?' He said, 'OK'. So nothing happened. The next morning, he said, 'I'd like you to let out some chickens I've got over there'. He went to let them out. But as he opened the door, all the chickens fell down on the ground, dead. As things fell, he would take something and just kill them right off. It didn't bother him if things fell. This was a kid who wasn't hurt by anything. He'd just cut things down. He'd just cut it down and kill it.

The king said, 'Well, my boy. In the morning you'll go and open a duck pen I've got over there'. He opened it. Whoosh!! Flap!

They just kept on coming out and falling down. That finished every one of them off, just cut them up, dead! He went back and said, 'My king, those ducks I went to let out, well, such-and-such a thing happened'. He said, 'Well, my boy, did it hurt you?' He said, 'My king, it didn't hurt me'. 'Oh', he said. Well, this kept going on and on until there was nothing left in that place. I don't need to list all that was gone. There was absolutely nothing left. He'd killed everything. All that was left was some pigs he had.

So he said, 'Well, my boy. Go open up the pig pen over there'. So he went to let out the pigs. The pigs all fell down. So he jumped out and he clubbed them all to death. Cut them all up. Cut off their tails and took them. Then he buried those tails. He took the rest of the pigs' bodies and hid them off in the underbrush. He just buried those tails till all that was left above ground was a tiny bit, the tips were barely sticking up.

He just did it to make a problem with the king. He killed absolutely all of them. Then he came out and he ran to him. He went straight to his king. 'My king, my king!' he said. 'I went to go let out the pigs, and all of them burrowed down under the ground! So I ran back to tell you!' [laughter] The king said [very agitated], 'Where?' He said, 'Over there!' The king said, 'Let's go!' He ran off and when he arrived he looked around. Now, the way they were buried, the pig's tails went deep into the ground, and only a little piece was sticking up. You couldn't grab it to pull it out. They grabbed them as tight as they could. The king said, 'This won't work. You know what we'll do?' 'What?' said the boy. 'Run back to my wife, in the house over there. [laughter] Go have her give you a shovel. Quick! Bring it back'. The kid ran back there. He really ran fast to get there, and he said, 'Quick! Hurry up, as fast as you can. My king says to!' 'All right', she said. So then he told her – 'My king says to tell you – Well, he just says that I should "live" with you'. [exclamations and laughter] 'What did you say?!!' she asked. 'Yes', he said. '"Quick! Quick! Quick!" That's what he said!' She said, 'No way!' The king turned and shouted back to her, 'Quick! Give it to him quick! Give it to him quick! Give it to him right away!' She said, 'OK, I understand'. The king said 'Give it to him! Give it to him! Give it to him! Fast! Fast!' [hysterical laughter] That's what he said. 'Give him! Give him! Give him! Give him! Give him!' The boy took the wife and threw her right down on the bed. And then he went to work.

Well, that shovel that the king sent the boy back for, in a rush, so they could dig up the pigs – Well, the boy didn't bring it back very quickly. He was gone for quite a while, and finally the king said, 'something's wrong'. He ran on back to the house, looked in, and the boy was on top of his lady. [exclamations] He fell backwards and just lay there. The boy said, 'My king, did this hurt you?' He said, 'Yes, this hurt me'. The boy said, 'Bring your butt over here!' [wild laughter] The king turned his butt toward the boy and approached him. He brought his butt over. The boy lopped off a kilo. And then the king died. That's why things are the way they are for us. Otherwise, it would have been that whenever you asked for work from a white man, a king, he'd kill you. The boy took care of all that for us. That's as far as my story goes.

Refusing to accept the white man's definition of the situation, the boy triumphed in the end. And today, however hard it is for Saramaka men to retain their inner strength and dignity while submitting to humiliating work and treatment in coastal wage labour situations (cleaning out toilets at the French missile base at Kourou, for example), tales like this – and First-Time memories of heroic eighteenth-century events – help them keep going.[37]

Meanwhile, Saramaka subsistence labour – making and tending gardens, hunting and fishing, preparing food – has (and had) a wholly different tone. In the eighteenth century, as today, the most routine subsistence tasks of men and women were deeply infused with social and cultural meaning. As Sally Price writes of the strong positive feelings held by modern Saramaka women toward their gardens, located several hours from the villages,

> They view the [garden] camp as a bounteous storehouse: the whole range of domestic crops is readily available; useful forest products, from edible palm fruits to roofing materials, are close at hand; the trees felled for garden sites provide a convenient supply of firewood; and the yields for every kind of fishing and hunting are many times greater than they are around villages ... [And in terms of the symbolic meaning of food preparation:] It is perhaps not surprising that women often include a bottle of [labour-intensively produced] cooking oil in formal gift presentations to their husbands, even though men do not use it themselves, for oil rendering (like a smoothly mounded bowl of rice) epitomizes women's work, and the final product is viewed by Saramakas as an important symbol of wifely devotion and conscientiousness.[38]

Likewise, Saramaka men spend (and spent) large portions of their lives off in the forest, fishing and hunting, and these pursuits represent the very height of masculine values. To reiterate: Saramaka subsistence activities are embedded in complex webs of social and cultural meaning. Being engaged in them, as well as talking in great detail about

them, remain central to what it means to be Saramaka. And the
sharpness of the Saramaka conceptual dichotomy between, on the
one hand, slavery and wage labour, and, on the other hand, their
subsistence activities at least suggests that – from the slaves' perspectives – provision grounds and field labour may have represented even
greater polarities than many scholars, attending more to 'practical' and
economic than to ideological or cultural concerns, might have us think.

NOTES

1. This paper was written in Martinique, overlooking a large tropical garden (containing yams, tania, sweet potatoes, maize, sugar cane, okra, cucumbers, bananas,
   peppers, and pumpkins, among other crops) that stretches down to the sea. Though
   most of the relevant ethnographic and historical data about eighteenth-century
   Suriname were available to me there, in the form of notes, much comparative
   literature that might have enriched the discussion was not. For the same reason, I
   cite scientific names only when necessary for clarity – in many cases, the texts that
   would have been needed for identification were not available to me. And, in any
   case, as John Gabriel Stedman wrote for his more ambitious foray into the flora and
   fauna of Suriname, 'the Linaen names may easily be added by the Connoisseurs'.
   (John Gabriel Stedman, *Narrative of a Five Years Expedition against the Revolted
   Negroes of Suriname* ed. by Richard Price and Sally Price (Baltimore, 1988), 8).
2. Sidney W. Mintz and Douglas Hall, *The Origins of the Jamaican Internal Marketing
   System*, Yale University Publications in Anthropology No. 57 (New Haven, 1960),
   3–26, and various papers collected in Mintz, *Caribbean Transformations* (Chicago,
   1974). Studies of provision ground cultivation have increased in recent years (see,
   for example, several papers in this volume), as have analyses of Caribbean
   peasantries in historical perspective (see, for an excellent example, Michel-Rolph
   Trouillot, *Peasants and Capital: Dominica in the World Economy* (Baltimore,
   1988)).
3. For detailed discussion of these sources, and for examples of such discursive
   texts, see Richard Price, *Alabi's World* (Baltimore, 1990). In this article, I have
   eliminated diacritical marks from Saramaka words, in accordance with the rules of
   Slavery & Abolition.
4. See Richard Price, 'To Every Thing a Season: The Development of Saramaka
   Calendric Reckoning', *Tijdschrift OSO*, 3 (1984), 63–71.
5. The previous year, Alabi's people had found it necessary to abandon an extensive
   already planted set of new gardens (at Tutu Creek) because of difficulties with
   the site. The missionaries claimed that these problems concerned drainage (F.
   Staehelin, *Die Mission der Brüdergemeine in Suriname und Berbice im achtzehnten
   Jahrhundert* (Herrnhut, 1913–19), IIIi, 180); but it seems more likely to me that
   difficulties with local gods were the proximate cause. Saramaka Captain Gome, in
   1978, described for me the domestication of the god that 'owned' Tutu Creek, as
   it finally took place during the mid-nineteenth century, allowing his ancestors
   (Alabi's descendants) finally to settle in the area.

> Tata Waimau Amosu, his wife Pelamma, and his brother Uwii. They came into
> the creek to cut gardens. But the creek didn't want people to come inside it, the
> *apuku* [forest spirit] who lived there called Masikweke. It fought with them.
> Surrounded them with a hundred [evil] things. Well, they made a shed ...
> [Waimau went hunting and returned] He said, 'I went hunting and killed only
> one bird!' She [his wife] said. 'Go to the Afoompisi people [the people who

today inhabit Tjalikonde, at Tutu Creek]. They have Baimbo [an *obia*]. Go to them. Beg them for help'. So he went. ... They told him what to prepare. He assembled: *nyanyan buka nyanyan* [a combination of various raw foods used in certain sacrifices], cane drink, parrot feathers, cowrie shells, a white-cloth hammock sheet, a white cock. Then they 'killed the chicken' [in divination]. To ask whether the place would accept them now. And they were able to come on over. ... That *apuku* had been so baad! If you tried to cross the creek in a canoe, it would sink you! So, they did it all [the ceremony]. Killed the chicken. Its testicles were pure white! [indicating that the god was pleased]. They raised the flag [the hammock sheet, planted on a pole]. They poured the sugar-cane libations [at its foot]. The *apuku* had said they could work the land there!

Saramaka techniques of site-divination, getting the *apuku* 'who-has-the-place' to agree to the use of the land, and to encourage its productivity, vary in detail. Some are as simple as placing a calabash with particular leaves and water on a forked stick for a week, after the fields have already been cleared, felled and burned, for the god's final approval; others involve the technique that I describe for Alabi's people, carried out before the land is desecrated at all. As with almost all Saramaka ritual, different people know and use different techniques and formulae. But every potential field site, especially in an area that has not previously been used for gardens, must be approached with respect and caution, and the local gods must be brought into the process of preparing it, planting it and harvesting it at every stage. And the process of interaction with the local gods is a central part of all horticultural activity, today as in the eighteenth century.

6. For examples of twentieth-century Saramaka axe songs, see Richard and Sally Price, *Music from Saramaka* (New York, Folkways Records, 1977).
7. R. Price, *Alabi's World*, Ch. 5.
8. C.L. Schumann, 'Saramaccanisch Deutsches Worter-Buch', in Hugo Schuchardt, *Die Sprache der Saramakkaneger in Surinam*, *Verhandelingen der Koninklijke Akademie van Wetenscappen te Amsterdam*, 14(6) (Amsterdam, 1914), 46–116, s.v. grun.
9. In Saramaka, cooked rice is called *nyanya*, also the generic noun for food; as a verb, *nyan* means 'to eat'.
10. For a recent discussion, with useful bibliography, of Caribbean subsistence cultivation, see Riva Berleant-Schiller and Lydia M. Pulsipher, 'Subsistence Cultivation in the Caribbean', *New West India Guide*, 60 (1986), 1–40.
11. Schumann, 'Saramaccanisch', s.v. *jammesi*.
12. During the 1960s, we were told by Peter Kloos, who was then studying the Galibi (Carib) – Suriname's largest group of Amerindians – that they no longer bothered to make cooking oil, buying imported oil instead. Meanwhile, he observed Saramaka women, using the technology their ancestors had learned from Indians two and a half centuries before, patiently manufacturing their own oil.
13. Details of eighteenth-century housebuilding are described in R. Price, *Alabi's World*, Ch. 3.
14. Schumann, 'Saramaccanisch', s.v. *seli*. Today, egg-bearing females boiled with water and salt are much appreciated.
15. For contemporary comments about similar tastes among Suriname slaves, see Stedman, *Narrative*, 338.
16. Staehelin, *Die Mission*, IIIii, 42.
17. Ibid., 47.
18. Gerhard Lindblom, *Afrikanische Relikte und Indianische Entlehnungen in der Kultur der Busch-Neger Surinams* (Gothenburg, 1924), represents the most detailed analysis of Indian and African influences in these realms, but it is based solely on the morphology of the relevant items of material culture and on extensive library research, rather than on field experience with their actual use.
19. For an illustration, see Stedman, *Narrative*, 497, where it is labelled 'the Spring-Basket'.

20. See Charles J. Wooding, *Winti: een afroamerkanse godsdienst in Suriname* (Meppel, 1972).
21. Richard and Sally Price, *Two Evenings in Saramaka* (Chicago, 1991).
22. See Schumann, 'Saramaccanisch', s.v. *domonnu, neku,* and *fissi.*
23. See ibid., s.v. *possinja.*
24. See ibid., s.v. *timba, trapu, mo,* and *awitti.*
25. Charles Joyner's descriptions of rice processing among South Carolina slaves (though involving wet, rather than dry, highland rice) are nearly identical, the main differences being that Saramakas used wooden rather than basketry 'fanners' for winnowing and that Saramaka mortars and pestles, which are otherwise similar to those in South Carolina, are – like all Saramaka wooden articles – much more finely made (Joyner, *Down by the Riverside: A South Carolina Slave Community* (Urbana, 1984), 45–50; Sally and Richard Price, *Afro-American Arts of the Suriname Rain Forest* (Berkeley, 1980)).
26. The introduction of iron griddles (modern Saramaccan *tjubenge*) was a major symbolic event, closely tied in the minds of modern Saramakas to the coming of Peace with the whitefolks after 100 years of war. A late-eighteenth century griddle still stands today on a special pedestal outside the doorway of the Tribal Chief, to commemorate a series of whitefolks–Saramaka transactions dating from this period (R. Price, *Alabi's World,* 423).
27. Johann Andreus Riemer, *Missions-Reise nach Suriname und Barbice* (Zittau and Leipzig, 1801), 205–7. As S. Price has written,

> Today [in Saramaka] ... visual isolation [of men and women eating] continues to be the critical variable. To Saramakas, one of the most exotic features of western culture is the custom of women eating within sight of their husbands. The segregation of the sexes is as strongly embedded in Saramaka concepts of propriety for meals as it is in western notions about public bathrooms. [*Co-wives and Calabashes* (Ann Arbor, 1984), 45]

For Riemer's more general discussion of eighteenth-century Saramaka meals, see *Missions-Reise,* 276–8; for S. Price's twentieth-century counterpart, *Co-wives,* 46, passim.
28. A historical and comparative study of Afro-Caribbean cuisine has yet to be undertaken. African-derived names for a number of dishes were (and in many cases are) widespread throughout the region, though the same name sometimes designated rather different dishes in different places. Etymological dictionaries of creole languages (such as F.G. Cassidy and R.B. Le Page (eds.), *Dictionary of Jamaican English* 2nd edn (New York, 1980)) would be one useful starting place for such comparisons.
29. Stedman, writing of cuisine among contemporaneous Suriname slaves, noted that '*Tom-Tom* is a verry good Pudding Composed with the Flour of Indian Corn, and boild with Flesh, Fish, Cayenne pepper and the Young Pods of the *Ocro* or *Althea* Plant' (*Narrative,* 536).
30. Stedman, in contrast, described slave '*Doquenoo*' as 'Composed of the Flour of Maiz ... eat with Molasses &c' (ibid., 536).
31. Cited in Eugene D. Genovese, *Roll, Jordan, Roll. The World the Slaves Made* (New York, 1974), 546.
32. See, for twentieth-century equivalents, S. Price, *Co-wives,* 27–8.
33. These late eighteenth-century realities form the backdrop to R. Price, *Alabi's World,* where they are described at length.
34. Because the internal organization of eighteenth-century Saramaka labour was very similar to that of today, and because the latter has already been described in detail (R. Price, *Saramaka Social Structure* (Rio Piedras, 1976); S. Price, *Co-wives*), it is unnecessary to dwell on it here. Suffice it to say that horticulture was based on matrilineal (family) workgroups but that men played a somewhat larger role in horticultural tasks than today; men often exchanged labour directly for the hardest, tree-felling portion of garden-making; and certain tasks – roof-tying, hauling

canoe-logs out of the forest to the river – involved communal (village-wide) labour parties. Because for the past century, since the abolition of slavery on the coast, men have spent large portions of their lives in wage labour outside of Saramaka territory, women not only do more garden work than in the eighteenth century but a greater share of food preparation in general. For example, in the eighteenth century, cassava processing – according to Brother Schumann (s.v. *kassaba*) – proceeded as follows: 'the man digs up [the roots], carries them home, and peels them; the woman washes and grates them; the man squeezes out the juice and mashes the pulp; the woman sifts it and bakes it; the man checks that it's done'. But today this whole process, from digging out the roots to stacking the cooked cakes, now finely decorated on their surfaces with typically female designs, is carried out by women.

35. Saramaka folktales are told as part of funeral rites. Dynamic and filled with performative nuance, they are – in their natural settings – supremely interactive, with the teller engaging the listeners in an ongoing give-and-take as the tale unfolds. R. and S. Price, *Two Evenings*, presents English translations of two full evenings of Saramaka tale-telling, recorded during wakes in 1968. The tale presented here was told by a man in his late twenties to an enthusiastic group of relatives, friends and neighbours of the deceased. As presented here, it is a truncated one-person narrative, abstracted from the fuller communal version presented in that book.

36. R. Price, *First-Time: The Historical Vision of an Afro-American People* (Baltimore, 1983).

37. It is worth noting that none of the other versions of this folktale known to us from non-Maroon sources – from the Cape Verde Islands, Puerto Rico, the Dominican Republic, coastal Suriname and Haiti – contain the same, prototypically Maroon, central message. (See, for these other versions, Manuel J. Andrade, 'Folklore from the Dominican Republic', *Memoirs of the American Folklore Society*, 23 (1930), 48–9; Melville J. Herskovits and Frances S. Herskovits, *Suriname Folk-lore* (New York, 1936), 368–75; J. Alden Mason and Aurelio M. Espinosa, 'Puerto-Rican folk-lore', *Journal of the American Folklore Society*, 35 (1922), 44–7; Elsie Clews Parsons, 'Folk-lore from the Cape Verde Islands', *Memoirs of Am. Folklore Soc.*, 15 (1923), 112–6, and 'Folklore of the Antilles: French and English', ibid., 26 (1933–43), Pt II, 572). These others focus on explicit contests or wagers between a boy and a king (sometimes a boy and a devil) to see who can keep from getting angry the longest. In this comparative context, what is striking about the Saramaka version of the tale is that it describes an ongoing, long-term labour situation – indeed, alienated labour itself – and that, rather than a particular, explicit 'contract' about not getting angry, the story hinges on the hero figuring out (after many of his fellows have already been killed in the attempt) that the only way to triumph is to question the very nature of the system itself, not to accept the boss's definition of the labour situation, be it slavery or servile wage labour.

38. S. Price, *Co-wives*, 31, 33.

MAINLAND NORTH AMERICA

As 'A Kind of Freeman'?: Slaves' Market-Related Activities in the South Carolina Upcountry, 1800–1860

John Campbell

In principle, slaveowners enjoyed unfettered access to slave labor; in practice, they commonly allowed slaves to use a portion of their labour on their own account. As many scholars have long noted, slaves not only engaged in a variety of subsistence-related tasks, such as cooking and tending their garden plots, but they also performed remunerative work which thrust them into the market economy of their masters.[1] As market participants – who produced, sold and purchased their own property – slaves temporarily experienced one of the central attributes of freedom: the purchase and sale of labour power and the enjoyment of its fruits. Presumably the slaves' presence on the terrain of freedom wrought important consequences for slaves and slaveowners alike. Yet it is only recently that scholars have come to grips with the nature and implications of slaves' independent production and related market activities. In his work on the Georgia–South Carolina lowcountry Philip Morgan shows how rice slaves used their opportunities for independent production to accumulate considerable wealth, expand their autonomy, and strengthen bonds of community among themselves. Participation in the market facilitated slave theft of the master's property, argues Alex Lichtenstein, and thus enabled slaves to better their economic position, while damaging that of their masters. Indeed, the very process of exchange empowered slaves, suggests Lawrence McDonnell, simply because masters and slaves 'confronted each other ... as bearers of commodities, stripped of social dimensions'. In short, the emerging portrait of slaves' independent production and related market activities highlights, on balance, the positive implications of these economic activities for slaves.[2]

The cumulative experience of slaves living in the cotton regions of the South Carolina upcountry supports this view in part.[3] Participation in the market economy enabled upcountry slaves to better themselves materially, possess and assert greater control and independence in their lives, create and strengthen social relationships among themselves as well as with non-slaveholding white people, and challenge the interests and power of slaveholders. However, these benefits were not

131

evenly distributed over time. Changes in the way that slaves earned and spent their incomes altered the impact and implications of slave market activities during the nineteenth century. In the century's first decades slaves worked as wage earners; in the late antebellum years they earned their income primarily as commodity – most notably, cotton – producers. This transformation heightened conflict between slaves and masters which resulted, eventually, in a number of 'reforms' designed to reduce slave independence, and hence subversive activity, within the marketplace. As a result of these reforms slaves enjoyed relatively less control over their economic affairs in the 1840s and 1850s than did their predecessors; at the same time the last generation of cotton slaves derived greater material rewards from their market-related activities. An examination of these developments during the nineteenth century reveals the complex and contradictory nature of market participation for slaves living in upcountry South Carolina.

*   *   *

By the time Eli Whitney's cotton gin opened the South Carolina upcountry to large-scale, market-oriented cotton production in the 1790s, South Carolina slaves had already won the right to participate in the market. In 1740 South Carolina lawmakers set aside Sunday as a day when slaves did not have to work for their owners but instead could engage in their own pursuits.[4] During the course of the eighteenth century slaves living on the coastal rice plantations used the prevailing organization of work – the task system – to expand their independent economic activities. The organization of labour by tasks, in which each slave was assigned a measurable quantity of work, encouraged slaves to work quickly. Once finished the remainder of the day belonged to them and they used it to produce and sell a range of goods including rice, corn, tobacco, pumpkins, canoes and baskets.[5] By the late eighteenth century rice planters had grudgingly conceded such arrangements; indeed, a 1796 South Carolina law implicitly ratified the custom of slaves selling and buying their own goods when it attempted to regulate, rather than prohibit, such market activities.[6]

On the emerging cotton plantations of the upcountry slaves also participated extensively in the market economy. However, the special conditions of upcountry life structured the slaves' income earning in distinct ways. The slaves' commodity production – whether crops or manufactured items – was constrained by the amount of time and land available to slaves and, to a lesser extent, by their subsistence needs. First, slaves labouring on both new and established cotton plantations did not have free time in the afternoon to work for themselves; for rather than work by the task upcountry cotton slaves laboured in gangs. Gang labour invariably meant that slaves remained in the fields until sundown. As a consequence, cotton slaves could pursue their own economic activities only at night, on Sundays, or on the occasional day when poor weather kept them from their owners' fields. A persistent feature of upcountry cotton agriculture, the gang system permanently restricted the amount of time available for slaves to pursue their own economic interests.[7]

Yet the first generation of cotton slaves faced an additional constraint on their productive activities: a shortage, if not outright absence, of tillable farm land. During the first decades of settlement there was simply little land available for slaves to cultivate. It would take years of repeated tillage before there was a sizable quantity of cleared – if also worn out – land that slaveowners could cede to slaves. With farm land scarce, at least from the perspective of slaves, it was difficult for individual slaves or slave families to gain access to the one or two acre plots that slaves regularly controlled in the 1840s and 1850s.[8] Instead, in the early years of the nineteenth century slaves made do with the small garden patches around their cabins or land 'in some remote and unprofitable part of the estate, generally in the woods'.[9]

Restricted access to time and land automatically limited the independent economic production of upcountry slaves and their potential involvement in the marketplace as sellers of commodities, reducing the scale of their activity below that of rice slaves. The size of the food allowance which slaves customarily received from their masters also limited the scale of slave commodity production. According to Charles Ball, a slave who lived on an upcountry plantation during the first decade of the nineteenth century, the quantity of corn and meat that slaveholders provided was insufficient to sustain him and his fellow slaves. As a result they used their patches of land to grow food crops such as corn, potatoes, pumpkins and melons.[10] Because slaves raised these crops as supplements to their subsistence allowance, they consumed – rather than sold – most of what they produced.

None the less, even with these constraints, slaves still produced commodities for the market. When slaves grew food crops primarily for subsistence they sometimes sold their surplus. In 1803 slaves living on the plantation of Gabriel Guignard, located near present-day Columbia, sold 18 bushels of corn for 42 shillings or roughly $9. Some slaves also used their time and land to grow non-food crops, like tobacco, and sold them at market. In addition to selling crops, slaves peddled a variety of useful articles, such as baskets, brooms, horse collars and bowls, which they manufactured when inclement weather kept them out of the fields.[11]

Producing and selling commodities was not the only means by which the first generation of South Carolina cotton slaves earned income. They also worked for wages; and – in light of the history of cotton slaves' independent economic activities – wage work constituted a most distinctive development. The prominence of wage work during the early nineteenth century reflected shortages of labour and capital in the upcountry. Determined to maximize their profits, the first generation of cotton planters drove their slaves from sun-up to sun-down, six days a week. Despite this relentless pace, slaveowners still required additional labour. This need was especially pronounced among aspiring planters who, in the process of building their estates from scratch, had to lay out fields, clear trees, uproot rocks, and erect farm structures – all while getting a crop in the ground. But after 1800, when the price of cotton abruptly fell, even established planters needed additional labour if they hoped to offset the adverse economic consequences of lower cotton prices with increased production.[12]

The process of harvesting cotton created an even more acute demand for – or, perhaps more accurately, persistent shortage of – plantation labour. The short-staple cotton grown in the pioneer upcountry was difficult to pick 'as the pods did not open widely'. Problems in separating the cotton from the pods meant that slaves could harvest relatively little cotton in a day.[13] Between 1801 and 1804 slaves on the Guignard plantation picked an average of 30 pounds per day and only 50 pounds on the best days of the harvest. (In contrast, slaves commonly picked 100 pounds in a day during the late antebellum period[14]). To increase productivity, especially after 1800, cotton planters sought – and would eventually find – a more pickable and productive variety of short-staple cotton. In the meantime the only way that slaveowners could increase production was by acquiring additional workers, work time or work effort during the harvest.

The slaveowners' labour needs spelled economic opportunity for slaves. To increase the amount of cotton slaves harvested slaveowners frequently paid their slaves directly for each pound of cotton that they picked above a targeted amount, generally at the rate of a penny a pound. Rather than spend their free time tending their own crops, some slaves found it advantageous to work for wages. According to Charles Ball, it was 'universal amongst the slaves on the cotton plantations' to work as wage-earners on the Christian Sabbath. During the Guignard harvests, for example, slaves picked cotton for wages on Sunday. In other seasons of the year, they earned cash clearing land, splitting rails, ploughing and hoeing cotton and potatoes.[15]

Slaves not only worked for their master but also travelled off the plantation on Sunday to work elsewhere. Charles Ball recalled how he and other slaves customarily left their home plantation to clear land and pick cotton for wages on neighbouring estates. Individual slaveowners tried to stop this labour haemorrhage by offering their slaves more than the customary daily wage of 50 cents if only they would work on the home plantation. But even with the possibility of earning a higher wage slaves 'often [left] the fields of their master ... to go to the field of some neighbouring planter .... [During the harvest] it is a matter of indifference to the slave, whether his master gets his cotton picked or not'.[16]

As an income-earning activity, wage work carried contradictory consequences for slaves. In working for wages slaves unavoidably strengthened the very system that oppressed them. Where slave-produced commodities, such as cotton or tobacco, provided no direct economic benefit to slaveowners, slaves who provided additional labour as wage earners helped insure the economic success of individual slaveowners and, thus, the slaveholders' continued commitment to slavery as a system of organizing and extracting labour. Yet participation in the Sunday labour market also gave slaves a temporary taste of freedom. In leaving the plantation, slaves sold their labour power to whom they chose and became, if only briefly, someone else's employee and not their slave. Slaves themselves were impressed with the way that the Sunday labour system blurred the boundary between slavery and freedom. As Charles Ball put it, slaves who left the plantation to sell their labour power became 'a kind of freeman on Sunday' as they 'exercised [their] liberty on this day'.[17] Thus wage work both reinforced slavery and undermined it by allowing slaves to experience a kind of freedom and to see themselves as something other than slaves.

With their wages and other earnings some slaves did quite well as participants in the market economy. Charles Ball took special note of two diligent slaves, a man and a woman, who earned $31 and $26 respectively as cotton pickers. Ball earned a comparable amount, both from wage work and from the wooden trays and vessels he made in his spare time and sold to local merchants and planters. The experience of other slaves suggests Ball's achievement was exceptional. Slaves on the Guignard plantation earned, on average, approximately $3 annually, during the period between 1802 and 1804. Overall, the typical field hand probably earned from $3 to $8 in a year.[18]

These earnings, whatever the size, enabled slaves to improve their lives in two ways. With their earnings slaves purchased 'little articles of necessity or luxury', such as sugar, molasses, coffee, tobacco and clothing, augmenting the all too bland and meagre subsistence allowance they received from their masters.[19] Perhaps even more importantly, especially in light of future developments, slaves received their earnings in cash rather than credit or in kind. With cash in their pockets slaves could buy the goods they wanted when they wanted them. Slaves found cross-roads shopkeepers were more than willing 'to rise at any time of the night to oblige [their slave] friends' by trading. Such service was much less likely, Charles Ball suggested, if slaves paid, as most white people did, by credit alone. Indeed, the possession of money itself encouraged slaves to leave the plantation surreptitiously at night to spend their earnings as they desired, and thereby assert their independence. In this context, money became synonymous with independence and control over their lives for many slaves.[20]

*   *   *

If the nature of short-staple cotton – particularly the difficulties in separating cotton from the pod – served as a surprising ally in slave efforts to carve out their own economic niche, it remained the bane of pioneer cotton planters. Keenly aware of how this variety of short-staple cotton shackled their economic aspirations, cotton planters attempted to develop more pickable varieties. During the second decade of the nineteenth century planters in the lower Mississippi Valley cross-bred common short-staple cotton with a Mexican variety. The resulting strain served the needs of planters marvellously: the bolls were noticeably larger than those of the common variety and, more significantly, they were much easier to separate from the pod.[21]

'Mexican' short-staple cotton reached the Carolinas about 1816 or 1817 and, within a few years, many upcountry planters had adopted it.[22] Given that Mexican cotton enabled slaves to pick far more cotton in a day, planters had fewer reasons to pay slaves for extra cotton picked during the regular work day or, more importantly, to hire slaves to pick on Sunday. Having established their plantations planters also felt less pressure to expand the work week by hiring slaves on Sunday. Thus the arrival and adoption of Mexican cotton in the second decade of the nineteenth century signalled the demise of the Sunday wage-work system. Although masters would continue to pay slaves for performing a variety of plantation chores on Sunday, wage work would no longer constitute a central or predictable means by which slaves could earn independent income.

Slaves themselves may have endorsed, if not initiated, the collapse of the Sunday wage system by choosing to spend their Sundays growing their own Mexican cotton. In early years the low productivity of the older varieties of cotton and the difficulties picking it had discouraged slaves from planting cotton along with their food crops. Instead slaves believed their time could be more fruitfully spent working for wages. With the arrival of Mexican cotton they too had at their disposal a variety whose weight and picking properties perhaps offered more financial rewards than wage work. In short, slaves may have withdrawn from the Sunday labour system on their own in order to plant, cultivate and harvest their own cotton.

In any case, with the introduction of Mexican cotton into South Carolina after the War of 1812 cotton grown independently by slaves became an important feature of the upcountry economy. In 1819 slaves living on five Darlington District plantations produced over 1,600 pounds of their own cotton. In the mid-1820s 52 slaves living on 27 different Laurens District plantations produced well over 10,000 pounds of their own seed cotton. In the following decade 53 slaves living on 16 plantations produced and sold a comparable amount of cotton to the Society Hill merchant, Leach Carrigan.[23] During the 1840s and 1850s slaves on four plantations independently raised seven per cent of all cotton produced. When projected to the entire upcountry or the South as a whole this level of production suggests that independent production by slaves played a direct role in making cotton king.

When viewed in its entirety the slaves' independent production and associated market activities during the 40 years between 1820 and 1860 constitute a distinct period in the history of slaves' income-earning activities in the upcountry. The era did not reach its apogee, however, until late in the antebellum years. This delay reflected the fact that two important features of the 'wage-work era' persisted into the 'cotton era': autonomy in work and relative access to and freedom within the marketplace.

In the first years of the nineteenth century upcountry slaves worked their crops after sundown or on Sunday, outside of the master's supervisory presence. Slaves who began growing their own cotton maintained a similar regimen. Before the onset of independent cotton cultivation, slaves travelled off their home plantations, unaccompanied by owners or overseers, to sell their labour power, crops and manufactured goods, and to buy various consumer goods. In the very last years of the 1790s, for example, slaves from local farms and plantations in Laurens District traded at John Black's general store. Slaves who began to grow their own cotton maintained a similar degree of mobility. In 1819, for example, slaves from five Darlington District plantations carried their own seed cotton to the merchant firm of Law and DuBose, and, at the point of sale, decided whether to receive their payment in cash or goods. A few years later, in the mid-1820s, dozens of slave men and women regularly left Laurens District plantations to sell and buy with merchant Black.[24] These trans-plantation market activities were neither exceptional nor illegal; state law allowed slaves to leave the plantation and participate in the market as long as they had their master's permission.[25]

During the first third of the nineteenth century slaves used their access to the marketplace to pursue their own social and economic interests and, in the process, challenged those of their masters. Once away from the plantation slaves sought out men and women, most commonly non-slaveholding whites, who would sell them liquor 'and other trashy goods' normally denied to them by their masters. When accompanied by drink, gambling and an overall spirit of conviviality these transactions laid the basis for important – and, from the perspective of slaveowners, dangerous – relationships between slaves and their white trading partners.[26] For when 'the poison of the one, invigorated by copious draughts of the inebriating beverage, [was] poured into the ready ear of the other ... new and pernicious ideas' seeped into 'the susceptible mind of the African'. Under these poisonous influences formerly contented slaves became despondent and, eventually, insubordinate and incapable of obeying 'any domestic regulation' on the plantation.[27]

More subversive yet, these relationships of 'perfect equality', as the planter Whitemarsh Seabrook called them, sometimes threatened slaveowner interests more directly. 'Low [white] fellow[s]' encouraged 'negro[s] to steal and bring to [them] – easing the poor fellow's conscience by making him believe what he takes is the fruit of his own labour and he is therefore entitled to it'.[28] As John Brown, a slave, put it, 'when these poor whites cannot obtain a living honestly, which they very seldom do, they get the slaves in their neighborhood to steal corn, poultry, and such like, from their masters, and bring these things to them ...'.[29] While Brown may have overlooked the degree to which slaves acted on their own, without coaxing from white co-conspirators, slaves employed these social relationships to better themselves materially – often at their masters' expense. It was precisely because slaves travelled – and with their masters' permission – that they could develop and sustain relationships with poor white people in the first place.

However much the wage-work and the cotton eras had in common in terms of labour patterns and market participation, the transition to independent cotton production changed the slaves' economy. Attached to the plantation as cotton producers, slaves no longer experienced the independence that derived from their ability to leave the plantation to work elsewhere on Sunday. Indeed, as long as slaveowners respected the slaves' right to move freely, even *threatening* to leave the plantation enabled slaves to strike better wage agreements with their master. With the eclipse of wage work this expression of the slaves' power disappeared.

The emergence of independent cotton production also reduced the liberating quality of slaves' market-oriented work. As cotton growers slaves no longer enjoyed the sense of freedom that Charles Ball associated with participation in the Sunday labour market, simply because their work occurred on their masters' plantation. While work itself, especially outside the masters' immediate purview, still offered slaves a sense of independence, the context of work – the plantation – precluded slaves from acting like 'a kind of freeman'. For when the geographical domain of slaves' income-earning activities became coterminous with the boundary of the plantation, the liberating quality of slaves' work experience shrank sharply.

The geographic and economic shift in slave income-earning work heightened tensions between masters and slaves. Within production, slaves pursued interests which invariably clashed with those of the master. Unwilling or unable to confine their work on their own crops – both cotton and provisions – to the early evening hours, slaves tended them late into the night; and, as slaveowners well knew, night work made slaves ill-fit for labour in the masters' field the following day. Moreover, slaveholders claimed that slaves, in tending crops outside of their presence, misused and damaged plantation equipment and work animals. After 1830, when masters attempted to shape the moral and religious beliefs of their slaves, the slaves' Sunday work was also seen as interfering with proper religious development and moral deportment. All in all the advent of cotton made production itself a terrain of escalating conflict between slaves and masters.[30]

Independent cotton production by slaves expanded old and created new opportunities for slaves to assert themselves, much to the dismay and detriment of their masters. With cotton seemingly everywhere slaves could steal with greater ease and thus with greater impunity than ever before. During the wage work era slaves sold stolen goods illicitly, at night and under the cloud of possible detection and punishment. In September 1802, for example, two slaves in Edgefield District were caught selling pilfered cotton and tobacco at 'about 12 or 1 o'clock in the night'.[31] The dangers of selling stolen goods diminished considerably, however, once slaves earned their income primarily as producers and sellers of crops. For when slaves left the plantation to sell their own cotton and other crops they could hide stolen property amid their marketable goods. In this way, slaves were able to fence stolen property conveniently, during the day and as part of their 'legitimate', master-sanctioned marketplace activity. Indeed, such a safe and direct way of disposing of stolen goods encouraged slaves to steal with greater frequency. As one South Carolina overseer put it, 'by permitting [slaves] to leave the plantation with the view of selling and buying, more is lost by the owner than he is generally aware of'. Much to the slaveowners' chagrin, such market-related theft became all the more pronounced *because* slaves had their own cotton to sell. Compared to corn, for example, cotton offered more temptations to theft because it was more easily carried, less easily detected and of greater value. 'A negro that would take one hundred pounds of cotton, in seed worth two dollars', observed an upcountry planter in 1832, 'would hardly venture on the same weight of corn worth only seventy-five cents'. For this planter, as for many others, slave theft could be reduced by restricting the slaves' independent production to corn and by preventing them from using their marketing activities as a cover for selling stolen crops. Instead, slave crops should be 'disposed of by [the master]'.[32]

Slaveowners began searching for ways of reducing, if not eliminating, behaviour they found disruptive, if not subversive. To this end, between 1830 and 1860 slaveowners adopted two strategies to reduce the problems foisted upon them by their slaves. Most drastically, some slaveowners simply prevented slaves from growing and selling their own cotton or other cash crops. James Henry Hammond, who entered the planter ranks in the 1830s, allowed his slaves to grow food crops solely for their own subsistence. In 1851 another planter reported how he 'formerly gave [his slaves] crops' but had discontinued this practice 'of late'. Instead of crops, he paid his slaves a bonus at the year's end, the size of which depended upon their behaviour during the year. W. H. Evans of Darlington District argued that, as an alternative to producing their own cotton, slaves should be paid 25 cents for extra cotton picked on specially designated days during the harvest. Other slaveholders advocated less manipulative, instrumental replacements for 'negro crops' (as they were sometimes called), such as giving gifts of cash or material goods that would equal 'what their crop (if they had one) would [have] yield[ed]'.[33]

A second group of slaveowners continued to allow their chattel to grow marketable crops such as cotton. But in order to reduce the subversive impact of slaves' market-related activities, these planters exerted greater control over the entire range of slaves' independent production, selling and buying activities. Within this new context slaves no longer experienced as much independence as they once had in the conduct of their economic activities. As a result, the social, psychological and other non-economic rewards of slaves' market-oriented activities narrowed considerably in the late antebellum period.

During the 1840s and 1850s the cotton era of slave market-related activities took its fullest form. Within production slaveowners made two important changes in the slaves' economy. First, hoping to discourage night-time – or even Sunday – work by their slaves, masters gave them additional time during daylight hours to work their crops. For some slaves this extra time came regularly on Saturdays, a day that slaves had previously spent working on their owners' crop. According to Mary Johnson, a former slave of Newberry District, she and her fellow slaves 'had Saturday afternoon off to do anything we wanted to do'. Sylvia Cannon, a slave in Marion District, used this free time to work 'dey extra crop'. For slaves such as Johnson and Cannon, having Saturday to work their crops or engage in other activities became a customary feature of plantation life during the late antebellum years.[34]

While some planters systematically reduced the slaves' work week from six to five-and-a-half or even five days, others gave their slaves an occasional Saturday or even weekday for tending their crops. On the estate of Thomas C. Law, a Darlington planter, slaves had a combination of Saturdays and weekdays for planting, hoeing and ploughing their own crops (see Table 2). Similarly, on the Caleb Coker plantation slaves received a few days late in the year to harvest their cotton. In 1859, for example, they picked their cotton on Friday 2 December and on Saturday 3 December. The following year, on the Darlington plantation of H. G. Charles, slaves tended their owner's crop on Saturday but still received two weekdays to pick their cotton in late November, after the bulk of the owner's cotton had been harvested.[35]

Rather than allow slaves to manage these special workdays as they saw fit, masters supervised the slaves' supposedly independent activities. As long as masters permitted slaves to grow cash crops they 'should superintend the planting, working and gathering ... and strictly forbid all working after dark', admonished one cotton planter. Likewise, Thomas Law argued in an address to the Darlington Agricultural Society in 1852 that slave crops should be 'ploughed, under the owner's direction, as regularly as his own'.[36]

Such oversight was intended to keep slaves from mishandling work animals and equipment. Harvest-time supervision, whereby slaves picked their cotton under the watchful eye of their owner or overseer, might discourage if not prevent slaves from stealing the owners' cotton. Not leaving anything to chance, slaveowners also weighed slave-grown cotton once it had been picked. By monitoring this procedure each master would be able to 'detect theft if there should be any, as he is better able to judge of the quantity each would probably make from the ground cultivated, when it is submitted to his measurement'.[37]

The masters' active, supervisory role unleashed a host of adverse consequences for upcountry slaves. Slaves lost some of the independence that came when they worked their crops on Sunday or furtively at night. Diminished independence, especially at harvest, made it harder for slaves to supplement their own crops with their masters'. Moreover, the slaveowners' supervision of Sunday work impinged on long-established rights, jeopardizing customary practices. Work thus became less of a means by which slaves demonstrated their independence and asserted control over their lives and more of a means to generate income.

Even so, slaves still controlled aspects of their market-related work. Despite the owners' efforts to wean their slaves of evening work, slaves continued to labour 'dat crop in de night, dat crop wha' dey buy dey Sunday clothes wid'.[38] Slaves also helped determine when they received their special workdays. On the Thomas Law plantation, for example, the timing of such days depended in large part on the current status of Law's crop: that is, slaves received time to plant and plough only after they had finished planting or ploughing their owner's cotton. On Monday 19 April 1841 slaves planted their cotton after having completed work on Law's crop the preceding Saturday. Similarly, on 25 May 1850 slaves ploughed their own crop after they had finished ploughing Law's earlier in the day. Conversely, the timing of when slaves worked their cotton determined, in effect, the subsequent work on their owners' crop, such as in May 1851 when Law's slaves began the second round of ploughing only after they had ploughed their crops once over.

The regularity described by Thomas Law in his 1852 speech was thus not in terms of frequency or priority but predictability: that slaves would plant, hoe and plough their crops only after they had finished performing the equivalent task on the masters' crop. Aware of the functional relationship between when they worked their crops and when they worked their masters' crop, slaves worked the masters' crop more rapidly, thereby hastening the day when they could tend their own crops. Like rice slaves, cotton slaves exercised some control over when they worked their crops in daylight hours. Their control, unlike that enjoyed by rice slaves, was asserted collectively, with the entire field force working together to complete the masters' work in a timely fashion.[39]

Slaves benefited from these special work days in a number of ways. They provided a brief respite from endless toil for their masters. As episodic as they were, these work days gave slaves the choice of whether to use evening or Sunday hours for activities other than tending their crops. They also enabled slaves to tend their crops more

efficiently than allowed by night work. During the fall special workdays helped slaves harvest their cotton in a timely fashion, thereby
preserving the quality and value of their cotton. For, as all cotton
growers – black and white, slave and free – well knew, prompt picking
was essential if the ripe cotton bolls were to be spared damage by
sudden frosts, rain or even snow.[40]

Special workdays no doubt helped slaves increase their production
and earnings. On four Darlington District plantations individual slaves
raised and sold roughly 200 to 350 pounds of seed cotton annually,
while slaves living and working in family units produced considerably
more.[41] The size of the cotton crop in any one year determined, in large
part, the size of slave earnings. While slaves on these and other
plantations produced and sold other commodities (corn, fodder, fowl,
baskets, mats, tar, coal and lumber) along with their cotton and
performed miscellaneous labour for pay (dig ditches and wells), the
sale of cotton constituted the bulk of their incomes. Overall, the
earnings of individual slaves ranged from $4 to $9 annually, although
families might earn more.[42] It would appear that slaves earned more
in the late antebellum era than they had earlier in the nineteenth
century.[43]

* * *

Slaveowners were no less diligent in asserting their control over slave
market activities as sellers of commodities. As a South Carolina
overseer put it in 1836, 'Negroes should in no instance be permitted to
trade, except with their masters'. In 1834 this position was echoed in the
South Carolina legislature which made it illegal for anyone to trade
with slaves, day or night, Sunday or weekday, with or without permission from the slave's owner.[44] By outlawing inter-plantation trade
between slaves and anyone else, the 1834 law compelled slaveowners to
oversee the disposal of their slaves' crops, whether as purchasers or
factors. For without the owners' intercession slaves would have had no
legal means of disposing the crops which they had produced with their
masters' approval in the first place.

Some slaveowners and merchants, for whatever reasons, failed to
comply with the 1834 law. In publicly offering $500 for evidence
that would convict anyone of buying 'produce from my negroes
without a special order from me in my own handwriting', one planter
unabashedly admitted that he still allowed his slaves to trade on their
own accord outside of the plantation.[45] None the less, during the 1840s
and 1850s slaveowners tended to supervise the disposal of the crops
slaves produced on their own. On some plantations change came

slowly, but it came nevertheless. Still purchasing large quantities of slave-grown cotton in the late 1830s, the Carrigan firm of Society Hill bought but one bale during the 1850s, perhaps because its former slave trading partners now sold their cotton to their masters (or did not even grow cotton any more). Although Thomas Law allowed his slaves to sell their 1844 cotton crop off of the plantation, by the late 1840s Law had changed his ways. Thereafter, Law purchased his slaves' cotton directly.[46]

Regardless of economic standing or locale, slaveholders, such as Thomas Law, evicted slaves from the marketplace as sellers and asserted direct control over the sale of slave-grown crops. Men such as Peter S. Bacot, who managed over 100 slaves, bought their slaves' cotton, as did slaveholders of more modest means. Bacot's fellow Darlington planter, Peter S. Wilds, planted with 30 slaves and purchased his slaves' cotton in the early 1840s. To the northwest of Darlington, York District, John Bratton bought his slaves' corn and cotton in the 1850s, as did Thomas C. Perrin, who lived even further west along the Georgia border in Abbeville District. When slave-owners did not purchase slave cotton themselves they still arranged to have it sold and shipped to someone else, as did the Darlington planter William Law.[47]

In short, during the last years of slavery slaveowners – partly in response to slaves' independent marketplace activity – overturned the long-standing custom of allowing slaves to leave the plantation and sell on their own account. By keeping slaves out of the marketplace slaveowners implicitly acknowledged the power that slaves had earlier wielded. By preventing such independence slaveowners eliminated one central means by which slaves challenged their authority. With one swift stroke upcountry masters shored up their hegemony on the plantation and throughout the surrounding countryside.

According to masters, slaves benefited from these new marketing arrangements. In purchasing slave-grown crops masters sometimes claimed that they did their slaves a favour by protecting them from 'unprincipled men ... who might cheat them out of their earnings'. By buying the slaves' crops 'more justice will be done them than if disposed of by themselves, which is always at a less price than can be obtained by the master'. Thomas Law believed that the master should 'always *purchase* what they have to *sell*' and to always pay the 'highest market price, whether he needs it or not, since it convinces [slaves] of your doing them justice and induces them to prefer you as the buyer'.[48] This need to elicit the slaves' goodwill and the *de facto* acceptance of the master as purchaser worked to the economic advantage of Law's slaves. In November 1859 Thomas Law paid them eleven and a half cents per pound of ginned cotton, an amount that exceeded the local market price of a little more than ten cents, which was paid to the slaves of William Law, who had sold their cotton to a local merchant.[49] Indeed, the price received by Thomas Law's slaves reflected the higher prices of the Charleston cotton market (see Table 3).

Yet the experience of Thomas Law's slaves was not typical. On balance, the available evidence suggests that slaves failed to receive Charleston market prices and thus were underpaid for their cotton. Some planters, like Peter Bacot, deliberately short-changed slaves when buying their cotton. Throughout the 1850s Bacot's slaves received a price that was consistently below the local market price, as exemplified by the transactions of William Law's slaves during these years. In 1854, for example, Bacot paid his slaves less than seven cents per pound of ginned cotton, while Law's slaves received eight cents when selling to a local merchant; the difference became even more pronounced in 1856, when Law's slaves received nearly twice as much for their cotton as Bacot's.

Rather than set his price according to market fluctuations, Bacot simply paid his slaves a set price of roughly six and a half cents per pound. He did so despite the fact that his slaves produced a good quality cotton.[50] The prices realized by Bacot when he sold cotton were well within the range of market prices and thus it can be reasonably inferred that the cotton which he purchased from his slaves and then sold along with his own was of a good quality, or it did not depress the prices he received from Charleston factors (see Table 3). In short, Peter Bacot's slaves received a low price not because their cotton was of a poor quality but because Bacot wanted to profit at his slaves' expense.[51]

Apart from deliberate gouging by their masters, slaves' earnings were reduced simply because their owners did not let them receive the benefit of market prices in Charleston. The prices received by masters when they sold their cotton in Charleston usually exceeded those paid to slaves when they sold to the master or to local merchants (see Table 3).[52] In 1841, for example, Peter Wilds paid his slaves slightly more than two cents per pound of seed cotton (or, roughly seven cents per pound of ginned cotton); then, when he sold this cotton – along with his original cotton – in Charleston, he received almost nine cents per pound of ginned cotton or roughly 22 per cent more than what he paid his slaves. Similarly, the slaves of William Law received a fair local market price of eight cents in 1854 when they sold their cotton to a nearby merchant; yet this price was still 34 per cent less than the average price of about 12 cents that Law himself earned when he sold his cotton in Charleston in that year.[53]

There was no guarantee that slaves would have always received a better price if they had sold their cotton in Charleston, however. If the slaves of William Law, for example, had sold their 1858 crop on 30 April 1859, when Law sold a portion of his cotton, they would have received the same price per pound (11 cents) that they eventually got from a local merchant. Indeed, in this instance Law's slaves would have earned less from the Charleston than from the local sale. In selling locally slaves did not incur the various marketing expenses – freight, insurance, bagging and baling, weighing, storage and factor's commission – that typically accompanied a sale in Charleston; and presumably Law would have made his slaves pay these charges if they had sent their cotton to be sold in Charleston.[54] When these expenses were taken into account the resulting net price (as opposed to the gross price of 11 cents) slaves would have earned – the price received by Law (11 cents) less marketing expenses (5.6 per cent) – would have been slightly more than ten cents per pound or 5.6 per cent less than what they received.

Yet more often than not the various marketing expenses would not have made a Charleston sale less profitable than a local one. Of the 74 different instances (price–date combinations) in which the cotton of Bacot, William Law and Wilds was sold by their respective Charleston factors, there were 59 occasions when slaves on these plantations would have received a better price, even after marketing costs were taken into account. Overall, selling in Charleston would have increased slave incomes, on average, by roughly 18 per cent. In actuality, of course, it was the master or local merchant who pocketed the extra earnings after they purchased and resold the slaves' cotton in Charleston.[55]

Thus the new marketing arrangements instituted in the 1840s and 1850s brought considerable hardship on slaves. The one possible benefit slaves could have received – higher market prices – was lost as masters refused, by and large, to pay slaves the Charleston price or to market slave-grown cotton in Charleston. Instead of receiving the highest prices available, slaves bore the double burden of receiving local prices without, at the same time, being able to sell their cotton themselves. Confined to the plantation, slaves of the late antebellum era thus lost a valuable means for developing and sustaining relationships with merchants of their own choosing, even if they happened to be 'unprincipled men'. No longer able to market their own goods independently meant, in turn, that they could no longer expropriate their owners' cotton and other property with the same impunity.

Indeed, aside from the fact that slaves had something to sell and were paid, there was precious little in 'selling' to the master that bespoke a market experience. Inasmuch as marketing refers to the processes of selecting a buyer and haggling over price, slaves did neither. As for the market itself, it appeared in a distorted fashion, embodied in the master who, as merchant, either purchased the goods or, as factor, arranged to have someone else purchase them. Rather than become levelling experiences, where blacks were raised and 'whites were lowered', these transactions, predicated as they were on the master's monopolistic control of the disposal of slave crops, reflected and reinforced the unequal distribution of power among masters and slaves. In selling to or through the master, as opposed to travelling the countryside seeking their own customers, slaves found their dependence on their master reinforced rather than reduced. Instead of being an important moment of temporary independence for slaves, selling became a sharp reminder of their limited independence.

*   *   *

The long arm of the master also shaped the way slaves spent their earnings. Just as slaveowners of the late antebellum period reduced the slaves' participation in the marketplace as sellers of commodities, so they restricted slaves' activities as consumers. First, slaveowners gave their slaves fewer opportunities to leave the plantation as potential buyers by selling them consumer goods directly. William Law, for example, maintained a supply of molasses and tobacco which his slaves purchased throughout the year. Other individuals went further and, as one overseer advised in 1836, kept 'a [plantation] store of such articles as slaves usually purchased elsewhere'. When such a well-stocked store existed, as it did on the plantation of Thomas Law, slaves had little opportunity to shop elsewhere. By serving as retail merchants to their slaves, masters limited the extent to which slaves participated in the market place as consumers and thus helped put slaves 'out of the way of the temptation to roguery'.[57]

However, even when they doubled as merchants some upcountry planters allowed their slaves to travel off the plantation to spend some, if not most, of their earnings. Yet when these slaves left the plantation unaccompanied their owners tried to control the goods slaves purchased. They did so by giving their slaves credit, rather than cash, when they purchased their slaves' crops or when they compensated them for other economic endeavours. Thus, when buying goods from a local merchant slaves bought against their credited earnings. Eventually the master received a bill for the amount of each slave's purchases and then used the slaves' earnings to pay the merchant. In 1859, for example, William Law received a draft of credit for $305 for his slaves' cotton, which had been purchased by merchant R. A. Kendall of Cheraw. Later, Law used this money to pay the Darlington firm of Huggins and Brunson for goods that his slaves had purchased from that firm.[58] In effect, slaveowners such as Law served as factors to their slaves: first crediting slaves with the value of their independent economic endeavours and then deducting from each slave's account the cost of his or her purchases. Such transactions reduced the amount of money handled by slaves far below their earnings.

Both the relative absence of money among slaves and their use of credit enabled masters to police and regulate slave purchases, even when they were beyond the owners' immediate surveillance. Carrying little money with them, slaves had few means to buy liquor or other contraband from white traders they might visit as they travelled to and from the marketplace. At the same time, the use of credit – as either dispensed or withheld by the master – *dictated* where slaves had to spend their earnings. Cash poor, credit rich, slaves could only purchase merchandise from merchants who would sell on credit (where slave-owners had arranged to reimburse them for the amount of the slaves' purchases). For their part, slaveowners only made such arrangements with 'reputable' men who would not sell contraband to slaves. In short, just as the use of a plantation store guaranteed that slaves would not acquire liquor or firearms, so the credit system enabled masters to prevent their slaves from purchasing such goods when they spent their earnings off the plantation.

The use of credit helps explain why many slaveowners and merchants violated the 1834 law which had outlawed any commercial exchange between slaves and shopkeepers. With the credit system, masters and merchants achieved a central goal of the 1834 law – preventing slaves from buying contraband – without needlessly compromising or sub-verting their own interests. The credit system enabled slaveowners to avoid, if they so desired, the potentially irksome chore of operating a plantation store, while allowing merchants to keep their slave customers.[59] Moreover, in permitting slaves to leave the plantation as consumers slaveowners did not jeopardize the law's second objective – the prevention of slave theft – because slaves, as consumers, presum-ably left the plantation empty handed; any slave attempting to do otherwise naturally aroused suspicions. If some masters and merchants failed to comply with the substance of the 1834 law, they none the less found a workable means of respecting the spirit of the law.

Even within the constraints imposed upon them by the credit system, buying away from the plantation still proved beneficial and rewarding for slaves. Travelling off the plantation unchaperoned by a master or some other white person was no doubt a liberating experience just as it had been earlier in the century. Not surprisingly, slaves exploited the owner's absence to pursue their own interests, spending more than their master wanted or expected. In late 1853, for example, the slaves of

William Law bought $200 worth of merchandise from the merchant, F. W. Cooper. Apparently Law's slaves took advantage of their owner's absence for Cooper later informed Law that the 'amount of [the] Negroes indebtedness ... is not as you desired[,] owing ... to not having recd. your letter in time. ... [Although] most of them got what they wanted on Christmas Day or the[ir] accounts would not have been so large'. Law's slaves were able to purchase as much as they wanted to because Cooper, as he claimed, failed to receive Law's letter of instructions on time or, as one might suspect, ignored the instructions in order to sell more. Either way, it was purchasing outside of the masters' presence that enabled Law's slaves to spend as they desired and contrary to the master's wishes.[60]

As the above episode suggests, slaves sometimes went into debt while participating in the market.[61] Although slaveowners such as William Law frowned upon slave indebtedness, they did little to discourage or prevent it. Rather than punish slaves for going into debt, Law and other slaveholders simply made their slaves pay their debts with future earnings. This mode of repayment, and hence indebtedness itself, benefited slaveowners because it insured that at least some of slaves' future time would be spent in income-earning, and not other, possibly disruptive, activities on the plantation. Perhaps with this benefit in mind, slaveowners in the upcountry tolerated indebtedness as a normal feature of slave market participation.

This tolerance – combined with year-round spending, buying on credit and the advantages of overspending for slaves – made it easy for slaves to fall into debt. Slaves who bought consumer goods months before they harvested and sold their crops ran the risk of spending more than they would eventually earn. Year-round spending helps explain, for example, why the slaves of Peter Bacot went into debt more frequently than did the slaves of Thomas and William Law, who spent most of their earnings only after they had harvested and sold their cotton.[62] Indebtedness also loomed large when slaves purchased consumer goods from local merchants on credit. Merchants such as F. W. Cooper had little reason to care about, much less encourage, careful spending by their slave customers. If anything, it was in their economic interest to encourage overspending, since they would sell more goods without running the risk of not being paid. For, according to South Carolina law, slaveowners were the legal owners of slave property, thus they were also responsible for any debts incurred by their slaves when purchasing consumer goods. As long as masters were financially healthy merchants were assured of repayment even when slaves spent more than they had earned.[63]

Slaves did not have to be seduced into spending beyond their means, however. Overspending was attractive to slaves because it allowed them to own and use more goods for a longer period of time than if they had avoided indebtedness; conversely, not going into debt and remaining solvent meant that slaves deferred the purchase and use of desired goods. Unwilling, perhaps, to make such short-term sacrifices, some slaves on the plantations of Thomas and William Law deliberately overspent, even though they knew how much they had earned and had available for spending.[64]

But overspending carried significant costs for slaves. By going into debt, slaves consigned themselves to work in the future, whether they wanted to or not. Debts from one year also meant reduced purchasing power in the next, as slaves used a portion of their future earnings to balance their accounts. Moreover, indebtedness exposed some slaves to an additional possible loss of future income: namely, the possibility of having to pay interest. Such was the experience of slaves living on the Bacot plantation. From 1852 to 1860 some men and women incurred interest charges ranging from eight to 88 cents. An average charge of 33 cents meant forsaking, for example, three yards of calico or three pounds of sugar – no small sacrifice for slaves whose annual income was $5.42.[65]

Overall these disadvantages, as well as the attractions of remaining solvent, encouraged most slaves to avoid indebtedness. Even with year-round spending, Peter Bacot's slaves generally avoided indebtedness; indeed, more slaves on this plantation would have remained solvent if Bacot had paid them more fairly for their cotton. Buying primarily after the harvest of their crops helped seven out of ten slaves on the Thomas and William Law plantations to avoid debt. By staying out of debt slaves on these latter two plantations also saved roughly 15 per cent of their earnings when buying on credit from either the master or local merchant.

By avoiding debt slaves acquired more control over their own affairs. Solvency allowed slaves to decide whether to earn incomes in the future, while the possession of a surplus (unspent earnings) gave them the option of reducing their work effort without limiting their future purchases. With a surplus slaves could also buy from one another or make loans to each other. The resulting web of economic and social interdependence could be dense indeed. During the 1850s the slaves of Peter Bacot, for example, initiated dozens of financial loans amongst themselves. While these loans did not necessarily involve cash transfers as Bacot simply moved credit from one account to another, these transfers were no less significant as a means of strengthening bonds of community among slaves.[66]

With a surplus slaves also acquired one of the most illusive – and powerful, objects – money. Although slaves generally received their earnings as credit to be spent on merchandise, the unspent portions were frequently given to them as cash. In contrast to receiving their surpluses as credit, which carried a heavy residue of dependence when dispensed by the master, the receipt of money increased slaves' independence. With money slaves could circumvent the master altogether when making loans to fellow slaves, thereby making these exchanges – unlike credit-based loans, which involved the banker-like services of the master – direct relationships between individual men and women. With money slaves could purchase from each other, itinerant peddlers or even illicit traders whom they might visit when they travelled off the plantation to shop with 'legitimate merchants'. Finally, with money slaves could make loans or financial gifts directly to slaves living on other plantations, thereby creating or cementing relationships between different slave communities. In 1859, for example, Serena, a woman owned by Thomas Law, gave Excell, a slave man living on another estate, a $3 coat. Later, when it became obvious that Serena had gone into debt, Excell reimbursed Serena.[67] In short, just as the possession of money empowered slaves in the early nineteenth century, so too did it give slaves such as Excell and Serena control over their economic affairs in the late antebellum years. That money and control accrued to slaves in the late antebellum years only because they decided to avoid year-end indebtedness underscores the significance of such financial decisions.

Without minimizing the control that slaves exercised over their own lives during the 1840s and 1850s, slaves still enjoyed less independence as consumers in the late antebellum years than they had earlier. Not only did they possess far less money but they had to avoid the snares of the credit system. In contrast, slaves in the early nineteenth century routinely received money, and the potential power that came with it, as payment for their wage work or other economic endeavours. Moreover, in the late antebellum years slaves enjoyed far less freedom of movement. Whereas their predecessors customarily left the plantation to buy where and even when they pleased, later generations of upcountry slaves did not enjoy comparable mobility. Some spent most of their earnings on the plantation and rarely left it as consumers. Others, who did leave, faced the restrictions imposed by the credit system which, as manipulated by their masters, dictated where slaves spent their earnings and what they could or could *not* buy.

However, during the late antebellum years slaves enjoyed two distinct advantages over their predecessors. First, they had greater spending power per dollar. In the course of the nineteenth century the price of consumer goods fell dramatically. While the index of consumer prices averaged 162 from 1800 to 1812, it hovered around 94 during the last 20 years of slavery.[68] This long-term decline in the price of consumer goods meant that each dollar earned by a slave in 1850 had roughly one and a half times as much buying power as a dollar earned in 1810.[69] Such deflation enabled slaves of the late antebellum period to buy more consumer goods than their predecessors.

Slaves were able to put their greater spending power to good use. The passage of time also witnessed an explosion in the variety of goods produced in the burgeoning manufacturing centres of the United States and Europe. Slaves of the 1840s and 1850s were able to take advantage of these economic changes simply because they, like their forebears, did not have to use their earnings to pay for their basic subsistence, did not face a slaveowner ultimatum of either pay for food and clothing or go without, and thus did not have to spend their earnings on subsistence.[70] Instead, they were relatively free to buy – within the limitations of their incomes – a wide variety of goods for themselves and their families.

Slaves with direct access to full-time retail merchants acquired a broad range of merchandise. In 1852 Toney, a slave of one Mrs Brockington of Darlington District, used his income of $38 to purchase 31 different items from the merchant firm of Charles and Milling. The goods acquired by slaves when buying from the master were no less diverse. On an income of $25, Elleck, a slave owned by Thomas Law, purchased 21 items from Law's plantation store in 1859.[71] Overall, the slaves on Law's plantation purchased roughly 60 types of consumer goods in 1859, including tobacco, sugar, dishes, finished clothing such as shoes, dresses and coats, and 24 varieties of fabric.

When slaves could not find what they wanted either in the plantation store or even at the shops of local merchants, they sometimes requested that their master buy the goods in distant cities. Throughout the 1850s, for example, the slaves of Peter Bacot acquired, through Bacot's intercession, coats, shawls, and dress patterns from Charleston shops. Even the retail establishments of South Carolina's leading city were within the reach of common field slaves living on upcountry cotton plantations.[72]

*   *   *

In allowing slaves to produce marketable crops, earn their own incomes, acquire property and participate in the market, slaveowners hoped these opportunities would permanently transform slave values, attitudes and behaviour. 'If slaves are industrious for themselves, they will be so for their masters', waxed one confident master defending slave market-related activities. The crops grown and goods purchased with their earnings would also 'impress on [the slaves'] minds the advantages of holding property' and, presumably, respect for the owner's property as well.[73] Instead of making obedience or diligence a *sine qua non* of cash-crop production and related activities, masters believed that participation itself would eventually transform slaves into an obedient, property-respecting and hard-working labour force. Where the system of Sunday wage work had, for masters, the clear short-term purpose of providing additional labour for necessary plantation work, producing and selling cash crops had the more fundamental, long-term purpose of socializing slaves in the masters' image.

From one perspective, participation in market-related economic activities did transform slaves, or at least promoted diligence, intentionality and responsibility. In order to increase the size of their crops and earnings, slaves pooled the labour of family members when they worked their crops and purchased Peruvian guano, the fertilizer of choice among late antebellum cotton planters. Concerned with protecting their personal possessions, slaves sometimes purchased padlocks.[74] Unwilling to buy and accumulate cavalierly, slaves spent their earnings carefully, thereby avoiding year-end indebtedness. All in all, slaves could not have disappointed their masters, as they were industrious in their work, respectful of property and prudent in their financial affairs.

Yet when it came to the masters' crop, property and interests this seeming exercise in social engineering failed miserably. Despite their opportunities to buy and sell, produce and consume their own property, slaves remained a disobedient and troublesome labour force. Slaves who grew their own cotton for the market still disrupted the masters' work regime, as did three slave men owned by H. G. Charles – Aron, Boston and Andrew – who ran away at various times in 1860, though not in the fall when they harvested their own cotton. Even in the late antebellum years, when masters had asserted greater control and supervision over slave economic affairs, slaves still stole, and proclaimed their right to do so. Mose, a slave living near Camden, who, along with his fellow slaves, produced and sold corn to their overseer, was suspected of stealing and 'leaving bags full of something at certain houses in Camden'. Fed, a slave living on the Bacot plantation, was a member in good standing of the Mechanicsville Baptist Church until December 1847, when he was excluded for stealing and adultery.[75]

To add insult to injury, slaves not only mocked the putative power of their market-oriented activities, but invoked the masters' own

Christian ethics to justify continued depredations on the masters' property. As a slave of Thomas Law brazenly asserted to Law, he and other slaves could take what they worked for (even if it was nominally owned by the master) because 'the Bible says a man has the right to the sweat of his eyebrows'. The failure of independent economic activities to reform slaves was implicitly acknowledged by the slaveholding members of the Black Creek (Darlington District) Agricultural Society who, at their May 1860 meeting, debated without resolution the 'general management of slaves and particularly their government so as to prevent their thieving from their masters'.[76]

Despite this failure, slaveowners still reaped rewards from slaves' economic endeavours. By underpaying slaves for their crops slaveowners realized a profit on the resale of slave cotton. By situating slave workdays within the overall agricultural work regime cotton planters benefited from more diligent work from their slaves, who tended their master's crops more speedily in order to hasten the day when they tended their own. More importantly, the very fact that slaves engaged in a plethora of production, selling and buying activities meant that slaves had less time to engage in other, possibly subversive behaviour on the plantation. These income-related activities filled time which, as one planter put it, 'otherwise would be spent in the perpetration of some act that would subject [slaves] to severe punishment'.[77] In effect, participation in the market economy channelled the slaves' time, energy and attention into 'safe' and non-threatening activities and thus helped masters maintain order and stability on the plantation. These objectives were advanced all the more as slaveowners increased their control over the full range of slaves' market-related activities. Although this supervision was ultimately a rearguard action designed to overcome years of slave independence and disruptive activity as market participants, it none the less helped slaveowners maintain their power and authority in the upcountry.

Thus for slaves of the late antebellum era participation in the market came at a high price: diminished control over their own affairs and additional exposure to slaveowner dictates. Slaves who did not participate enjoyed more day-to-day independence and escaped master interference in yet another aspect of their lives. Rather than make these slaves into 'a kind of freeman', market participation in the 1840s and 1850s reinforced, in many ways, slaves' position of dependence and limited control over their lives. As a result upcountry slaves derived relatively few non-economic rewards from their involvment in the market; in contrast to their early nineteenth century predecessors the last generation of cotton slaves enjoyed fewer opportunities to forge social relationships beyond the plantation and to challenge the authority of their masters. Yet despite the restrictive nature of their market activities, these slaves still benefited from their economic pursuits. They enjoyed improved material conditions, especially in contrast to their predecessors. Market participation itself created new and important ways in which slaves asserted control over their affairs, such as determining when they worked their crops, choosing whether to go into debt, or deciding how to use their unspent earnings. Indeed, participation in the market helped black people to confront the opportunities and obstacles of the market once they were freed. It was during slavery, however, that many black people first experienced the contradictory nature of market participation.

NOTES

I would like to thank Karen Anderson, Ira Berlin, Stanley Engerman, Sara Evans, Stephen Gudeman, Colette Hyman, Barbara Laslett, Russell Menard, Philip Morgan and Stuart Schwartz for reading and commenting on earlier versions of this essay.

1. Orville V. Burton, *In My Father's House Are Many Mansions: Family and Community in Edgefield, South Carolina* (Chapel Hill, 1985), 161–2; Eugene D. Genovese, *Roll, Jordan, Roll: The World the Slaves Made* (New York, 1976), 535; Jacqueline Jones, *Labor of Love, Labor of Sorrow: Black Women, Work, and the Family, From Slavery to the Present* (New York, 1985), 36; Allan Kulikoff, *Tobacco and Slaves: The Development of Southern Colonies in the Chesapeake, 1680–1800* (Chapel Hill, 1986), 392; Leslie Howard Owens, *This Species of Property: Slave Life and Culture in the Old South* (New York, 1976), 53–4; Kenneth M. Stampp, *The Peculiar Institution: Slavery in the Antebellum South* (New York, 1956), 164; Deborah Gray White, *Ar'n't I a Woman? Female Slaves in the Plantation South* (New York, 1985), 155–6.
2. Philip D. Morgan, 'Work and Culture: The Task System and the World of Lowcountry Blacks, 1700 to 1880', *William and Mary Quarterly*, 3rd series, 39 (1982), 563–99; 'The Ownership of Property by Slaves in the Mid-Nineteenth Century Low Country', *Journal of Southern History*, 49 (1983), 399–420. Alex Lichtenstein, '"That Disposition to Theft, with Which They Have Been Branded": Moral Economy, Slave Management, and the Law', *Journal of Social History*, 21 (1988), 413–40; Lawrence T. McDonnell, 'Money Knows No Master: Market Relations and the American Slave Community' in Winifred B. Moore Jr, Joseph F. Tripp and Lyon G. Tyler (eds.), *Developing Dixie: Modernization in a Traditional Society* (Westport, CT, 1988), 31–44.
3. In this essay, the term 'upcountry' has two connotations: the bulk of South Carolina located inland from the lowcountry of the coast and, more importantly, that vast area where short-staple cotton – as opposed to rice and long-staple cotton – was cultivated. My use of 'upcountry' joins together the middle country – the area south of the fall line and inland from the coastal rice districts – and the 'real' upcountry – that area north of the fall line.
4. John Belton O'Neall (ed.), *The Negro Law of South Carolina* (Columbia, 1848), 21.
5. Morgan, 'Work and Culture', 566, 573–4.
6. The 1796 act attempted to regulate slaves' marketing activities by increasing to $200 the maximum penalty for trading with a slave who did not carry a permit to trade from the master. The goal of the stiffened penalty was to discourage individuals from trading illicitly with slaves. Howell M. Henry, *The Police Control of the Slave in South Carolina* (Emory, VA, 1914), 81–2; Lichtenstein, '"That Disposition to Theft"', 429–30.

7. Robert W. Fogel and Stanley L. Engerman, *Time on the Cross: The Economics of American Negro Slavery* (Boston, 1974), 1: 203–6; Lewis C. Gray, *History of Agriculture in the Southern United States to 1860* (Washington, DC, 1933), 1: 550–56; Philip D. Morgan, 'Task and Gang Systems: The Organization of Labor on New World Plantations' in Stephen Innes (ed.), *Work and Labor in Early America* (Chapel Hill, 1988), 189–220; U.B. Phillips, *American Negro Slavery* (Gloucester, Mass., 1959 (1918)), 247.

8. George Rawick (ed.), *The American Slave: A Composite Autobiography* (Westport, CT, 1977), 2, pt. 1: 191 (Sylvia Cannon); 3, pt. 4: 221 (Genia Woodberry).

9. Charles Ball, *Slavery in the United States: A Narrative of the Life and Adventures of Charles Ball, A Black Man* (New York, 1969 (1837)), 166.

10. Ibid., 166.

11. Plantation Volume, 1801–12, 53, Guignard Family Papers, South Caroliniana Library, University of South Carolina, Columbia (hereafter, SCL) (Guignard began planting in 1801 with 16 slaves); McDonnell, 'Money Knows no Master', 36; Ball, *Slavery in the United States*, 190, 195.

12. Cotton prices averaged roughly 35 cent per pound of ginned cotton from 1790 to 1800. From 1800 to 1801, the price dropped from 44 to 19 cents. For the next 20 years, the price would remain below 20 cents, with occasional exceptions. Gray, *History of Agriculture*, 2: 681, 682, 1027 (Table 41).

13. Ibid., 2: 689–90. Long-staple (sometimes known as sea island) cotton was even more difficult to pick. See Phillips, *American Negro Slavery*, 224.

14. John Campbell, 'The Gender Division of Labor, Slave Reproduction, and the Slave Family Economy on Southern Cotton Plantations, 1800–1865', Ph.D. Diss. (University of Minnesota, 1988), Ch. 2.

15. Ball, *Slavery in the United States*, 187, 189, 217, 271–3; Plantation Volume, 1801–12, 48, 53, 54, 63, 64, 69, 71, 76, 136, Guignard Family Papers, SCL.

16. Ball, *Slavery in the United States*, 273, 187. Ball himself worked for 20 different employers.

17. Ibid., 273.

18. This range reflects the differing experience of slaves living on the Guignard plantation and those with whom Charles Ball was acquainted. Although Ball did not indicate how much the typical slave earned, it may be conjectured that, at 50 cents per day, they might have earned $8 in the fall (50 cents times 16 Sundays during the four-month period running from September to December). Of course, this amount was probably less for some slaves who, as Ball says, 'would not work constantly on Sunday'; ibid., 272. Future research may well revise these estimates, however.

19. Ibid., 108, 167, 188, 190, 202, 270. The Guignard slaves typically received, as part of their allowance, shoes, blankets, hats, cloth and, thus, presumably used their earnings to supplement these subsistence goods; Plantation Volume, 1801–12, 36, 67, 75, 88, 118, 136, 137, 146, 148, 160, Guignard Family Papers, SCL.

20. Ball, *Slavery in the United States*, 191.

21. John Hebron Moore, *Agriculture in Ante-Bellum Mississippi* (New York, 1971), Chs. 1, 2.

22. Gray, *History of Agriculture*, 2: 689; James L. Watkins, *King Cotton; A Historical and Statistical Review, 1790–1908* (New York, 1969 (1908)), 75.

23. Law-DuBose Cash and Barter Book, 1818–20, William Law Papers, Special Collections, Perkins Library, Duke University (hereafter, DUKE); Slave Account Book, 1824–27, John Black Papers, SCL; Leach Carrigan Records, 1836–38 vol., SCL; McDonnell, 'Money Knows No Master', 33.

24. Ball, *Slavery in the United States*, 190, 191, 195; Ledger, 1796–99, John Black Papers, SCL; Law and DuBose Cash and Barter Book, 1818–20, William Law Papers, DUKE; 'Slave Account Book, 1824–27, John Black Papers, SCL.

25. The law allowed slaves to trade away from the plantation as long as they had a written permit from the master. An updated law, passed by the General Assembly in 1817, continued to allow slaves to trade on their own but increased the penalties for those individuals convicted of trading with slaves who did not have their owner's

permission. The new maximum fine was $1,000 and no less than one month, but no more than a year, in jail. O'Neall, *The Negro Law*, 46.

26. Ball, *Slavery in the United States*, 167, 191, 192, 291, 307–8; A Practical Farmer, 'Observations on the Management of Negroes', *Southern Agriculturalist*, 5 (1832), 181–4; 'On the Management of Slaves', ibid., 6 (1833), 281–7; Tattler, 'Management of Negroes', *Southern Cultivator*, 8 (1850), 162–4.

27. Whitemarsh B. Seabrook, *An Essay on the Management of Slaves* (Charleston, 1834), 8.

28. Ibid., 8; undated speech, 4, Thomas Cassels Law Papers, SCL. This speech may have been an early version of an address given by Thomas C. Law on 10 Aug. 1852 to the Darlington Agricultural Society, entitled 'The Report on the Management of Slaves – Duty of Overseers and Employers'. The final version omits the quoted phrase on slave theft.

29. F.N. Boney (ed.), *Slave Life in Georgia: A Narrative of the Life, Sufferings, and Escape of John Brown, A Fugitive Slave*, (Savannah 1972 (1855)), 47–8. Among these poor whites were the apparently underpaid civil servants of antebellum America, such as Robert McQueen, postmaster at Cheraw, SC, who supplemented his salary by purchasing stolen cotton from slaves, and who was eventually convicted of this crime in 1832; Laurence Prince to Stephen Miller, 12 Apr. 1832, Box 3, Folder 3, Chestnut Family Papers, State Historical Society of Wisconsin (hereafter, SHSW).

30. A Practical Farmer, 'Observations on the Management of Negroes', 181–4; Tattler, 'Management of Negroes', 162–4; Thomas C. Law, 'On the Management of Slaves', 10 Aug. 1852, Thomas Cassels Law Papers, SCL. These tensions within production, as well as in other aspects of slaves' market-related activities, existed throughout the South. See, for example, A Mississippi Planter, 'Management of Negroes upon Southern Estates', *De Bow's Review*, 10 (1851), 621–7.

31. Folder Nos. 184–93, Thomas Waties Papers, SCL; in the same collection, see also Folder Nos. 283–92 for another example of slaves selling stolen goods at night.

32. An Overseer, 'On the conduct and Management of Overseers, Driver, and Slave', *South. Agric.*, 9 (1836), 225–31; A Practical Farmer, 'Observations on the Management of Negroes', 181–4.

33. Drew Gilpin Faust, *James Henry Hammond and the Old South: A Design for Mastery* (Baton Rouge, 1985), 74; James M. Townes, 'Management of Negroes', *South. Cultiv.*, 9 (1851), 87–8; W.H. Evans, 'Report of the Committee on Cotton: Read before the Darlington (South Carolina) Agricultural Society, at its Last Meeting', *The Rural Register*, 2 (1860), 180; Tattler, 'Management of Negroes', 162–4; A Mississippi Planter, 'Management of Negroes Upon Southern Estates', 621–7. Like South Carolina and Mississippi cotton planters, those in Georgia also became disillusioned with slave crops and market-related overtime. According to one Georgia planter,

> 'It was at one period much the custom of planters to give each hand a small piece of land to cultivate on their own account, if they chose to do so; but this system has not been found to result well ... It is much better to give each hand, whose conduct has been such as to merit it, an equivalent in money at the end of the year'.

Robert Collins, 'Essay on the Treatment and Management of Slaves', *South. Cultiv.*, 12 (1854), 205–6.

34. Rawick (ed.), *The American Slave*, 3, pt. 3: 56 (Mary Johnson); 2, pt. 1: 185 (Sylvia Cannon).

35. Farming Books, 1841–2, 1843–4 (but actually up to 1852), 1853–54, 1854–55, 1856–57, 1856–59, 1860–63, Thomas Cassels Law Papers, SCL. Data missing for some years in Table 2 probably reflects Law's failure to describe plantation work, whether performed on his crops or his slaves' crops, with the same amount of detail from year to year. From 1859 to 1861 slaves on the Caleb Coker plantation received four Saturdays and five weekdays to harvest their own cotton: 2, 3 Dec. 1859; 12, 15,

29 Sept. 1860; 9, 10 Nov. 1860, 16 Sept. and 29 Oct. 1861, Caleb Coker Plantation Book, 1856–61, SCL; 13 and 14 Dec. (Thursday and Friday), H.G. Charles Plantation Volume, 1860, Charles and Company, Darlington Merchant Records, SCL. In addition, slaves on the William Law plantation commenced planting their cotton on Friday 23 Apr. 1858, the day after they finished planting Law's cotton: 'A Minute of Farming Operations-Year 1858', Folder 1857–59, William Law Papers, DUKE.

36. Hurricane, 'The Negro and his Management', *South. Cultiv.*, 18 (1860), 276–7; Thomas C. Law, 'On the Management of Slaves'.

37. Thomas C. Law, 'On the Management of Slaves'. See also, A Practical Farmer, 'Observations on the Management of Negroes', 181–4.

38. Rawick (ed.), *The American Slave*, 3, pt. 4: 221; see also 2, pt. 2: 143–4.

39. The same work pattern existed on the Chester District plantation of John Strong. In his plantation record book, Strong recorded on Wednesday 12 May 1852 that: They 'finished ploughing middles today ... the Negroes ploughed their crop this evening'. A month later, on Tuesday 15 June, Strong wrote: 'ploughed the hillsides over at James got done about half past ten o'clock ... ploughed part of the Darkies' corn'. Folder 4, unbound plantation volume (15 April 1852–17 Aug. 1852), Strong Family Papers, SCL.

40. Cotton damage due to snow was a very real possibility. On the H.G. Charles plantation, slaves finished harvesting their 1860 cotton crop on 13 December – a scant one day before snow fell. H.G. Charles Plantation Book, Charles and Company Records, SCL.

41. The owners of these plantations were Peter S. Bacot, Thomas Law, William Law and Peter S. Wilds; see Campbell, 'Gender Division of Labour', Ch. 6.

42. Income inequality within and between plantations – as well as between different regions, such as the rice lowcountry and cotton upcountry, in South Carolina – indicates another way in which slaves' income-earning activities played an ambiguous role in slave life. Inequality created, at a minimum, a source of economic difference among slaves, and, more significantly, possible discord within plantation slave communities. Although I consider the possible implications of income inequality in my dissertation, 'Gender Division of Labor', a more systematic discussion is outside the scope of this essay.

43. Fogel and Engerman, *Time on the Cross*, 1: 148, report that some slaves in Texas earned as much as $100 annually from their cotton crops.

44. An Overseer, 'On the Conduct and Management', 225–31. Under this new law, the penalties for trading illegally with a slave remained as they were under the 1817 law, see n.25 above; O'Neall, *The Negro Law*, 46, and Henry, *The Police Control*, 82.

45. Quoted in Henry, *Police Control*, 83.

46. McDonnell, 'Money Knows No Master', 33; for Law, see sources cited in n. 35 as well as Negro (Accounts) Book, 1859–60, Thomas Cassels Law Papers, SCL.

47. Slave account books, Peter S. Bacot Papers, SCL; Peter S. Wilds cotton picking records, Wilds Family Papers, Darlington (South Carolina) Historic Commission (hereafter, DHC); Ledger 1847–62, Bratton and Rainey Ledgers, SCL; Folder 2: 1840–49, Folder 3: 1850–56, Folder 4: 1857–59, Folder 5: 1860–80, Folder 6: Undated, Thomas C. Perrin Papers, Southern Historical Collection, University of North Carolina-Chapel Hill (hereafter, SHC); Folders 1837–39, 1843–45, 1848–49, 1850–53, 1854–56, 1857–59, 1860–62, 1863–66, Undated, William Law Papers, DUKE. For other planters who purchased slave crops, see also Caleb Coker Plantation Book, SCL; McRrae to Mr Christmas, 5 March 1858, vol. 7, John McRae Letterbooks, SHSW; Cotton Book, 1858, Mary Hart Means Papers, SCL; Witherspoon Plantation Record Book, 1839–59, Witherspoon Family Papers, SCL.

48. A Practical Farmer, 'Observations on the Management of Negroes', 181–4; Law, 'The Report on the Management of Slaves', Thomas Cassels Law Papers, SCL.

49. In his analysis of the Carrigan cotton records, McDonnell found that slaves earned the same prices received by white people who sold their cotton to the Carrigan firm.

Thus, for the present purposes, I am assuming that when the slaves of William Law sold their cotton locally under Law's auspices they received a fair local price.

50. Although Bacot did not describe the quality of his slaves' cotton, his peers were quick to note any deficiencies, and paid accordingly. In 1841, for example, Peter Wilds paid his slaves two cents per pound of yellow (that is, inferior) cotton as opposed to two and two-tenths for their better cotton. Such careful pricing was understandable given that Charleston factors judged cotton strictly when *they* determined price and reminded planters that mixing low and high quality cotton in the same bale reduced the value of the entire bale. In 1824, for example, the Charleston factorage firm of Parker and Brailsford wrote to Stephen Miller of Statesburg, advising him to 'direct your overseer not to mix the prime cotton in the same bale with the inferior ... as it not only injures, but renders it difficult to accomplish a sale to advantage'. Folder 7: 1824, Chesnut Family Papers, SHSW. In light of these meticulous grading standards, it is reasonable to assume that, because the prices received by Bacot were generally in line with Charleston prices, the cotton produced by his slaves was not yellow or otherwise inferior.

51. When selling consumer goods to his slaves, Bacot did not exploit his slaves by charging excessive or extortionate prices. A comparison of the prices he charged and the prices he paid when buying the same consumer goods revealed no differences. Overall, the Bacot slaves spent 30 per cent of their earnings on the plantation.

52. This analysis is made possible because factor invoices for the sale of the owner's cotton exist for all four plantations studied in this section. These invoices provide information on the number and weight of the owner's balls of cotton, the price received by the owner and the various marketing costs, such as freight, insurance, weighing, storage and factor's commission, incurred in sending cotton to Charleston.

53. The prices in the distant Charleston market were higher than those in the local area – all other things being equal – for two reasons. First, producers who delayed the sale of their cotton by sending it to a distant market received a risk payment as part of the price that they eventually received. For in refusing to accept a price that they were certain of in the local market, these producers took the risk that the prices of the distant market would fall between the time that they could have sold their cotton locally and when the cotton was actually sold in Charleston. Secondly, by delaying the sale of their crop – for up to six months after the harvest in some instances – planters also received an interest payment as part of the price, since in not selling their cotton immediately, they deprived themselves of the possible interest on the income earned when their cotton was sold soon after it was harvested. In short, the price structures of distant, centralized marketplaces were automatically higher than those of the local marketplace.

54. On one occasion (1857), Law's slaves did have to pay shipping expenses of $1.605 per bale ($1.00 for freight, 48 cents for bagging and rope, and 12.5 cents for weighing) when selling their cotton to an upcountry merchant who lived a slight distance away from them in Cheraw, S.C. Revealingly, these costs were standard, regardless of how far one shipped one's cotton. Throughout the 1840s and 1850s, Law paid these amounts when he sent his bales to Charleston. In effect, then, Law's slaves paid some of the cost of shipping their cotton to Charleston, but without sending it there and thus possibly receiving a higher price as a result.

55. Overall, a Charleston sale would have increased slave incomes by 15.9 per cent, 12 per cent and 24.5 per cent for slaves living on the Wilds, William Law and Bacot plantations, respectively.

56. McDonnell, 'Money Knows No Master', 35.

57. William Law Papers, DUKE, Folders 1857–9, 1860–62. The William Law slaves generally spent most of their incomes off the plantation, as did the slaves of Peter S. Bacot. Negro Book, 1859–60, Thomas Cassells Law Papers, SCL; An Overseer, 'On the Conduct', 225–31 (both quotations).

58. Folders 1857–59, 1860–62, William Law Papers, DUKE.

59. Keeping their slave customers was no trivial matter to merchants in the post-1834 period. In an editorial that attempted to alleviate the concerns of merchants, the *Charleston Daily Courier* argued that the point of the new 1834 law was to limit slaves' illicit trade in stolen goods and possession of liquor and, as a result, 'we can see no good reason why it [slaves' legitimate, master-approved trade] cannot still be innocently indulged in'. Quoted in Henry, *The Police Control*, 82. Clearly, many other planters and merchants also tolerated such indulgences – but, as the credit system indicates, not mindlessly or recklessly.

60. Folder 1850–53, William Law Papers, DUKE.

61. Unfortunately there are no records which indicate how much Law's slaves earned from their crops in 1853 and, thus, there is no way of determining how many slaves went into debt and by what amount.

62. The findings in Table 4 are based on my reconstruction of each slave's economic and financial affairs in a given year. To determine a slave's year-ending financial status I subtracted his or her total expenditures in a year – goods purchased, money loaned out, interest payments made and so on – from the slave's total income – crop and other earnings, money received from other slaves, credit for consumer goods returned and so on. The results in this table present the aggregated experience for all of the slaves on the plantation in each year. Technically, the unit of analysis is not individual slaves per se but, rather, discrete slave producing–selling–buying consumer units. For slaves who operated as individuals, outside of a family context, the selling–buying unit was each individual slave. For other slaves, who lived in identifiable family units on the plantation, the unit of analysis is the family. Each family's overall financial status includes the buying and selling activities of all of its members. Typically, more than one family member appeared in the records as buying and selling – most commonly, both the husband and wife each had their own separate accounts of their economic activity. I am assuming that even though spouses, for example, may have had separate accounts, they none the less earned their incomes, spent their earnings, used consumer goods, and made economic decisions within the context of the family, and not as discrete, solitary individuals who just happened to live in families. For an initial analysis of the extent and implications of slave participation in market-related activities, by gender, see Campbell, 'Gender Division of Labor', Ch. 6.

63. 'A slave may, by the consent of his master, acquire and hold *personal* property. All, thus acquired, is regarded in law as that of the master. ... A slave cannot contract, and be contracted with'. O'Neall, *The Negro Law*, 21–2.

64. Table 4 presents slaves' year-end financial status in terms of the year in which slaves produced their crops, which was not necessarily the same year in which slaves made their purchases once they were paid. The slaves of William Law, for example, appear to have spent their 1857 earnings in January or February of the following year. Rather than treat these purchases as part of their 1858 financial affairs, I include them as part of their 1857 economic activities, just as Law himself did when balancing slaves' accounts in February of 1858. Overall, William Law and his brother, Thomas Law, noted when slaves made their purchases and thus make it relatively easy to determine which purchases should be included in which year when calculating slaves 'year-ending' financial status. The same cannot be said, however, for Peter Bacot, who did not always indicate when slaves made their purchases or whether their purchases were bought with unspent earnings from the previous year or bought against future earnings for crops not yet harvested and sold. As a result of these ambiguities, I may have assigned purchases to the wrong years, thereby misstating the year-end financial picture for individual slaves and, hence, for the entire Bacot slave community as a whole. With this in mind, it is best to view the Bacot findings as good approximations of slaves' year-to-year financial status on this plantation.

65. Calculations made from data in Slave Account Books, Peter S. Bacot Papers, SCL.

66. Ibid. Of course, loans between slaves may also mask tensions stemming from income inequality within the slave population.

67. Negro (Accounts) Book, 1859–60, Thomas Cassels Law Papers, SCL. It is unlikely that the slaves studied here saved a portion of their earnings each year in order to buy their freedom at a later date. The amount of money earned, much less saved, by these slaves was far too small to finance their 'self-purchase', even after years of savings.
68. Glenn Porter (ed.), *Encyclopedia of American Economic History* (New York, 1980), Table 1, 234. The base period is 1910–14, with 100 as the base. Index values less than 100 signify lower consumer prices (deflation) than in the 1910–14 period; values greater than 100 indicate higher prices for consumer goods.
69. For example, a yard of flannel cost 75 cents in 1819 but less than 30 cents in the 1850s; Folder: 1811–19, Thomas Waties Papers, SCL; and Campbell, 'The Gender division of Labor', 279–80.
70. For examples of late antebellum planters who gave slaves subsistence goods, thereby enabling slaves to spend their incomes on an array of 'luxury', non-subsistence goods, see Peter S. Bacot Papers, SCL; William Law Papers, DUKE; Witherspoon Family Papers, SCL; Thomas C. Perrin Papers, SHC; Mary Hart Means Papers, SCL.
71. Charles and Company, Merchant Records, SCL; Negro (Accounts) Book, 1859–60, Thomas Cassels Law Papers, SCL. Actually, Elleck purchased $27 worth of goods and thus, went into debt by $2. But given the size of his income he would have still purchased, in all likelihood, a large number of different goods even if he had not overspent.
72. Campbell, 'The Gender Division of Labor', 278, 2790 Slave Plantation Books, Peter S. Bacot Papers, SCL. For the extent and implications of slave participation in market-related activities, by gender, see Campbell, 'Gender Division of Labor', Ch. 6.
73. R. King Jr, 'On the Management of the Butler Estate and the Cultivation of Sugar Cane', *South. Agric.* 1 (1828), 523–9.
74. On guano and padlock purchases see Negro (Accounts) Book, 1859–60, Thomas Cassels Law Papers, SCL; for padlocks, also see Slave Plantation Books, Peter S. Bacot Papers, SCL.
75. H.G. Charles Plantation Volume, 1860, Charles and Company Merchant Records, SCL; McRae to Christmas, vol. 7, 479, John McRae Letterbooks, SHSW; Mechanicsville (Darlington District) Baptist Church Records, 83, SCL.
76. 'On the Management of Slaves', Thomas Cassells Law Papers, SCL; Black Creek Agricultural Society Minute Bok, 5, SCL. Although the various measures adopted by late antebellum slaveowners to reduce slave theft – from greater supervision in production to control of the marketing of slave crops – no doubt made it harder for slaves to steal, slaves still stole. Indeed, the incidence of slave theft seems to have reached epidemic proportions by the late antebellum period. Although South Carolina slaveowners and their allies continued to press the legislature to pass even sterner laws against individuals who traded illicitly with slaves, theft and illicit trade continued unabated. Eventually, slaveowners throughout South Carolina took the law into their own hands leading, in extreme cases, to bloodshed, as in March 1858 when 60 or so members of the Darlington Vigilante Committee assaulted and killed two white men who were known traders with slaves. Campbell, 'The Gender Division of Labor', Ch. 5. For other discussions of slave theft and slaveowner response to it in the late antebellum period, see also J. William Harris, *Plain Folk and Gentry in a Slave Society: White Liberty and Black Slavery in Augusta's Hinterlands* (Middleton, CT, 1985), 52–61; Henry, *The Police Control*, Ch. 8; Michael Stephen Hindus, *Prison and Punishment: Crime, Justice, and Authority in Massachusetts and South Carolina, 1767–1878* (Chapel Hill, 1980), Ch. 6; Lichtenstein, '"That Disposition to Theft"', 426–33; McDonnell, 'Money Knows No Master', 35–7.
77. James O. Breeden (ed.), *Advice Among Masters: The Ideal in Slave Management in the Old South* (Westport, CT, 1980), 267.

TABLE 1

SLAVE COTTON PRODUCTION ON FOUR SOUTH CAROLINA UPCOUNTRY
(DARLINGTON DISTRICT) PLANTATIONS, 1841–1861

	Cotton Production By Slaves	Total Cotton Production	Proportion of Cotton Production By Slaves
Peter S. Wilds			
1841	5,141 lbs.	98,014 lbs.	5.2%
1842	5,930	106,084	5.6
Total	11,071	204,098	5.4
Thomas C. Law			
1849	1,928	61,596	3.1%
1858	7,679	124,035	6.2
1859	5,749	103,037	5.6
1860	4,750	103,687	4.6
Total	20,106	392,355	5.1
William Law			
1852	10,017	76,839	13.0%
1854	9,112	84,181	10.8
1855	7,380	66,980	11.0
1856	7,902	56,750	13.9
1857	7,436	67,440	11.0
1858	5,940	61,634	9.6
1859	9,156	86,949	10.5
1860	6,066	58,560	10.4
1861	10,426	75,661	13.8
Total	73,435	634,994	11.6
Caleb Coker			
1858	9,640	125,640	7.7%
1859	6,850	134,751	5.1
1860	4,238	131,075	3.2
1861	1,348	104,679	1.3
Total	22,076	496,145	4.4
All Four			
Total	126,688	1,727,59	27.3%

Note: All cotton measured in pre-ginned pounds.

Source: Wilds Family Papers, Darlington (South Carolina) Historic Commission;
Thomas Cassels Law Papers, South Caroliniana Library, University of South
Carolina; William Law Papers, Perkins Library, Duke University; Caleb Coker
Plantation Book, South Caroliniana Library, University of South Carolina.

TABLE 2

THE TIMING OF SLAVE WORK ON THEIR OWN CROPS, THOMAS C. LAW
PLANTATION DISTRICT, DARLINGTON, SOUTH CAROLINA, 1841–1858

Date	Activity
1841	
4/17 Saturday	"plant my [Law's] cotton"
4/19 Monday	"finished planting negro cotton-- begin to shave cotton with scrapers"
5/15 Saturday	"gave Negroes day to work their crop"
1843	
7/8 Saturday	"gave Negroes day to work their crop"
1844	
3/24 Sunday	"planted Negro cotton; finished 3/25"
6/22 Saturday	"given to Negroes to plow and hoe their crops"
1846	
5/16 Saturday	"ploughed negro crop"
1847	
4/30 Friday	"finished planting my crop"
5/1 Saturday	"planted negro crop"
1848	
4/26 Wednesday	"planted negro crop"
4/27 Thursday	"begin to plough cotton"
6/17 Saturday	"ploughed negro crop"
1849	
5/5 Saturday	"planted negro crop"
6/21 Thursday	"ploughing negro crop and finished fresh land cotton"
1850	
5/6 Monday	"finished planting cotton for myself"
5/7 Tuesday	"planted negro cotton"
5/25 Saturday	"finished ploughing cotton first time and ploughed negro crop"
7/3 Wednesday	"ploughed negro crop 2nd time"
7/6 Saturday	"begin to plough [my] cotton 3rd time"
1851	
5/26 Monday	"finished plouging corn 2nd time and ploughed negro crop"
5/27 Tuesday	"begin to plow [my] cotton 2nd time"
6/21 Saturday	"ploughed negro corn"
1852	
4/17 Saturday	"stopped after dinner for hands to prepare their own lands"
5/1 Saturday	"let negroes have 1 1/2 days to plant their crop on the plantation"
7/5 Monday	"ploughed negro cotton"
7/10 Saturday	"gave all hands the day to work their own crop"

TABLE 2 (continuted)

Date	Activity
1853	6/18 Monday	"finished hoeing and putting to a stand cotton in 58 acres ploughing over negro crop"
	7/2 Saturday	"ploughed negro corn"
	7/9 Saturday	"ploughed negro cotton"
1854	4/1 Saturday	"Negroes mostly working for themselves to plant their corn"
	6/12 Monday	"ploughed negro cotton"
1855	5/19 Saturday	"planting negro corn"
	6/19 Tuesday	"ploughed negro corn"
1857	8/14 Friday	"finished ploughing [my] cotton"
	8/15 Saturday	"ploughed negro cotton"
1858	4/23 Friday	"finished planting cotton for self today"
	4/24 Saturday	"worked Negroes land"

Source: Thomas Cassels Law Papers, South Caroliniana Library, University of South Carolina.

TABLE 3

ACTUAL VERSUS POSSIBLE PRICE FOR COTTON GROWN
INDEPENDENTLY BY SLAVES, ON FOUR DARLINGTON DISTRICT,
SOUTH CAROLINA, PLANTATIONS, 1841–1861

Owner/Date	Average Price[a]	Owner's Price[b]	Net Price[c]	Slaves' Price[d]	Percent Difference in Price[e]
Peter Wilds					
12/11/1841	8.625	8.75	8.29	7.13	+16.4%
Wilds 1842					
10/29/42	7.875	7.0	6.40	4.87	+31.4%
12/24/42	6.25	6.25	5.67	4.87	+16.4
03/14/43	5.875	5.0	4.66	4.87	-4.3
Wilds 1843					
11/03/43	7.5	7.0	6.45	6.31	+2.2%
01/09/44	9.25	9.0	8.42	6.31	+33.4
William Law					
04/26/1845	6.19	6.125	5.617	4.0	+40.4%
04/29/45	6.10	5.25	4.78	4.0	+19.6
W. Law 1846					
12/06/47	7.5	6.75	5.62	8.625	-34.8%
W. Law 1852					
03/15/53	9.8	9.25	8.56	8.29	+3.2%
06/07/53	11.0	10.75	10.10	8.29	+21.4
06/07/53	11.0	8.75	8.12	8.29	-2.0
W. Law 1854					
12/30/54	8.125	7.25	7.189	8.0	-10.1%
03/22/55	8.625	8.25	8.22	8.0	+2.8
05/18/55	9.9	10.125	10.188	8.0	+27.4
W. Law 1855					
04/15/56	10.8	9.0	8.35	8.25	+1.2%
04/15/56	10.8	10.5	9.89	8.25	+19.9
06/22/56	11.12	10.625	9.99	8.25	+21.1
W. Law 1856					
12/08/56	12.0	11.5	10.74	12.25	-12.3%
05/23/57	13.87	13.5	12.66	12.25	+3.3

TABLE 3 (continued)

Owner/Date	Average Price[a]	Owner's Price[b]	Net Price[c]	Slaves' Price[d]	Percent Difference in Price[e]
W. Law 1857					
10/08/57	12.375	13.375	12.64	8.0	+57.9%
02/17/58	11.4	11.55	10.83	8.0	+35.4
04/21/58	12.125	13.0	12.24	8.0	+53.0
05/20/58	12.375	12.0	11.26	8.0	+40.8
06/12/58	12.06	10.625	9.57	8.0	+19.6
W. Law 1858					
09/22/58	12.06	12.375	11.72	11.0	+6.5%
10/26/58	12.06	11.0	10.39	11.0	-5.5
04/30/59	12.25	11.0	10.38	11.0	-5.6
04/13/59	12.25	12.165	11.47	11.0	+4.3
W. Law 1859					
10/05/59	11.0	10.625	10.33	10.25	+.5%
01/09/60	11.06	10.625	10.30	10.25	+.5
04/24/60	11.125	10.875	10.5	10.25	+ 2.4
W. Law 1860					
10/26/60	10.9	10.875	10.252	9.0	+13.9%
10/26/60	10.9	10.75	10.13	9.0	+12.6
10/26/60	10.9	10.375	9.76	9.0	+8.5
02/02/61	f	11.0	10.256	9.0	+14.0
Peter S. Bacot					
11/04/1852	9.25	9.54	8.86	8.05	+10.1%
12/03/52	8.8	8.75	8.176	8.05	+1.6
12/03/52	8.8	8.5	7.87	8.05	-2.2
02/17/53	9.5	8.0	7.33	8.05	-8.9
03/10/53	9.8	8.0	7.39	8.05	-8.2
03/10/53	9.8	8.165	7.57	8.05	-6.0
06/08/53	11.0	9.0	8.13	8.05	+1.0
06/08/53	11.0	11.0	10.09	8.05	+25.3
06/08/53	11.0	10.165	9.29	8.05	+15.4
Bacot 1853					
11/23/53	9.68	10.25	9.626	6.63	+45.2%
11/24/53	9.68	9.625	9.018	6.63	+36.0
11/16/54	9.68	10.125	9.481	6.63	+43.0
01/16/54	9.44	8.75	8.147	6.63	+22.9
02/23/54	9.19	9.25	8.645	6.63	+30.4
03/11/54	9.18	7.75	7.2	6.63	+8.6
03/11/54	9.18	9.125	8.55	6.63	+28.9
06/ /54	9.0	7.0	6.41	6.63	-3.4
06/ /54	9.0	6.5	5.885	6.63	-11.2
06/ /54	9.0	9.75	9.07	6.63	+36.8

TABLE 3 (continued)

Owner/Date	Average Price[a]	Owner's Price[b]	Net Price[c]	Slaves' Price[d]	Percent Difference in Price[e]
Bacot 1854					
12/26/54	8.125	6.75	6.22	6.58	-5.5%
10/16/54	8.875	9.5	8.91	6.58	+33.5
11/29/54	8.93	8.125	7.545	6.58	+14.7
11/30/54	8.93	7.75	7.255	6.58	+10.3
02/19/55	8.18	7.25	6.70	6.58	+1.9
02/26/55	8.18	7.25	6.748	6.58	+2.6
03/13/55	8.625	8.125	7.557	6.58	+14.9
Bacot 1855					
11/26/55	8.93	9.125	8.261	6.58	+25.5%
01/10/56	9.06	8.75	8.097	6.58	+22.8
03/05/56	10.06	10.00	9.432	6.58	+43.3
03/05/56	10.06	9.0	8.47	6.58	+28.7
05/24/56	10.875	10.0	9.369	6.58	+42.4
Bacot 1856					
10/28/56	12.0	11.375	10.77	6.58	+63.7%
01/04/56	11.68	12.0	11.42	6.58	+73.5
12/02/56	12.0	11.5	10.82	6.58	+64.5
12/12/56	12.0	11.25	10.55	6.58	+60.3
12/30/56	12.0	12.00	11.39	6.58	+73.1
02/ /57	13.125	11.75	11.1	6.58	+68.3
Thomas C. Law					
11/ /1859	10.94	10.69	10.05	11.5	-12.6%

Explanation:

Owner/Date:	Slaveowner, crop year, and date when owner's cotton was sold in Charleston, S.C.
Column A:	Average price per pound of cotton in the Charleston market during the month the owner's cotton was sold in this market.
Column B:	Price per pound of lint cotton (cents) received by the owner for his cotton.
Column C:	Price in Column A minus the percentage going to marketing expenses. Thus, the net possible price slaves would have received if they had sold in Charleston.
Column D:	The actual price received by slaves in selling to their owner or, in the case of William Law's slaves, to a local merchant.
Column E:	The net possible price (Column C) minus the actual slave price (Column D) divided by the actual slave price. That is, the percentage increase or decrease of the possible price over the actual slave price.

f = no data available

Sources: Data in Column A are calculated from Alfred Glaze Smith, *Economic Readjustment of an Old Cotton State, South Carolina, 1820–1860* (Columbia, 1958), Table 2, 224, 225. Smith provides the low and high cotton prices for each month; the price in Column A for any given month is the average of Smith's low and high prices for that month.

Data on slaveowner and slave cotton are derived from the following collections: Peter S. Wilds Cotton Picking records, Wilds Family Papers, Darlington (South Carolina) Historic Commission; William Law Papers, Special Collections, Perkins Library, Duke University; Peter S. Bacot Papers, South Caroliniana Library; Peter S. Bacot Papers, Southern Historical Collection University of North Carolina; Thomas Cassels Law Papers, South Caroliniana Library.

TABLE 4

NUMBER AND PERCENTAGE OF SLAVES ENDING EACH YEAR WITHOUT
A DEBT, AND AVERAGE PERCENTAGE OF INCOME SPENT EACH YEAR
BY SLAVES, THREE DARLINGTON DISTRICT, SOUTH CAROLINA PLANTATIONS,
1853–1860

Year	Number of Producing/ Consuming Units With Accounts	Units With No Debt	Average Spending Rate for Units With Accounts
W. Law Plantation			
1854	18	9 (50.0)%	94.5%
1856	14	14 (100.0)	82.5
1857	16	14 (87.5)	82.0
1858	16	9 (56.2)	97.5
1859	19	18 (94.7)	58.0
1860	18	13 (72.2)	91.0
Total	101	77 (76.2)	82.0
Bacot Plantation			
1852	61	33 (54.1)%	78.1%
1853	71	35 (49.3)	156.0
1854	49	34 (69.4)	77.2
1855	39	12 (30.8)	159.8
1856	44	34 (77.3)	3.3
1857	32	17 (53.1)	100.0
1858	38	19 (50.0)	112.1
1859	21	6 (28.6)	296.3
1860	23	8 (34.8)	573.2
1861	33	18 (54.5)	44.7
Total	411	216 (52.6)%	99.9%
T.C. Law Plantation			
1859	24	16 (66.7)%	86.0%
1860	22	15 (68.2)	56.0
Total	46	31 (67.4)%	85.0%

Note: Spending Rate is the percentage of a slave's total income spent on consumer goods in a given year. It is simply Value of Total Expenditures/Value of Total Income. The lower the percentage the more the slaves saved. A percentage greater than 100% indicates indebtedness.

Sources: See Table 3

The Internal Economy of Slavery in Rural Piedmont Virginia

John T. Schlotterbeck

When historians first explored the day-to-day world of slaves, they emphasized the creation of an independent domestic, religious and recreational life in the plantation quarters. Several recent studies have shown that many slaves also engaged in independent productive labour. Caribbean sugar planters, for example, found it cheaper to have their slaves raise their own food and livestock rather than supply them with purchased rations. These slaves fed themselves and their families and sold surpluses to their owners and in village markets. Slaves purchased consumer goods with their earnings and, over time, created an internal economy of barter and trade with each other and with planters and non-slaveholding whites. By becoming independent producers with ties to off-plantation markets, Caribbean slaves, some historians believe, undermined the plantation regime and reduced the planters' authority. Another kind of internal economy emerged in the South Carolina lowcountry where, under the task system of labour organization, slaves worked for themselves after they had completed their daily assignment. Slaves thus controlled part of their work day and engaged in productive activities that enabled them to accumulate capital and property and become familiar with markets. These experiences proved vital in enabling lowcountry blacks to escape the plantation system following emancipation. Similar circumstances also permitted slaves to engage in independent production in sugar and cotton producing areas in the antebellum south. Complex internal economies encouraged slave enterprise and strengthened slave family and community life while, masters believed, reducing slave rebelliousness.[1]

Internal economies were not limited to slave regimes that had provision grounds or task systems. An examination of northern piedmont Virginia between the Revolution and the Civil War reveals that an internal economy – albeit in a more attenuated form – existed even under the most unfavourable conditions.[2] Laws, mixed agriculture, the gang labour system and small slaveholdings all tended to limit slaves' control over their time and their access to land and markets. The existence of an internal economy testified to the determination of Virginia slaves to exact concessions from their owners for their productive labour, to enlarge their personal independence and to seize opportunities for individual advancement. A close look at the origins and organization of the internal economy in Orange and Greene Counties in Virginia's northern piedmont demonstrates the ways Virginia slaves were able to work for themselves, how they disposed of surplus production, and what they did with their earnings.[3] The internal economy created by Piedmont slaves also illuminates aspects of master–slave relationships, resistance and accommodation to slavery, contacts beyond home plantations, and the impact of slavery on post-emancipation behaviour.

The internal economy never received legal recognition in Virginia. Legislators believed that allowing slaves to engage in independent economic activity would undermine the masters' authority and threaten the institution. The 1792 slave code included a provision that 'No person whatsoever shall buy, sell, or receive of, to, or from a slave, any commodity whatsoever'. Six years later both slaves and free blacks were prohibited from vending 'goods, wares or merchandise'. These laws were designed to suppress trade off the plantation and apparently were never applied to bartering between slaves and owners. The internal economy thus emerged from informal exchanges between masters and slaves and was extended to a large range of underground trade in the neighbourhood.[4]

Northern piedmont Virginia was an unlikely place for the creation of an internal economy. In the 1730s and 1740s tidewater planters sent overseers with small gangs of slaves into the upcountry to carve tobacco quarters out of the wilderness. By the American Revolution planters and slaveowning farmers dominated the region and had created their own economy based on diversified agriculture that combined staple crops of wheat and tobacco for export with production of corn, grasses, fruits, vegetables, livestock, animal products and home manufactures for local consumption.

Diversified agriculture with its gang labour system minimized slaves' control over day-to-day work routines and land use and reduced personal time to work for themselves. Successful tobacco cultivation required careful management to raise and process the crop, so slaves were usually divided into small groups or squads under the supervision of an overseer or slave driver. Wheat cultivation, introduced in the third quarter of the eighteenth century, lengthened the work day. The 'laying-by' time, after tobacco planting and following the harvest, could now be devoted to corn and wheat cultivation. As specific tasks were completed during the day, gangs were regrouped for new assignments. Work continued from sunup to sundown throughout the year and, occasionally, at night. Even during rainy days slaves were kept busy working indoors. Owners with only a few slaves were often shorthanded at critical phases of the cultivation cycle and drove their slaves harder than did large planters. Because the labour needs of mixed farming varied enormously during the year, masters frequently hired out surplus or underemployed slaves to their neighbours. Finally, the predominance of small scattered holdings in the Piedmont – most slaves lived on units of less than 20 – isolated slaves from each other.[5]

The pressure on slaves' work time increased in the late ante-bellum period. The spread of 'improved' agriculture – especially soil restoration, crop rotation, planting grasses, manuring and fertilizing and better livestock husbandry – increased the amount of work that had to be done. Better farm machinery, used extensively by planters after 1850, enlarged the amount of land each field hand could till, speeded up the work pace and required more routinized labour.[6]

Despite the determination of owners to control their slaves' time and labour, by 1780 Virginia slaves had won important concessions that gave them access to garden plots, hunting and foraging privileges, time off on Sundays and holidays and the right to travel between neighbour-ing plantations. These gains provided the foundation for the internal economy and were the results of struggles between individual masters and their slaves. While some rights – that Sunday was the 'slaves' time', for example – were universally acknowledged by both parties, many other rights – such as time on Saturday to work slave gardens – were not. The specific rights and privileges slaves enjoyed thus varied from place to place.

The origins of both customary and plantation-specific privileges remains to be discovered. Some were undoubtedly brought to the piedmont by Tidewater creoles. Yet many blacks on the frontier were Africans, and only gradually did masters and slaves reach under-standings of what to expect of each other. African men and women toiling in small gangs on isolated tobacco tracts could scarcely com-municate with their overseers or, indeed, with other slaves. After 1750, as the slave population grew and the number of men and women became more balanced, slaves on adjoining holdings were able to form ties of marriage and friendship. As long as slaves performed the work expected of them and did not collectively challenge their masters' authority, their personal time was their own. Mingling on weekends and holidays, slaves exchanged news, held religious gatherings, aided runaways, planned acts of sabotage, traded goods and simply enjoyed each others' company. The neighbourhood, not the plantation, became the unit of the slave community.[7]

At the same time the growth of some large estates provided slaves with a variety of new work roles as artisans, house servants and teamsters and with a greater likelihood of being hired out to local farmers or in nearby villages. Greater variety of work experiences and exposure to different overseers and hirers enabled slaves to develop a clearer sense of what constituted a fair day's labour and proper treatment. Revolutionary ideas and evangelical Protestantism also eroded slavery's harsh edges and nurtured an idealized domestic slavery among masters. Encouraging slave families or religious conversions or declaring a holiday for slaves fulfilled paternal responsibilities and created, many masters believed, a more contented and productive work-force. Over time community standards concerning hours of labour, rations, housing and various privileges were established between masters and their slaves and among local planters. But, unlike provision grounds in the Caribbean or the task system in the Carolina lowcountry, these arrangements were never institutionalized and were subject to renegotiation as circumstances and owners changed.[8]

The internal economy developed from the most widely acknowledged slave privileges: garden plots, hunting and foraging rights and time off on Sundays and other holidays. Most slaves were able to raise vegetables, keep chickens, fish, collect nuts and hunt small game. For slaveowners these activities reduced ration costs and shifted much of the subsistence burden onto their slaves' free time in the evenings and on weekends. They also believed these practices deterred clandestine raids on storerooms and theft of livestock and market crops. Older slaves who were no longer productive workers were 'retired' to support themselves by raising corn and vegetables and keeping chickens. Some owners used gardens as part of their reward system. Silas Jackson, a former slave who had lived in Ashby's Gap in northern Virginia, recalled that each family was given three acres to raise chickens and vegetables and families who produced their own food received a ten dollar bonus at Christmas. Other masters gave newly married couples cabins and garden patches. Gardens created opportunities for slaves to work for themselves and provide for their families. They could supplement the quantity and add variety to the often meagre and monotonous rations of corn meal and bacon. The products of this labour – chickens, eggs, fish, ducks, melons, vegetables, berries, hay, seed, potato slips and nuts – were also traded between slaves or sold to slaveowners and white yeomen.[9]

Most subsistence labour was done on the slaves' personal time. Masters rarely required their slaves to work for them on Sundays and the week between Christmas and New Year, Whitsunday, and – with no sense of irony – Independence Day were generally recognized holidays. Slaves were sometimes given a day off after completing especially arduous tasks, like corn planting or the wheat harvest. Less common were owners like Francis Taylor who permitted his slaves one or two days each year to plant watermelon and potato patches. Rarer still, some slaves were allowed part or all of Saturdays for their gardens. Silas Jackson was required to work on Saturdays only during the wheat harvest; otherwise he was free to tend his garden or earn money from extra work.[10]

While encouraging their slaves' subsistence activities masters usually prohibited raising market products, especially tobacco and hogs. They feared, with ample reason, the difficulty of distinguishing between their slaves' goods and their own, particularly since slaves found ready purchasers among poor whites and country merchants. Masters who did allow their slaves to cultivate tobacco usually required that it be sold to them. Catlett Conway, for example, purchased over 300 pounds of tobacco from seven of his slaves in 1840. William Daniel bought several hundred pounds of tobacco in 1852 from his own and from his neighbours' slaves. Only the most privileged slaves could keep livestock. Noah Davis' father, who was the slave miller for a Fredericksburg merchant, kept a cow and a horse and also fed his chickens and hogs meal from the mill. Poultry and fowl, on the other hand, were raised exclusively by slaves on many plantations. In 1854 one planter's wife remarked that it was impossible to have her own turkeys and chickens because 'all the servants have them and they would get so mixed up'. Chickens and eggs were by far the most common items slaves sold.

Slaves were always paid for extra work done in their own time at night and on Sundays and holidays. Moses, Frances Taylor's slave carpenter, received five shillings (about 85 cents) for four days work in December 1792. William Daniel paid his slaves seven dollars for getting wood and fixing his ice pond over the Christmas holidays in 1853 and he also hired a neighbour's slave to haul plaster. Silas Jackson recalled earning as much as 50 cents per day working for neighbouring farmers. Planters who found themselves shorthanded paid their slaves to work extra hours and non-field hands received cash for helping with the harvest.[12]

Special skills or advantageous work assignments also provided slaves with opportunities to earn extra money. Their variety defies classification. Slaves made and sold mats, trays, baskets, brooms, utensils, gloves and farm tools. The Taylor family paid slaves for plastering, carpentry, cooperage and general construction and repair work during the 1780s and 1790s. Gusty, a slave belonging to William Daniel, earned between three and five dollars each year during the 1850s for prizing Daniel's tobacco. Ned, a slave owned by Herndon Frazier, made $30 for carpentry work in 1857, and James Barbour Jr paid slaves for tar and 'blacking' and for breaking a colt. Slave shoemakers made and repaired boots on their own time. Fiddlers were paid to play at dances and weddings. A slave overseer on a plantation near Orange Court House rented horses to whites. Wagoners expected tips for delivering goods or animals to planters in good condition. George Taylor, for example, had to pay a neighbour's slave about 20 cents for hauling goods from Fredericksburg in 1788 after Ned informed him that 'his master allowed such small matters'. Slave wagoners also hauled extra store goods that they sold for themselves on the side. Household servants received tips from white visitors and guests for extra services and for running errands. Slave women earned money by raising poultry, selling food to passengers at train stations, making baskets, candles and soap, doing extra laundering and weaving and serving as midwives.[13]

Slaves hired out to industrial and transportation firms had even greater opportunities to earn extra money. The task system was used extensively in Virginia's iron forges and gold mines, and labourers received cash payments for extra work beyond their assigned quota and for labouring on Sundays and holidays. Slave gold miners in eastern Orange County hired themselves to local planters to dig ditches. Most industrial slaves also had gardens and raised poultry. Slave earnings were so large that some industrialists maintained company stores where their slave workers traded goods for cash and for store credit.[14]

Stealing was another source for goods, especially in the underground internal economy. Most thefts were primarily protests against short rations. Slaves believed they had a 'moral right to a fair proportion of the proceeds of their labour', one former slave declared, 'and that any means are excusable towards securing that portion. Hence, theft from the master [was] generally deemed a light offense, if not strictly justifiable. They think the master defrauds them publicly, and they will steal from him privately'. Stolen goods were frequently sold; however, unlike trade between slaves and masters, these items were more often obtained through collaboration. Many robberies involved several slaves of different owners and the alleged victim was often not any of their masters.[15]

Slaves developed sophisticated market behaviour in deciding about disposing of goods and selling their labour. While owners were the most frequent purchasers and hirers, slaves also had access to markets off their plantations. Planters often bought products or hired labour from slaves belonging to their neighbours or to relatives. Between 1787 and 1795 Frances Taylor purchased chickens and handicrafts from at least a dozen slaves belonging to ten different owners. Trade between individual slaves and whites often extended over several years. Taylor's blacksmith Moses had at least five transactions with him (totalling $2.75) during 1794 and 1795; most involved sales of chickens and fish. Neighbourhood slaves apparently sought Taylor out when they had goods to sell and recommended him to friends on their own plantations. This referral system enabled slaves to maximize their advantages in the internal economy. Slaves occasionally collaborated in money-making ventures, pairing up to raise tobacco or hire themselves or acting as selling agents for other slaves.[16]

Slaves also marketed their goods and labour services outside their neighbourhoods. Markets for slave goods, common in larger towns and cities, also existed in Virginia's rural villages. James Barbour Jr, for example, purchased ducks from slaves at Orange Court House in 1836. Slaves gathered on 'Court Sunday', the day before the monthly meetings of the Orange County Court, to conduct their trade. Whitsunday, the Monday after Easter, was another time when slaves bought and sold goods. 'It is astonishing to see', one diarist noted in the 1830s, 'how much more cheerful they are than the court day collection of whites'. Country churches were also convenient locations for slave bartering before and after (and sometimes during) services. Peter Randolph sold refreshments – cake, candy and rum – outside church. Slaves also traded directly with merchants using cash and credits due them from their owners and hirers. Sampson's account at Thomas Barbour and Benjamin Johnson's store in the 1780s was settled by cash payments and by credit and notes from three slaveowners. Herndon Frazier paid his slave Ned's account at Parker's store partially to settle a balance due to him for overwork. Peddlers also purchased slave goods, ignoring laws that prohibited this trade. Some slaves became marketing specialists for their plantation, accumulating goods from fellow slaves and then hauling them to town for sale.[17]

Slaves disposed of stolen goods and illicit handicrafts to other slaves and to yeomen. Ralph Roberts sold grains and tobacco taken from his master along with his own. Whites and free blacks caught in this illegal trading received swift punishment from slaveowner-controlled courts. Joseph Price, a white man, was whipped in 1786 for buying tobacco from slaves belonging to William Robertson. Nancy Lewis, a free black women, was given 15 stripes 'on her bare back' for receiving bacon, valued at six dollars, 'knowing it was stolen'. Slaves were also punished for dealing in stolen goods. In 1861 a local Piedmont court ordered that two slaves be given 39 lashes each for stealing meat worth $50. Three other slaves who had allegedly received the stolen food were punished with 20 lashes. Zion Baptist Church excluded Richard, a slave belonging to Garrett Scott, for concealing a hide of leather and also for conveying leather to Aggy, who was owned by Nelly Willis, that other slaves had stolen from Brother Thomas Hawkins. Illegal trade with whites entailed considerable risk for slaves, since they had no means of protecting themselves from being cheated. But on occasion they were able to strike back. William Grimes was able to escape whippings from the overseer, Mr Bennett, by threatening to tell his master that Bennett was secretly buying goods the slaves had stolen. Bennett well knew this information would lead to his immediate dismissal.[18]

Slaves also made independent decisions as consumers, choosing between saving and spending and determining what to purchase. In the late eighteenth century bartering was common between planters and slaves. After 1800 most transactions were on a cash basis. Although the amount involved only one or two dollars annually per person, over several years or a lifetime some slaves accumulated considerable savings. Herndon Frazier paid his servant Ned over $26 for extra work done during 1857 and 1858. Even more extraordinary was Aron Corbin, who in the mid-1850s gave his money to his owner F.M. Kendall for safe-keeping. Kendalll invested the money and by 1866 it had grown to over $600. Most slaves, however, found consumer goods safer and more desirable than cash. The latter had to be concealed as stolen money was almost impossible to recover. Both masters and slaves, on the other hand, recognized the slaves' rights to personal property. One slave, after learning that she might be sold to a slave trader, wrote to her husband that she would be unable to gather 'my things' which were scattered in several places across the state. The status of a deceased slave's property, in contrast, was less clear. Some masters assumed this property belonged to the heirs; slaves, however, apparently believed it reverted to the slave community as a whole.[19]

Most purchases by slaves were consumer goods that improved their standard of living or provided small opportunities to escape the harsh world of slavery. Frances Taylor sold old shirts, jackets and coats to neighbourhood slaves for cash, chickens or extra work. Slave women bought kerchiefs and scarves. Calico, sheeting, patterns, hats, linen, ribbons, thread and tableware were the most frequently purchased items by slaves at Barbour and Johnson's store in Orange County during the 1780s. The internal economy also provided a steady supply of alcohol, especially to slaves whose masters prohibited it on their plantations. Taylor gave Phil, a slave, brandy for mending his boots and shoes, and James Barbour sold to whites, free blacks, and his neighbours' slaves whisky from his distillery in the mid-1820s.[20]

Some purchases strengthened slave community life. Men brought treats – candies and cakes – and small gifts when they visited their families on weekends. Clothes and other apparel improved appearances at dances, picnics and barbecues. Slaves also sought counsel from fortune-tellers and conjurers and purchased magic hands or 'jacks' to ward off evil spirits. Some literate slaves forged passes, and slave burial societies collected small sums of money to provide coffins, new clothes and funeral services for their members.[21]

The varied ways slaves participated in the internal economy furnishes vivid testimony of their extraordinary initiative in exploiting opportunities to improve their day-to-day life. In exchange for labouring for their masters slaves exacted concessions that enlarged their sphere of independent economic activity. Still, the internal economy in Virginia never developed in ways that directly challenged the slaveowners' power or threatened the existence of slavery. Indeed, it was the diversified economy, firmly rooted in slave labour, that created the very openings the slaves seized to their advantage. The internal economy thus became both an accommodation to the masters' claims of time and labour and a form of resistance that set limits to those demands.

The internal economy also increased the range of experiences blacks had under slavery, many of which proved vital in the post-emancipation era. Slaves developed a dual work ethic. During the 'masters time' slaves slowed the work tempo and resisted unremitting routinized labour, but on their own time they exhibited the initiative and enterprise that would make the bourgeoisie proud. Slaves encountered some whites as producers and as consumers – roles that were not defined solely by the master–slave relationship. A few slaves even became familiar with the workings of a market economy, including the use of cash, role of credit and how to deal with storekeepers. Even slaves whose participation in the internal economy was limited learned that access to garden plots and foraging and fishing rights provided an essential foundation for economic independence. After emancipation, these provisions were included in virtually every labour contract. Because of the internal economy slaves had greater control over their personal time and more choices in their daily life. From the perspective of free labourers these were perhaps small gains, but for the slaves, whose lives were hemmed in at every point, they were indeed important victories.

NOTES

1. Philip D. Morgan, 'Work and Culture: The Task System and the World of Lowcountry Blacks, 1700 to 1880', *William and Mary Quarterly* 3rd series, 39 (1982), 564–99; Eugene D. Genovese, *Roll, Jordan, Roll: The World the Slave Made* (New York, 1974), pp.535–40. For studies of internal economies in sugar and cotton economies, see Roderick A. McDonald's and John Campbell's essays in this volume and Joseph P. Reidy, 'Slave Labor on Plantations and Farms in the Cotton

Economy of Georgia' in Ira Berlin and Philip D. Morgan (eds.) *Cultivation and Culture: Labor and the Shaping of Slave Life in the Americas* (forthcoming).

2. I am not arguing that *every* slave on *every* plantation was involved in bartering activities, yet most adult slaves in Virginia lived in settled communities and were aware of the existence of the internal economy.

3. This paper is part of a broader study of rural life and culture in Orange and Greene Counties, Virginia, between 1730 and 1900. This 500 square-mile area is located between Fredericksburg and the Blue Ridge Mountains. Because of the limited number of primary sources by slaves, I have supplemented local records with slave accounts from northern and central Virginia.

4. Robert McColley, *Slavery and Jeffersonian Virginia*, 2nd edn (Urbana, 1973), 102. The internal economy by its very nature left few written records of its existence. Trade between slaves and masters often went unrecorded, since the payments involved were usually under a dollar, and most planters, if they kept written records at all, were more concerned with their market crops. Most participants in illicit trading – slaves and poor whites – were illiterate and naturally left few records. Plantation account books did record purchases from slaves, but it is not always clear whether the persons named were slaves, free blacks, or whites.

5. John Schlotterbeck, 'The "Social Economy" of an Upper South Community: Orange and Greene Counties, Virginia, 1815–1860', in Orville V. Burton and Robert C. McMath Jr (eds.), *Class, Conflict, and Consensus: Antebellum Southern Community Studies* (Westport, Conn., 1982), 3–28. For labour routines and slave management in Virginia, see McColley, *Slavery*, 60–61; VA, WPA, Writers Program, *The Negro in Virginia* (New York 1969 (1940)), ch. 7; Charles Perdue Jr, Thomas Barden and Robert Phillips (comps.), *Weevils in the Wheat: Interviews with Virginia Ex-Slaves* (Bloomington, 1980 (1976)), 302–7; William Grimes, *Life of William Grimes, The Runaway Slave* (New York, 1825), 14–15; John F.D. Smyth, *A Tour of the United States*, 2 vols. (London 1784), 1: 44. James Madison noted that slaves preferred task work to gang labour because the former gave them more personal time; Madison to Dr Morse, 28 March 1823, James Madison, *Letters and Other Writings of James Madison*, 4 vols. (New York, 1884) 3: 310–15.

6. John Schlotterbeck, 'Plantation and Farm: Social and Economic Change in Orange and Greene Counties, Virginia, 1716–1860' (Ph.D. Diss., The Johns Hopkins University, 1980), Ch. 7.

7. Schlotterbeck, 'Plantation and Farm', Ch. 1; Allen Kulikoff, *Tobacco and Slaves: The Development of Southern Cultures in the Chesapeake, 1680–1800* (Chapel Hill, NC, 1986), 335–45, 381–2, 387–96; Philip Morgan and Michael Nicholls, 'Slaves in Piedmont Virginia, 1720–1790', *WMQ*, 3rd series, 46 (1989), 211–47; Philip D. Morgan, 'Slave Life in Piedmont Virginia, 1720–1800' in Lois G. Carr, Philip D. Morgan and Jean B. Russo (eds.), *Colonial Chesapeake Society* (Chapel Hill, NC, 1988), 433–44, 454–70; Gerald Mullin, *Flight and Rebellion: Slave Resistance in Eighteenth-Century Virginia* (New York, 1972), Chs. 1 and 2; Ira Berlin, 'Time, Space, and the Evolution of Slavery in British Mainland North America', *American Historical Review* 85 (1980), 69–77.

8. James Barbour, 'Presidential Address to the Albemarle Agricultural Society, Nov. 8, 1825', *American Farmer*, 8, No. 37 (2 Dec. 1825), 290; Willie Lee Rose, 'The Domestication of Domestic Slavery', in Willie Lee Rose, *Slavery and Freedom*, exp. edn, (New York, 1982), 18–36; Kulikoff, *Tobacco and Slaves*, 396–408, 421–3; Morgan, 'Slave Life', 479–83.

9. Norman Yetman (comp.), *Life Under the 'Peculiar Institution': Selections from the Slave Narrative Collection* (New York, 1970) 175–8; John Davis, *Travels of Four Years and a Half in the U.S.A. during 1798, 1799, 1800, 1801, and 1802*, 2 vols. (New York 1909), 1: 423; Perdue et al., *Weevils*, 45; Account Book of James Barbour Jr, 1828–66, James Barbour papers, box 7, University of Virginia, Charlottesville, VA; Frances Taylor Diary, 1786–99, Southern Historical Collection, Univeristy of North Carolina, Chapel Hill, NC, passim. See also: VA, WPA, *Negro in Virginia*, Ch. 8; Thomas Anbury, *Travels Through the Interior Parts of America, in a Series of*

Letters, 2 vols. (London 1789), 2: 331; Austin Steward, *Twenty-Two Years a Slave; Forty Years a Freeman* (New York, 1968 (1856)), 14; Peter Randolph, *From Slave Cabin to the Pulpit: The Autobiography of Rev. Peter Randolph...* (Boston, 1893), 158; Ralph Roberts, 'A Slave's Story', *Putnam's Monthly* 9 (June 1857), 618; Henry Box Brown, *Narrative of Henry Box Brown* (Boston, 1849), 25; Frederick Law Olmsted, *A Journey in the Seaboard Slave States* (New York, 1968), 108; George Washington to Arthur Young, 18 June 1792, *Letters from His Excellency George Washington to Arthur Young ... and Sir John Sinclair ...* (Alexandria, VA, 1803), 51–2. I have found no evidence that slaveowners eliminated rations and placed the entire subsistence burden onto their slaves. Olmstead believed that rations were so generous that slaves sold part of them, but slave testimony does not support this. Olmstead, *Seaboard*, 110.

10. Farm Diary of William T. Daniel, 10 May 1861, Daniel Family papers, University of Virginia; Taylor Diary, 4 June 1788, 5 April 1794, 5 May 1795 and passim; Yetman, *Peculiar Institution*, 175–8. See also: McColley, *Slavery*, 65; VA, WPA, *Negro in Virginia*, Ch. 8; Anbury, *Travels*, 2: 33, 34; Madison to Morse, 28 March 1823, Madison, *Letters* 3: 310–15; Hawfield Plantation Farm Diary for 1852, William G. Crenshaw papers, Box I, University of Virginia. Some masters required Sunday work as a disciplinary measure, but slaves universally condemned this practice. See Benjamin Drew, *A North-Side View of Slavery: The Refugees or the Narratives of Fugitive Slaves in Canada...* (New York, 1968 (1856)), 73–4, 161; James L. Smith, *Autobiography of James L. Smith* (New York, 1969 (1881)), Ch. 2.

11. Farm Book I: Farm Memo and Account Book, 1806–61, 27 April 1840, Conway Family papers, University of Virginia; Daniel Farm Diary, 27 Feb., 28 Dec., 1852, 18 Feb. 1860; Noah Davis, *A Narrative of the Life of Rev. Noah Davis* (Baltimore, 1859), Ch. 1; Miranda Sisson to her mother, 27 April 1854, Sisson Family papers, University of Virginia. See also: Account Book of James Barbour Jr, 1828–66, passim; Taylor Diary, 19 Aug. 1787 and passim; Olmsted, *Seaboard*, 110.

12. Taylor Diary, 31 Dec. 1792, 19 July 1795 and passim; Daniel Farm Diary, 28 March, 24, 26 Dec. 1853, 25 April 1859 and passim; Yetman, *Peculiar Institution*, 175–8. See also: Horace D. Taliaferro Diary, 1847–69, 20 May, 26 Dec. 1850, Va Hist. Soc., Richmond, VA; Peyton Grymes Jr to Peyton Grymes Sr, 13 Dec. 1847, Grymes Family papers, Va Hist. Soc.; James Barbour Cash Book 1828–40, 23 June 1830, James Barbour papers; James Barbour Jr Account Book, 1828–66, passim; Steward, *Slave*, 13; Olmsted, *Seaboard*, 58, 75, 89; McColley, *Slavery*, 62.

13. Taylor Diary 30 May 1788 and passim; Daniel Farm Diary. Jan. 1852, 29 Jan., 25 Feb. 1853; Herndon Frazier account with Ned, 1857–60, Sec. 7, Accounts and Memoranda, 1854–69, Herndon Frazier Papers, University of Virginia; James Barbour Jr Account Book, 1828–66, passim, Cash Book 1828–40, passim; Commonplace and Cash Book, 1816–25, passim, James Barbour papers, Box 5; David Hume to Frank D. Hume, 7 Jan. 1856, Hume Family Letters, University of Virginia; Fannie Page Hume Diary, 18 Feb. 1862, 3 Nov. 1863, Hume Diary, Southern Hist. Coll., University of North Carolina; Jacquelin P. Taliaferro Farm Diary, 14 July 1838, Taliaferro Diary, Va Hist. Soc.; Smith, *Autobiography*, Ch. 3; *Negro in Virginia*, 91; *Weevils in the Wheat*, 31, 120.

14. Richard C. Taylor and John L. Hayes, *Reports on the Woodville Gold Mine* (Washington, DC, 1850), 12–13; Taliaferro Diary, 1 Nov. 1850; Olmsted, *Seaboard*, 58. In 1850 about 100 slaves (about six per cent of adult male slaves) were employed in gold mines in eastern Orange County. Taylor and Hayes reported that slaves preferred mining to plantation work because of the overwork payments miners received. On industrial slavery in Virginia, see Charles Dew, 'Disciplining Slave Ironworkers in the Antebellum South: Coercion, Conciliation, and Accommodation', *American Historical Review* 79 (1974), 393–418 and Robert Starobin, *Industrial Slavery in the Old South* (New York, 1970).

15. Roberts, 'A Slave's Story', 617. See also, Morgan, 'Slave Life', 458–61. The fact that most burglaries involved slaves of different owners suggest prior planning. County courts held special tribunals, known as Courts of Oyer and Terminer, to

hear accusations against slaves. Blacks were provided legal counsel; in about half the cases they were acquitted or the charges were dropped for insufficient evidence.

16. Taylor diary, 28 June, 27 July, 6 Dec. 1794; 31 May, 13 Sept., 11 Dec. 1795, and passim. These conclusions about slave marketing behaviour are, of course, conjectural. But the Taylor Diary does indicate a pattern of slaves with the same owner selling goods to Taylor at different times, indicating a network of recommendations among the slaves.

17. James Barbour Jr, Account Book, 1828–66, 15 Oct. 1836; Jacquelin P. Taliaferro Diary, 25 March, 4 June 1838; Randolph, *Autobiography*, 197; Grimes, *Life*, 19–20; Barbour and Johnson account with Sampson, 1785–86, Daybook for Barbour and Johnson's store, James Barbour Papers, Box 7; Frazier account with Ned, 1857–60; Olmsted, *Seaboard*, 110. In the 1790s, Virginia passed a law to restrict slave marketing with peddlers; McColly, *Slavery*, 102.

18. Roberts, 'Slave's Story', 617; Taylor Diary, 13 Feb. 1786; Orange Co. Minute Book, 1830–33 (microfilm No. 39), 8 March 1833, Virginia State Library, Richmond, VA; Orange Co. Min. Book, 1856–67 (microfilm No. 42), 23 Sept. 1861, Virginia State Library; Zion Baptist Church, Orange Co., VA, Minutebooks, 1813–1912, entries for 20 Jan., 19 Feb., 17 March 1849, Va Baptist Hist. Soc., University of Richmond, Richmond, VA. See also Fannie P. Hume diary, 1 Sept. 1860; Grimes, *Life*, 19–20.

19. Frazier account with Ned, 1857–60; Affidavit of F.M. Kendell, c. March 1866, Records of the Bureau of Refugees, Freedman and Abandoned Lands (RG 105), Virginia, entry 4186, Nat. Archives, Washington DC; Maria Perkins to Richard Perkins, 8 Oct. 1852, in Willie Lee Rose (ed.), *A Documentary History of North American Slavery* (New York, 1976), 151; Taylor Diary, 10 April 1790 and 9 Dec. 1792; Olmsted, *Seaboard*, 102; Edward S. Abdy, *Journal of a Residence and Tour in the United States of North American, from April, 1833, to October 1834*, 3 vols. (London, 1835) 1: 217. Unfortunately, Kendall did not explain how Corbin had acquired his money. Sarah S. Hughes, in a study of a Tidewater county in the early nineteenth century, found that slaves owned utensils, furniture and cattle; Hughes, 'Elizabeth City County, Virginia, 1782–1810: The Economic and Social Structure of a Tidewater County in the Early National Years' Ph.D. Diss. (College of William and Mary, 1975), Ch. 5.

20. Taylor Diary, 7 June, 19, 26 July 1789, and passim; Barbour and Johnson Daybook, accounts with Sampson, Daniel, Paris, Phillip, George, Ibby, Betty and Margaret, 1785–86; Distillery Accounts, 1824–28, in Daybook, 1824–28, James Barbour papers, Box 5; Yetman, *Peculiar Institution*, 175–8; Roberts, 'Slave's Story', 617; Olmsted, *Seaboard*, 110, 112; Drew, *Northside*, 161.

21. Henry C. Bruce, *The New Man: Twenty-Nine Years as a Slave; Twenty-Nine Years as a Freeman* (New York, 1969 (1885)), 52; Grimes, *Life*, 250; John Blassingame (ed.), *Slave Testimony: Two Centuries of Letters, Speeches, Interviews, and Autobiographies* (Baton Rouge, 1977), 489; Perdue et al., *Weevils*, 166; *Negro in Virginia*, 76.

Independent Economic Production by Slaves on Antebellum Louisiana Sugar Plantations

Roderick A. McDonald

During the late antebellum period slaves on Louisiana sugar plantations organized extensive and integrated economic systems, accumulating and disposing of capital and property within internal economies they themselves administered. Such economic systems probably functioned on every sugar estate in Louisiana, and their importance far outweighed the often limited pecuniary benefits slaves derived. The internal economy not only reflected the ways in which slaves organized their efforts to earn and spend money, but also influenced the character and development of slave family and community life. The slaves' economy thus shaped patterns of slave life, providing the material basis for African-American culture in the sugar-producing region.

Louisiana was the foremost sugar-producing state in the antebellum South. Between 1824 and 1861 cane sugar – which was climatically unsuited to cultivation in most of the North American continent – became the principal crop in southern Louisiana. Sugar production quintupled to more than 500,000 hogsheads annually, and the number of sugar estates increased almost seven-fold, from 193 to 1,308. The slave population of the sugar region rose dramatically from just over 20,000 to around 125,000.[1]

Sugar production was confined to the southern part of Louisiana, the location of some of the largest and richest plantations in the South. Although only 24 of the state's 64 parishes grew sugar, and less than 50 per cent of their improved lands were ever in cane cultivation, the sugar region had a disproportionate number both of slaves and large estates. Louisiana's slave population numbered about 69,000 in 1820 and rose to 109,600 in 1830, 168,500 in 1840, and 244,800 in 1850. On the eve of the Civil War, it stood at 331,700. Slaves who worked on sugar estates numbered 21,000 in 1827 and by 1830 had reached 36,100 (about one-third of the state's total slave population). Thereafter the number of sugar plantation slaves increased to approximately 50,700 in 1841, 65,300 in 1844, and by 1852 and 1853 stood at some 125,000, or one-half of all slaves in Louisiana.[2]

Land consolidation and the growth of large estates paralleled the sugar boom. Small holdings were common in the 1820s, even in prime sugar land that fronted the rivers and bayous. After 1830, however, small farms gave way to large estates and by 1860 the average sugar plantation contained 480 improved acres compared to 128 improved acres for non-cane farms. With this consolidation, the number of slaves on each plantation increased steadily. By the Civil War plantations with slave populations numbering in the hundreds were commonplace. Sugar production soared and the great estates, where most southern Louisiana slaves lived and worked, dominated the sugar economy.[3]

The cultivation of sugar was a race against time. Sugar cane cannot withstand the frosts which occur annually in Louisiana. Consequently, the sugar cane harvest came but nine or ten months after the date of planting (compared to the fourteen to eighteen months necessary for full maturation). Yet the longer the crop stayed in the ground, the higher its sugar content. Louisiana planters thus sought to plant the sugar crop as early as possible in the year and to harvest it at the last conceivable moment. Crucial to the determination of when to start the harvest were the planter's estimate both of the speed with which the crop could be cut and processed, and the date of the first killing frost.

The work routine of Louisiana sugar plantation slaves reflected the intensity of the sugar crop's cycle. Immediately following their annual Christmas and New Year holidays slaves ploughed the fields in preparation for planting the canes, opening furrows some six to eight feet apart into which they placed seed cane set aside from the previous year's crop. Usually Louisiana planters allowed a given cane plot to ratoon for no more than two years before replanting.[4] Ratoons yielded less sugar than cane grown from seed, but ratooning also demanded less labour than planting, and thus permitted cultivation of many more acres. After two years low sugar yields required that the ratoons be dug up and the cane replanted from seed. Slaves thus planted about one-third of the estate's acreage of cane every year.

Slaves usually completed planting by the end of February and, after the plant cane and ratoons sprouted, tended the crop through the first months of its growth. Tending the canes involved hoeing and ploughing between the rows to keep the cane piece free of grass and weeds. By late June or early July the cane had grown tall enough to withstand weeds. Slaves then ploughed and hoed – 'threw up' – the rows of cane in ridges to permit better drainage from the plant's roots. The cane was then 'laid by' and left to grow untended until harvest time.

Tending the crop required less work than either planting or harvesting, which monopolized the time of the estate's labour force. During spring and early summer planters diverted some labour to such tasks as growing provisions and secondary cash crops, preparing for the sugar harvest and maintaining and improving the estate. Through spring and summer slaveholders had the slaves plant one or two crops of corn, as well as perhaps potatoes, pumpkins, sweet potatoes and other vegetables. Slaves harvested these crops and cut hay for fodder before the sugar harvest began. Slaves also mended roads and fences, built and repaired levees, made bricks for the construction and refurbishment of plantation buildings, dug and cleaned ditches, and gathered wood both for fuel and for use by the estate's coopers.

After the sugar crop was laid by slaves also began preparing for the sugar harvest. Before its commencement planters sought to have everything ready to see them through the harvest: sufficient wood to fuel the sugar mill, enough barrels and hogsheads to hold the crop and adequate roads to transport the cane from field to works. Out of crop (the non-harvest stage of production), slaves worked from sunup to sundown, with half-an-hour off for breakfast and a dinner break at noon, for five-and-a-half to six-and-a-half days per week, with time off on Saturdays and Sundays.

The sugar harvest usually began by mid-October. Once underway, the work of cutting canes and processing the crop continued without stop until completion. Slaves first cut and mat-layed (seed cane was literally laid out in mats and covered with a layer of earth to protect it from frost) the cane that was to be set aside for the next year's seed. Thereafter the harvest began in earnest. Slaves worked 16 or more hours a day, seven days a week, although factors such as bad weather, impassable roads and breakdowns at the mill could disrupt this schedule. In addition to their tasks in the fields slaves performed all the labour involved in processing the crop, from feeding and stoking the mill to loading hogsheads of sugar and barrels of molasses onto the river steamers at the plantation wharf.

Because of the threat of frost, harvest proceeded at a furious pace with slaves working in shifts through the night every day from late October through December. Freezing temperatures were most likely in the first couple of months of the new year, so planters tried to finish the crop by Christmas, at which time the slaves had their annual holidays. Often, however, harvest continued until January. Thomas Hamilton, a British military officer who visited Louisiana in 1833, noted that 'the crop in Louisiana is never considered safe till it is in the mill, and the consequence is that when cutting once begins, the slaves are taxed beyond their strength, and are goaded to labour until nature absolutely sinks under the effort'.[5]

The gang system prevailed on Louisiana sugar plantations. Planters organized gangs according to the capacity of the slave labour force, incorporating their notions of the appropriate sexual division of labour. All adults worked in the fields, but the two most burdensome tasks on the estate, ditching and wood-gathering, were men's work. Slave children also worked in gangs. Supervised by female slave drivers, they performed such light tasks as cleaning-up around the sugar works and picking fodder. The work schedule of women with unweaned children accommodated their babies' feeding routine. Such women either had additional time off from labour in the gangs, or worked in a 'suckler's gang'.

The combination of agriculture and industry required in sugar cultivation and processing placed tremendous demands on slave workers. Louisiana sugar plantations earned a dreadful reputation throughout the South. 'The cultivation of sugar in Louisiana', commented Hamilton, 'is carried on at an enormous expense of human life. Planters must buy to keep up their stock, and this supply principally comes from Maryland, Virginia, and North Carolina'. Frances Trollope, a committed abolitionist, claimed that 'to be sent south and sold [was] the dread of all the slaves north of Louisiana'. E. S. Abdy, an Englishman who travelled through the South in the early 1830s, related how planters in the seaboard South disciplined slaves by threatening to sell them 'down the river to Louisiana', while slaves incorporated the Louisiana sugar region's unenviable reputation in the chorus of a song:

> Old debble, Lousy Anna,
> Dat scarecrow for poor nigger,
> Where de sugar-cane grow to pine-tree,
> And de pine-tree turn to sugar.[6]

Sugar slaves suffered overwork often compounded by undernourishment, harsh punishment, inadequate housing and clothing, high infant mortality, ill-health and a life-span shortened by the grim plantation regime.

Slaves struggled to transcend the brutality of plantation labour, the planters and their agents. Slave community life throughout sugar's reign in Louisiana exhibited extraordinary creativity; the thousands of men and women who lived and died in bondage displayed resourcefulness, endeavour, dignity and courage – the full array of humanity's most prized attributes. The independence slaves displayed in their art and music, family and community development and religion was also manifest in their economic activities. As their houses, gardens and grounds provided the focus for slave family and community life, so too were they the base for their own economy.

While their independent economic activities had no basis in law, slaves secured the tacit assent and approval of the planters. In much the same way as slaves used what control they had over the processes of production – by withholding their labour or labouring inefficiently – to get the planters to accede, for example, to better working conditions and standards of food, clothing and shelter, planters also conceded to slaves the opportunity, during their time off from plantation labour, to work for themselves, to market the produce of their labour and to keep the proceeds. Although subject to constant negotiation, the internal economy developed by sugar slaves expanded steadily until the Civil War.

Agricultural endeavours were a central component of the slaves' independent economic production. On most Louisiana sugar estates slaves controlled some land, where they raised livestock and grew crops for their personal consumption and sale. Slaves almost always had a small patch surrounding their house where they tended gardens and kept some poultry and livestock. Travellers often commented on these gardens. 'In the rear of each cottage, surrounded by a rude fence', observed journalist T. B. Thorpe in 1853, 'you find a garden in more or less order, according to the industrious habits of the proprietor. In all you notice that the chicken-house seems to be in excellent condition.' Describing the slave village on a Louisiana sugar estate, London *Times* correspondent William Howard Russell noted 'the ground round the huts ... amidst which pigs and poultry were recreating'. A former slave, Elizabeth Ross Hite, confirmed Thorpe's and Russell's accounts, recalling that she and her fellow slaves 'had a garden right in front of our quarter. We planted ev'rything in it. Had watermelon, mushmelon, and a flower garden'. Similarly, ex-slave Catherine Cornelius remembered the 'garden patch, wid mustard greens, cabbage, chickens too'.[7]

Louisiana slaves put their kitchen gardens to diverse uses, raising fruits, vegetables, small livestock and poultry. The close proximity of these gardens to the cane fields meant that slaves could work them at odd times through the week, during the midday break and in the evenings. Moreover, elderly slaves, who had few responsibilities for plantation work, could spend considerable time in the kitchen gardens. One former slave recalled that her grandmother did not go to work in the fields but 'would tend to the lil patch of corn, raise chickens, and do all the work around the house'.[8]

Besides their kitchen gardens, slaves had more extensive allotments of land elsewhere on the plantation which were often known as 'Negro grounds'. There they generally cultivated cash crops, most commonly corn, although they also raised some minor crops such as pumpkins, potatoes and hay. While slaves consumed some of the kitchen-garden crops, they sold most of their provision-ground crops.

The 'Negro grounds' were less accessible than the kitchen gardens, and slaves normally could not spend time in them during the regular work week Often they were located on the periphery of the plantation, beyond the land in sugar, sometimes a great distance from the sugar works, cane fields and slave villages. Only on weekends (primarily on Sundays, but also sometimes on part of Saturdays) could slaves tend them. Russell observed that slaves had 'from noon on Saturday till dawn on Monday morning to do as they please'. On some estates, however, slaves did regular plantation work for six days and light work for part of Sunday. Ex-slave Elizabeth Ross Hite recalled that 'de Sunday wurk was light. Dey would only pull shucks of corn'. Sunday work usually entailed the performance of a specific task such as shelling corn, gathering fodder, branding livestock, or making hay, after which slaves had the rest of the day to themselves. Ex-slave Catherine Cornelius recalled that on the West Baton Rouge Parish estate where she lived the task work system applied to Saturdays, but slaves invariably had Sunday off except during the harvest: 'dat [Saturdays] was de day fo' ourselves', Cornelius explained. 'We all had certain tasks to do. If we finished dem ahead of time, de rest of de day was ours'.[9]

Slaves used their time off to cultivate their crops. Sometimes, generally just before the sugar harvest, slaves secured additional time off from the regular plantation schedule either to harvest or market their crop. For example, slaves on Duncan Kenner's Ashland Plantation 'gathered their corn, made a large crop' one Sunday in early October 1852. Two days later 'all but a few hands went to Donaldsonville', a nearby town, either to market their crop or spend their earnings. The next day the sugar harvest began. From mid-October until at least the end of December slaves harvested cane every day, including Sundays and Christmas.[10] The seven-day labour schedule, of course, precluded slaves from working in their grounds for the duration of the sugar harvest. Slaves, however, sometimes received compensation, getting days off at the end of the harvest equal to the number of Sundays worked.[11]

Slaves valued time off prior to the sugar harvest, since it allowed them to secure their own crops before labouring full-time cutting and grinding cane. Slaves on Isaac Erwin's Shady Grove Plantation in Iberville Parish spent the two days' holiday before the 1849 sugar harvest 'dig[g]ing their Potatoes & Pinders', while on Valcour Aime's St James Parish plantation on the day preceding the commencement of the 1851 sugar harvest the slaves had a 'free day to dig their potatoes'. When such free time was not available slaves did the best they could on their regularly scheduled days off. Slaves also worked for themselves during other annual holidays, which usually fell at Christmas and New

Year, as well as at the end of the cane planting and when the sugar crop was laid by in midsummer.[12]

The plantation was not only the source of the slaves' independent production but also the principal market for the goods they produced. The growing and retailing of corn was the most lucrative dimension of the internal economy on Louisiana sugar plantations and the one that involved the largest proportion of the slave population. Slaves marketed most of their produce on their home estate, as both they and the planters benefited from retailing the corn crop there. Planters wanted the crop since corn meal comprised a large proportion of the standard slave ration and by purchasing it on the plantation they were freed from the various fees attendant to buying through an agent, while slaves were saved the expense of shipping and marketing. Less frequently, slaves marketed their crop off the plantation. In 1849 Elu Landry recorded that he 'gave [the slaves] permission & pass to sell their corn in the neighborhood – lent them teams for that purpose', while slaves on a Bayou Goula plantation sold their 1859 crop of 1,011 barrels of corn to the neighboring Nottoway Estate of J. H. Randolph for $758.[13] Although in these years the price slaves got for their corn – from 37 1/2 cents to 75 cents a barrel – was somewhat below the commodity's market price in New Orleans, it was probably the equivalent of a local market price.[14]

Slave-grown corn was essential to the operation of many plantations. Because of its importance slaves sometimes managed to obtain protection for their crops in case of loss or damage. In 1859, Lewis Stirling's Wakefield Estate accounts recorded that 12 slaves 'lost all their corn' (a total of 47 barrels). They were, however, recompensed by the planter at the full price of 50 cents a barrel. When, in a similar instance two years previously, plantation hogs had destroyed their corn crop, six slaves received payment of $22 from the planter as compensation. Such arrangements document the importance to the plantation of the slaves' private agricultural endeavours and the extent of planters' commitment to the slaves' continued involvement.[15]

Slaves grew and marketed a number of other cash crops. Some slave-controlled land was put into pumpkins. Although they sold for only pennies apiece, pumpkins could bring in a tidy sum. On Benjamin Tureaud's estate a slave named Big Mathilda received $10 for the 700 pumpkins she sold to the plantation in 1858, while the accounts of slaves for the Gay plantation in Iberville Parish reveal that in 1844 seven of the 74 slaves derived part of their earnings from the sale of pumpkins. In the previous year the plantation's accounts record 'Pumpkins 4000 bought of our Negroes ... $80'.[16] Slaves also raised potatoes and their hay crops found a ready market on the plantation. In 1844 about the same proportion of the Gay plantation slaves as raised pumpkins sold hay to the estate at $3 a load, while a year previous the total crop was 10 loads or 3,000 pounds.[17]

Poultry and hogs, the animals most commonly raised by slaves in Louisiana, also found their principal market on the plantation. Raising poultry was ideally suited to the economy of the slave community, since it demanded little investment of time or effort, required minimal capital outlay, and provided a steady income through marketing both eggs and the birds themselves. Few travellers failed to comment on the slaves' proclivity to keep poultry, and their descriptions of slave villages on Louisiana sugar plantations invariably mention the chickens, ducks, turkeys and geese ranging through the quarters. The prices paid by planters for fowl varied little during the antebellum years. Chickens sold at anywhere from 10 cents to 25 cents each and the price of eggs was from 12 1/2 cents to 15 cents a dozen. On W. W. Pugh's Woodlawn Plantation in Assumption Parish, muscovy ducks fetched 37 1/2 cents each in the early 1850s.[18]

Judging from the scene which William Howard Russell witnessed, slaves showed a trading acumen consistent with their position as independent retailers. 'An avenue of trees runs down the negro street' on John Burnside's Houmas Plantation in Ascension Parish, Russell observed, 'and behind each hut are rude poultry hutches, which, with the geese and turkeys and a few pigs, form the perquisites of the slaves, and the sole source from which they derive their acquaintance with currency'. In the slaves' business transactions 'their terms are strictly cash. ... An old negro brought up some ducks to Mr. Burnside', Russell related,

> and offered the lot of six for three dollars. 'Very well, Louis; if you come tomorrow, I'll pay you'. 'No massa, me want de money now'. 'But won't you give me credit, Louis? Don't you think I'll pay the three dollars?' 'Oh, pay some day, massa, sure enough. Massa good to pay de tree dollar; but this nigger want money now to buy food and things for him leetle family. They will trust massa at Donaldsonville, but they won't trust this nigger'.

'I was told', Russell continued, 'that a thrifty negro will sometimes make ten or twelve pounds a year from his corn and poultry'.[19]

This exchange reveals the slave as a shrewd retailer with a knowledge both of the value of his commodity and the terms of the transaction. Indeed, Louis did not hesitate to contradict the planter in the course of the negotiations. The money Louis accrued from the sale was earmarked for purchases for himself and his family and, although he found a market for his goods on the plantation, Louis apparently planned to spend his cash off the estate in the nearby town of Donaldsonville, where, by virtue of his understanding of the terms demanded by the merchants there, he had traded before.

The sale of crops, poultry and livestock to the planter was not the only source of revenue for the slaves' independent economic activities on the plantation. Within the confines of the estate slaves had the opportunity to engage in various other money-making activities. Technological developments in the sugar industry that mechanized the grinding and milling of sugar gave slaves the opportunity to earn money, since the machines consumed huge quantities of fuel – almost without exception locally-felled timber. The vast amounts of wood required by the Louisiana sugar mills can be estimated, since it took from two to four cords of wood to make one hogshead of sugar, and twice in the decade preceding the outbreak of the Civil War the sugar crop topped 400,000 hogsheads. The amount of wood that could be collected during regular plantation hours rarely met the estates' needs, and contracting for wood off the plantation was expensive. Buying wood that slaves chopped on their own proved the most efficient means for planters to supplement their fuel supply. It also gave slaves the opportunity to earn substantial amounts of money. Payments to slaves for cutting wood on the Uncle Sam Plantation in St James Parish, for example, totalled over $1,000 in 1859. In July 1860 53 slaves received some $600 for wood-cutting and four months later $436 was paid to 58 slaves, while in the following year 61 slaves cut nearly 1,600 cords and were paid about $800 (the going rate in these years being 50 cents per cord). The most wood any one slave cut in 1861 was 80 cords and the least 3 cords, with the majority of slaves cutting between 15 and 40 cords.[20]

Slaves found advantages and disadvantages in lumbering. Although their compensation (from 50 to 75 cents per cord) was below the market price, slaves used the plantation's axes and saws, and also had access to the estate's flat-boats, work animals and the tackle necessary to carry the wood out of the swamp and back to the mill. Moreover, they felled trees on land owned by the planters. Thus, since planters covered most of the slaves' capital costs, the price paid for wood may have been more equitable than it appears.[21] Woodcutting, however, was onerous, unpleasant work, since the wood had to be carried from swamps and bayous abutting the river-front plantations. Slaves either worked from a flat-boat or stood in the water, and they had to float or boat the wood out. Invariably, only men did this work.

Woodcutting was just one of many services for which planters would pay slaves. Planters also paid slaves to dig ditches, since sugar estates needed well-maintained irrigation systems and the amount of ditching done as part of the regular plantation labour schedule usually proved insufficient. Planters were thus obliged either to contract ditchers or pay slaves on the plantation for any ditching done on their time off.[22] On W. W. Pugh's estate slaves made shingles, staves, pickets and boards, and Pugh bought slave-made shuck collars, barrels and hogsheads. Slaves were also paid to haul wood, as well as to do regular work for the plantation on Sundays or holidays.[23] Slaves on the Gay family's sugar estate in Iberville Parish similarly were paid for work done on their time off from plantation labour. The proliferation of jobs included sugar-potting, coopering, fixing and firing kettles, collecting fodder, forging iron hoops, mending shoes, counting hoop-poles and serving as watch-men. Skilled slaves, moreover, made money during sugar harvest. In the mid-1840s the plantation sugar-maker received $30 for his services at harvest, while his deputy received $15; the chief engineer and the kettle-setter each got $10. The firemen, kettle-tenders and the second engineer all received $5 for their harvest season work.[24] On his estate, Benjamin Tureaud paid slaves for making bricks, hogsheads, shuck-collars and baskets, while on the Wilton Plantation in St James Parish, estate accounts note cash payments to slaves for ditching, 'levying', and making rails and handbarrows.[25]

Skilled slaves had an especially wide range of opportunities to work for themselves. Slave carpenters, coopers and blacksmiths could use their training for their own profit, undertaking large-scale lucrative projects. For example, on the Gay family's plantation a slave named Thornton received $20 for making a cart.[26] On some estates slave tradesmen did piece-work, producing a specific quantity of items. On John Randolph's Nottoway Plantation coopers received cash payments for producing more than an agreed upon number of barrels. In December 1857 Cooper Henry received payment of $19.50 for making 26 barrels and 13 hogsheads above his quota, while his fellow tradesmen, Cooper William and Cooper Jack, earned $16 and $8 respectively for their extra production.[27]

Many paying jobs required physical stamina if not trained skills. Except for some tasks such as counting hoop-poles and collecting fodder, slaves lacking strength or skills had few opportunities other than making themselves available for day labour. Such work would take into consideration the abilities of the individual slaves since it was voluntary. Many slaves chose not to work for the plantation, however, preferring to tend to their farming, gardening, poultry and livestock-raising, and domestic crafts, while others combined working for themselves and for the plantation.

Cash could enter the internal economy from various other sources. Many sugar-plantation slaves found profit in nearby swamps and streams. Hunting and fishing supplemented the pork and corn ration supplied by planters, and also offered slaves an opportunity to supplement their income since they could sell or barter some of their catch to fellow slaves, traders or planters.[28]

At Christmas some slaves received cash payments as a holiday bonus. Such was the case for the 150 slaves on the Nottoway Estate where, through the early 1850s, John Randolph made regular payments to the slaves. Indeed, extant plantation manuscripts contain numerous references to cash paid to slaves. An 1854 memorandum from the Stirling family's sugar plantation lists 95 slaves, 50 women and 45 men, receiving cash payments totalling $314. Most payments compensated slaves for goods and services; some of the larger amounts went to two partners for wood-cutting. A similar list, probably dating from the following year, shows 78 slaves receiving a total of $258. Similarly, in the early 1840s there were a number of cash payments to slaves on the Gay family plantation. For example, between December 1841 and January 1842 34 men received a total of some $200, with individual payments ranging from $1 to $20. The money was probably paid either for slave crops or for harvest work, but may have included holiday or Christmas bonuses and gifts.[29] Within the confines of the plantation slaves thus had a wide range of opportunities to earn money which planter gifts supplemented.

Slaves also bypassed the plantation and sold their commodities elsewhere. Some were involved in marketing at major ports on the Mississippi River, as well as at local town markets and in the neighbourhood of the plantation. They also transacted business with the traders who plied the waterways and highways of southern Louisiana.

Throughout the sugar region slaves worked for themselves collecting and drying Spanish moss, a plant that grew in profusion. Picking moss from the trees was relatively easy, since with the assistance of a long staff the plant could readily be detached from a tree's trunk and limbs. After it had been dried in the sun slaves bound the moss into bales weighing 250 to 350 pounds ready for shipment. Hunton Love, who for the first 20 years of his life had been a slave on John Viguerie's sugar plantation on the Bayou Lafourche, testified to the importance of the collection and sale of moss. 'Once I heard some men talkin'', he recalled in the 1930s, 'an' one sed, "You think money grows on trees", an' the other one say, "Hit do, git down that moss an' convert it into money", an' I got to thinkin' an' sho' 'nuff, it do grow on trees.'[30] The records of various plantations show slaves exploiting this market for moss. On Robert Ruffin Barrow's Bayou Lafourche estates slaves spent Sundays working their moss crop, while the accounts of Magnolia

Plantation also recorded payments to slaves for moss.[31] Slaves consigned their dried moss to major entrepôts on the Mississippi, chiefly St Louis, New Orleans and Natchez, where they transacted business with the cities' retail agents.

The records of the Gay family's sugar estate contain rich documentation of moss-gathering, including the collection and marketing patterns, and payment schedules. In the mid-1840s Colonel Andrew Hynes and Joseph B. Craighead ran the plantation, while Edward Gay lived in St Louis and acted as agent for the estate's produce. In 1844 Gay wrote to Hynes and Craighead suggesting that the slaves pick moss and forward it to St Louis where he guaranteed it would sell for a good price. Thereafter, moss became an integral part of his slaves' internal economy. Within a few months the first shipment of dried moss sold in St Louis at 2 cents a pound with 22 slaves, two of whom were women, sending in all 9,705 pounds of moss and receiving a total of $162 ($196 less $34 freight and commission).[32] From 1844 to 1861 slaves on the Gay estate continued to send their moss to St Louis for sale, where the price per pound ranged from 2 cents to 1 1/4 cents. Mississippi steamers took an average of four or five shipments per year. Slaves paid for the cartage aboard ship and the agent's sales commission, which totalled from 75 cents to $1.25 a bale. When the receipts arrived at the plantation slaves received the total net proceeds, usually around $4 to $5 a bale.[33]

A record book documenting moss-gathering and sale on the Gay plantation between the years of 1849 and 1861 shows the extent of the slave community's involvement. During that period 160 slaves – 41 of whom were women – sold 1,101 bales of moss, with individual slaves selling between 1 and 48 bales. More than these 160 slaves were involved, however. Some of the shipments were sent jointly by husbands and wives, whose children and kin also assisted them in the project. Since the total slave population on the estate stood at 224 in 1850 and 240 in 1860, the great majority of adult slaves on the plantation were participating in this venture, from which, during the period, at least $4,000 entered the internal economy, an average of some $300 a year.[34]

Another commodity sold by slaves was molasses. On Duncan Kenner's Ashland Plantation the overseer recorded that in January 1852 he 'sold the negroes molasses' and bought flour for them with the proceeds. Slaves on the Gay plantation also regularly shipped molasses for sale in St Louis where it fetched $8 to $12 a barrel. One such shipment consigned 19 1/2 barrels which netted the 15 slaves involved a total of $148.[35]

Slaves on Louisiana sugar estates had other options for marketing their crops and goods. Some transacted business in the general locale of their home plantation. Slaves on the Ventress estate, for example, contracted with a neighbouring planter for the sale of their sizable corn crop of 1,011 barrels, while slaves on Elu Landry's plantation borrowed the estate's draft animals and wagons to peddle their crops throughout the neighbourhood.[36] Others who lived near towns could trade at the village markets that were held on Sunday, the slaves' traditional day off. In 1860 the Reverend P. M. Goodwyn, a resident on Edward Gay's plantation, was amazed and horrified at the prevalence of Sunday trading. He saw slaves 'going to and from the place of trade – wagons & carts, loaded and empty – servants walking and riding, carrying baskets – bundles – packages etc.', and asked,

> why all this? – Can it be possible that there is a necessity for it? – If so, then it is excusable – and, vice versa, – Has the Master gone, or is he going to the house of God today? – How will he – how *ought* he to feel – as the thought comes up while he is attempting to worship – My Servant, or Servants, have a *permit* from me, – and *now*, while I am here, they are trading and trafficking in the stores of the town.[37]

Despite the misgivings of Goodwyn and other men of the cloth, Sunday remained the principal trading day for slaves able to journey to nearby towns. These markets were important to slaves as places both to sell their wares and to spend their earnings. The slave Louis, who had sold his ducks to John Burnside, was obviously well acquainted with the retail outlets in the nearby town of Donaldsonville. He insisted on a cash payment for the poultry, since he intended spending the money in the town's stores where 'they will trust massa [with credit] ... but they won't trust [him]'.[38]

The market-day activities of Louisiana sugar slaves were not confined to retailing and purchasing goods. Some slaves used the day to shake the routine and restrictions of the plantation and at market spent some of their earnings on liquor, gaming and other pleasures. The Mayor of Plaquemine added his voice to that of other local officials when he complained that 'Several Negroes were lately caught in this town drunk and gambling on Sunday in the day time in the house of a Free Negro woman'. These illicit 'shebeens' were, no doubt, a feature of market towns throughout the Louisiana sugar region.[39]

Even when their Sabbatarian scruples proscribed Sunday trading, slaves still retailed their goods in town. In 1853 planter William Weeks reported that a slave named

> Amos has heard of the flat boats [trading vessels] being in New Town & has asked my permission to spend a portion of his crop on them – In consideration of his faithful services on all occasions,

and his really conscientious scruples about trading on Sunday, I have concluded to let him go tomorrow.

On Monday, a working day on the plantation, Amos went to town to trade on his own behalf.[40]

The vastness of Louisiana's sugar region and its paucity of towns meant that most slaves did not have recourse to urban markets for buying and selling goods. Nevertheless, by transacting business with itinerant peddlers slaves established trade networks over which planters had no control. Ex-slave Martha Stuart remembered the salesmen who 'come thru the country', while another former slave, Catherine Cornelius, recalled how the slaves on the plantation where she lived would 'git down to de ped'lers on de riber at nite tuh buy stuff'. In fact, river traders had more extensive contact with plantation slaves than highway traders. Inadequate roads made travel by land difficult, while the large sugar plantations had direct access to navigable waterways. Moreover, river traders could move quietly and quickly and thus trade clandestinely in illicit goods. On the eve of the Civil War a Canadian traveller, William Kingsford, left an excellent description of river traders. From the deck of a Mississippi steamer he observed

> the small vessels which, owned by pedlars, pass from plantation to plantation, trading with the negroes principally, taking in exchange the articles which they raise, or, when the latter are sold to the boats, offering to their owners the only temptations on which their money can be spent.

Kingsford related how 'now and then you come upon one of them, moving sluggishly down stream, or moored inshore, where the owner is dispensing his luxuries, in the shape of ribbons, tobacco, gaudy calicoes, and questionable whiskey'.[41]

Slaves found the independence the external trading network conferred extremely useful. It allowed slaves to divest themselves of the constraints of the plantation and engage in an independent economic system which they themselves controlled. Planters had influence over neither the form of the trade nor the goods being traded. Indeed, often the river trade was carried on in violation of both plantation regulations and state law. Clandestine trading provided slaves the opportunity to sell goods planters would not buy and to buy goods planters would neither sell nor order. For example, while slaveholders rarely sold slaves liquor, river traders did, despite laws banning its sale. In turn, traders purchased a variety of commodities, including stolen goods, not traded between slaves and planters.[42]

Sugar planter Maunsell White revealed the disparity of interests between planters and river traders on the one hand and the identity of interests between slaves and river traders on the other when some of his slaves 'were caught stealing molasses to sell to a Boat or "Capota"'. White kept them under surveillance until 'they were found on board the Boat, where they had hid themselves & were secreted by the owner; a man who called himself "Block", a German & another who called himself "Bill"'. (Block's German nationality was not unusual, since many of these traders were immigrants.) When White and his companions searched 'the Boat, an other negro was also found, who said he belonged to the Boat as did also the Men who owned it; but we soon found on arresting the whole of them, that the Boy confessed or said he belonged to [a fellow planter, George Lanaux]'. White interrogated Lanaux's slave the following morning, and he found that the man had been a runaway 'for 4 months; the whole of which time he said he spent in the City [New Orleans?] at work. Thirty five dollars and 50/100 was found on his Person, & a Silver Watch ... he afterwards said it was only 2 1/2 months'. River peddlers therefore not only gave slaves a means of enriching their lives in slavery, but also provided them with an opportunity to escape slavery entirely.[43]

Theft played an integral role in the internal economy. Many slaves had no compunction about taking the planters' property, since they believed that in appropriating plantation property they were taking what was rightly theirs. Transactions in stolen goods between slaves and peddlers were, according to Frederick Law Olmsted, common throughout the South. Olmsted noted, however, that there was a higher incidence of such trading in the Louisiana sugar region, because the sugar estates had navigable waterways and peddlers could more easily transport and conceal themselves. He observed that 'the traders ... moor at night on the shore, adjoining the negro-quarters and float away whenever they have obtained any booty, with very small chance of detection'.[44] River peddlers had few inhibitions regarding what they were willing to purchase. The character of the trade militated against bulky consignments, the loading of which would require time and therefore increase the likelihood of detection. If they could avoid such logistical problems, however, peddlers were willing to purchase whatever slaves had to sell. Few of the planter's possessions were safe from the depredations of those involved in the trade. According to Olmsted, one planter had 'a large brass cock and some pipe ... stolen from his sugar-works'. The planter 'had ascertained that one of his negroes had taken it and sold it on board one of these boats for seventy-five cents, and had immediately spent the money, chiefly for whisky, on the same boat'. It cost the planter $30 to replace the machinery. Another sugar planter informed Olmsted that he had lately caught one of his own negroes going towards one of the 'chicken thieves,' (so the traders' boats are called) with a piece of machinery that he had unscrewed from his sugar works, which was worth eighty dollars, and which very likely might have been sold for a drink.[45]

Plantation records reveal the prevalence of slave theft and profile its most popular targets. Most thefts involved the plantations' produce and livestock. Slaves on Maunsell White's plantation stole molasses to sell to river traders, and William Weeks grumbled about 'Simon that prince of runaways & troublesome negroes ... [whose] last offence was to go into the sugar house & steal a portion of the little sugar I had kept for home use'.[46] Livestock and poultry ranged free providing particularly easy prey for slaves. Joseph Mather, superintendent of Judge Morgan's Aurora Plantation, recorded the 'theft of chickens' and Ellen McCollam noted that she had 'had 8 hens stowlen out of the yard'. The threat of having his livestock stolen prompted Maunsell White to urge his overseer to make a picket pen 'in order to save our hogs, pigs & sheep from all sorts of "*Varmints*" two-legged as well as four'. Similarly, planter J. E. Craighead complained that 'the negroes steal our sheep as we have no safe place to keep them'. One can judge the extent to which stealing poultry was viewed as characteristic of slaves by a claim incorporated in the lines of a Louisiana song:

> Negue pas capab marche san mais dans poche,
> Ce pou vole poule –
> Negro cannot walk without corn in his pocket,
> It is to steal chickens –[47]

Slaves stole the slaveholders' personal property as well. Planter Andrew McCollam and his wife Ellen, for example, lost items from their laundry. Once they had '8 shirts stolen out of the wash', and later 'had a pair of sheets table cloth stolen out of the garden', whereas a visitor to Colonel Andrew Hynes' plantation had a trunk full of clothing stolen while his luggage was being loaded onto the steamer.[48]

Some stolen property supplemented the slaves' diet. Planter F. D. Richardson alluded to this in writing about slaves 'committing depredations in the way of robberies', and claiming that 'the whole matter is no doubt attributable to the high price of pork – for many planters will not buy at the present rates & depend upon a little beef and other things as a substitute'. Martha Stuart, formerly a slave on a Louisiana sugar plantation, recalled that 'ma Marster had a brother, they called him Charles Haynes and he was mean and he didn't feed his people ... he didn't give 'em nuthin; 'twas the funniest thing tho; his

niggers was all fat and fine cause dey'd go out and kill hogs – dey'd steal
dem from de boss'.[49] In addition to improving slaves' diet, clothing
and lodgings directly, goods stolen by slaves were traded for other
commodities or for cash. Theft made an important contribution both to
the slaves' economy and to their well-being.

Like the plantation economy, the slaves' independent economic
production varied with the seasons. Fall and winter saw the injection of
large sums of money into the internal economy, since slaves gained
most of their income when they sold their cash crops and when they
delivered wood prior to the beginning of the sugar harvest. Valcour
Aime, a St James Parish planter, paid $1,300 to slaves on his plantation
for their 1848 corn crop, and in October 1859 slaves on the Uncle Sam
estate received over $1,000 for cutting wood and making barrels and
bricks. The following year slaves on Uncle Sam earned about $500 for
wood, bricks and barrels, and the year after, the total paid was $843.
Similar payment schedules, involving sums from a few dollars to
hundreds, occur regularly in plantation records.[50]

Stealing from the sugar house also was seasonal, since it had to be
carried out between the time the crop was processed and was shipped
off the estate. Furthermore, gifts from planters were usually distributed at the end of harvest or at Christmas. Christmas, according to
T. B. Thorpe, was

> the season when the planter makes presents of calico of flaming
> colors to the women and children, and a coat of extra fineness to
> patriarchal 'boys' of sixty-five and seventy. It is the time when
> negroes square their accounts with each other, and get 'master'
> and 'mistress' to pay up for innumerable eggs and chickens which
> they have frome time to time, since the last settling day, furnished
> the 'big house'. In short, it is a kind of jubilee, when the 'poor
> African' as he is termed in poetry, has a pocket full of silver, [and]
> a body covered with gay toggery.[51]

Not all of the entry of cash occurred in late fall and early winter.
Poultry provided year-round earnings, as did theft, day labour, moss-
collecting and other commercial ventures. The sugar harvest, however, was another matter. The uninterrupted labour schedule left
slaves little, if any, free time to devote to their own economic interests.
At this time, slaves had to be preoccupied with the basic necessities of
survival – food and rest. Apart from those paid for their services during
harvest (such as kettle-men, firemen, sugar-makers and engineers),
and those able to 'appropriate' some of the sugar and molasses for
themselves, slaves had little opportunity to advance their economic

position. Additionally, they had little time to spend their money during harvest.

The internal economy, therefore, had a distinct seasonal profile. Earnings fluctuated considerably since the labour demands of sugar slavery, especially during harvest, overlaid the seasonal nature of income derived from growing and marketing crops. Earnings potential also varied from year to year, since the slaves' cash crops were subject to the vagaries of the weather. Poor growing years diminished profitability for the slaves as well as the planters.

Not all slaves participated in the internal economy equally and some may not have participated at all, although it was an integral part of community life on every sugar plantation in Louisiana. Considerable disparities existed in the earnings of slaves even within the same plantation. The money accumulated by individual slaves on Benjamin Tureaud's estate for 1858–1859 ranged from $170 to $1 (during this period, 104 slaves on the estate earned a total of $3,423, with most adult slaves earning between $15 and $50). Some slaves, including 22 of the 30 women and two of the 98 men, earned no money, although, since many received credit, there was the expectation of future earnings. Similarly, cash earned by slaves on the Gay family plantation in 1844 ranged from $82 to $1 with some slaves also getting credit: 66 slaves earned a total of $864 and ten slaves received $32 in credit in that year. The 23 slaves paid for cutting wood on the Stirling estate in 1849 received sums of from $10 to $1 as their share of the total of $103 paid, while an 1854 list records payments of from $15 to 10 cents in the total of $314 paid the 50 women and 45 men.[52]

Plantation records, however, provide only a partial reckoning of the slaves' earnings, containing payments for certain commodities or work performed. They do not record income earned off the plantation. Other earnings would also have been unevenly distributed, although they did not necessarily benefit the same slaves. Those slaves who derived the greatest profit from dealings with river traders or through theft, for example, may not have been the same slaves who made the most money in transactions with the planter.

The internal economy permitted slaves to enjoy substantial material benefits. Slaves used their earnings for self-improvement – to eat and dress better and to live in more comfortable homes, caring in these and other ways for themselves and for members of their families. Although earnings were often small and purchases modest – sugar plantation slaves could not, for example, expect to earn enough to purchase freedom for themselves or their families – they reflect the independent actions of slaves as consumers and offer insight into the way slaves dealt with their lives in bondage.

The purchases made by Louisiana slaves fell principally into six categories: food and drink, pipes and tobacco, clothing and other personal items, housewares, tools and implements, and livestock. Within these six categories, however, slaves chose from a wide range of goods. They bought such foodstuffs as flour, molasses, meat, fish, coffee, beans, rice, potatoes, fruit and bottles of cordial. They also purchased a variety of clothing and cloth from which they made their 'best clothing'. Among more elaborate purchases were 'Elegant Bonnets', 'fine Summer Coats', 'Fine Russian Hats', 'Chambray', white and coloured shirts, jackets and waistcoats, silk dresses, gloves, oiled-cloth and 'log cabin' pantaloons, and oiled-cloth winter coats. More usually, however, slaves purchased plainer goods: lengths of calico, checked, plain, and striped cotton, linen, cottonade, 'domestic', blue drilling and thread, as well as simpler ready-made clothing like dresses, hose, shirts, pants, hats, shoes and boots, kerchiefs, suspenders and shawls. Besides clothes, slaves bought such personal items as pocket knives, combs, fiddles and umbrellas. Patrick, a slave 'Engineer and Overseer' on the Gay family's plantation, even paid $15 for a watch. Slaves bought an equally diverse range of housewares. Their purchases included furniture, bedspreads, blankets, baskets, tin cups and buckets, copper kettles, chairs, bowls and pots, cutlery, locks, mosquito bars, soap and tallow, and spermaceti candles. Furthermore, Louisiana slaves made extensive use of chewing and pipe tobacco, which they bought along with pipes. Some of the purchases slaves made represented an investment in their economic activities, including various implements and tools, such as shovels, saddles, bridles and bits, wire, twine, fishing hooks and line, 'mud boots' and mitts. They also invested in pigs, shoats and poultry.[53]

Obviously not every slave bought such a wide range of goods. The foregoing derives from the records of purchases made by hundreds of slaves on some 20 Louisiana sugar plantations in the years between 1834 and the Civil War. This extensive listing, however, does indicate overall trends in slave purchases.

Slaves' buying practices underwent little change over time. Throughout the period they placed high priority on a limited number of commodities – specifically flour, cloth and tobacco – with other goods given primacy, including shoes and various items of ready-made clothing. This general pattern held not only over time but also from plantation to plantation. When slaves had only limited purchasing power they tended to buy these few staple commodities, whereas slaves with larger earnings purchased other goods in addition to the staples.

Rations distributed by planters could, in specific cases, alter slaves' buying habits; slaves obviously did not have to buy goods if they were given them by the planter. On the Gay plantation, for example, slaves received a regular ration of tobacco and hence an extensive itemization of purchases on that estate reveals them buying none.[54] The slaves' buying habits reveal that they wanted to enrich their diet, dress better, smoke tobacco and drink liquor. Slaves considered the purchase of the more elaborate personal goods, housewares and other items, of secondary import. They bought such goods only if they had money left over after buying the 'staples'.

Various plantation accounts provide evidence of this pattern. On one of Benjamin Tureaud's sugar plantations, for example, of the 93 men who bought goods through the plantation, 76 (82 per cent) spent part of their earnings on tobacco, 77 (83 per cent) bought shoes, and 70 (75 per cent) bought either meat or flour. In addition, the majority of the slaves (51 out of the 93 – 55 per cent) bought some cloth or clothing other than shoes. Conversely, a minority of slaves bought such items as mosquito bars, locks, buckets and sheet-tin. The records of the Weeks family's Grande Cote Island sugar estate substantiate this pattern. The principal commodities slaves bought there were striped cotton, handkerchiefs, tobacco, flour and coffee. Records of other Louisiana sugar plantations reveal similar purchasing patterns.[55]

Slaves managed their own earnings, purchasing needed goods and saving the rest. Planters co-operated with slaves in establishing plantation accounts which credited slaves for work or goods and which slaves could use as depositories for earnings made off the plantation. Planters also acted as intermediaries in many of the expenditures made by slaves; that is, slaves made their purchases through the planter, the cost being debited from the slaves' personal accounts. Similarly, any money accrued from intracommunity transactions, such as T.B. Thorpe alluded to ('the time when negroes square their accounts with each other'), could be deposited with the planter. Given the extent to which slaves withdrew and deposited cash, the plantation slave communities were familiar with the medium of hard currency, albeit in small denominations, and were acquainted with both a barter system and a cash economy.[56]

Slaves were also conversant with the operation of a credit economy. On the Gay plantation, for example, nine slaves received a total of $32 in credit in 1844. Six of the slaves used their credit to obtain flour and coffee, two withdrew theirs in cash, while one slave, Elias, spent part of his $4 of credit on a 'Fine Russian Hat bt. in N. Orleans' that cost him $3. The other dollar went to pay a previous balance he owed on clothes. Similarly, on the Tureaud estate two slaves, Nash and David Big, received flour, meat, handkerchiefs, check cloth, shoes and tobacco on credit, while another slave, Charles Yellow, who had earned only

$2 cutting wood, bought tobacco, flour, shoes, hose, meat, hand-kerchiefs, cotton cloth and a hat. Since the bill for these goods came to $15.50, the planter extended credit to Charles Yellow for the balance of $13.50.[57]

Debiting systems and purchasing patterns indicate that the slave accounts were family accounts designated under the name of the head of household, almost always a man. Few slave women had accounts listed in their own names. On the Tureaud estate, for example, 98 men all transacted business in their own names in 1858 and 1859, whereas of the 30 women listed in the ledger only eight accumulated any earnings; the other 22 had neither debits nor credits. Similarly, the Gay plan-tation records show only a handful of women with accounts in their own names, either in comparison to the number of men (six women and 70 men), or in comparison to the total number of 70 adult women living on the estate. That few women held accounts, of course, neither reflects their lack of involvement in the system nor suggests that they accrued fewer benefits from it.[58]

Wives had recourse to accounts listed under their husbands' names and made purchases through them. On John Randolph's Nottoway Plantation, for example, three slave women had their purchases of shoes deducted from the accounts of slave men. Two of these women, Mahala and Susan, each received a pair of shoes at the cost of $1, which was debited from the accounts of George and Gus respectively, while in another case, the journal records, 'Long William got one pr. Shoes (for Leana) – $1'. An 1864 'List of Negroes' shows that George and Mahala were husband and wife, and one may assume that Gus and Susan and Long William and Leana were also married or closely related, although it is also possible that they had some sort of non-kin working or contractual relationship. The accounts of slaves on the Gay plantation provide further evidence. In 1841 William Sanders had his account debited to pay for a 'White Cambrice dress for wife'. In 1839 Little Moses' account paid for shoes for his wife, Charity; five years later Ned Davis was charged for 'Coffee by your wife'. A slave named Willis bought children's shoes from his account on the Tureaud estate, while Kenawa Moses, a slave on the Gay estate, paid for 'meat for [his] children' from the money he earned. Other slaves on the Gay estate who were charged for goods for family members included Harry Cooper, who bought shoes for his wife and his daughter Tulip, and Alfred Cooper, who purchased calico for his daughter Louisiana and two 'Elegant Bonnets' costing $2 each, presumably for his wife Dedo and his daughter.[59]

The debiting systems and the purchasing patterns thus indicate that the slave accounts were family accounts to which the family of the account-holder had access. Purchases went to improve the lives and comfort not only of the slaves who were debited for the goods, but also of members of their families. Staple foodstuffs – meat and flour for example – fed the entire family, while the lengths of cloth bought through the accounts would have been sewn by the women of the family to provide garments for all. Similarly, furniture, cutlery and other tableware, cooking utensils, blankets, locks, mosquito bars, soap and candles would have been used by the household. Even where the records make no mention of kin-relationship, as in the debit of $12.50 from the account of Woodson, a slave on W. W. Pugh's estate, for a 'Silk Dress for Rachel', and in the 'cash [paid] to Aunt Julia' from Patrick's account on the Gay plantation, it seems likely that the men and women were kin.[60]

Records of the Gay estate reveal the familial basis of the slaves' accounts. A comparison of the 1844 slave accounts on the plantation with other slave lists compiled around the same time shows the family relationships of the account-holders. Seventy-six people earned money and held accounts, 70 of whom were men. Of these 70 male account-holders, 37 were heads of households, six were sons in male-headed households, three were sons in female-headed households and 18 were single males without family affiliation. (The status of the remaining six men is unclear.) Of the six women holding accounts, two were heads of households, one was a daughter in a female-headed household, and 1 a single woman. The two other women held joint accounts; Clarissa with her husband Toney (Toney also held an account with another slave, Ned Teagle, who was a son in a female-headed household) and Anna with William, neither of whom can be traced elsewhere in the plantation records. Some of the slaves recorded as single and without family affiliation nevertheless had families who drew on their accounts. The slave named Kenawa Moses, for example, who was listed as single, paid from his account for 'meat for [his] children'. The accounts held by sons in either male- or female-headed households suggests a 'coming of age' pattern. Young adults may have been listed individually, for example, when they assumed sole responsibility for a specific money-making endeavour.[61]

Slaves did not rely on the planters for all their purchases. Although they may or may not have kept accounts on the plantation, slaves frequently found reasons to buy elsewhere. Ex-slave Catherine Cornelius recalled that on the plantation where she lived the owner 'wouldn't gib us combs en brushes, but we got some from pedlin'.[62] Slaves also bought and traded for alcohol. Markets outside the plantation were usually the only source from which slaves could obtain liquor, since planters did not usually supply it (although they occasionally distributed it on holidays, like Christmas) and rarely allowed slaves to buy it through the plantation accounts.[63] Doubtless some of the cash slaves withdrew from their accounts went to purchase alcohol from river traders, illicit 'shebeens' and grog shops, or 'moonshiners', either on or off the plantation. Slaves also spent money gambling, as evidenced by reports of slaves 'drunk and gambling' on Sundays in Plaquemine township. Cultural and religious items and locally-crafted artifacts made by slave artisans were also purchased through agencies other than the planter.[64]

Participation in the internal economy offered slaves a number of less tangible benefits. Slaves who worked for themselves and accumulated money and goods not only supplemented their often meagre rations and compensated for deficiencies in food and other necessities, but also derived satisfaction from controlling a portion of their own lives. In assuming responsibility for structuring their independent economic activities, slaves chose the manner and extent of their involvement, decided which crops they would grow and how to distribute time between small-holding agricultural pursuits and work for which planters paid them, when to sell and what to buy: decisions not normally allowed them. Although the internal economy operated within the constraints imposed by chattel bondage, the opportunity for independent economic activity gave slaves a degree of control and independence at variance with the basic tenets of servitude. Slaves *qua* slaves operated within a structure of social and labour relations that deprived them of personal rights, autonomous actions, decision-making and self-motivated work regimes. As independent economic agents, however, they structured their own efforts, controlled 'their' land and the manner of its cultivation, and decided how to market produce and dispose of the accumulated profits.

The independent activities of slaves on Mavis Grove Estate in Plaquemines Parish provide a telling example of the disparity between the slaves' lives as slaves and their lives as independent producers. On Sunday 13 September 1857 the plantation journal recorded 'Boys not cutting wood today, resting from the fatigues of last night's frolic'. Although slaves on Mavis Grove normally spent Sunday chopping wood for sale to the planter, they themselves agreed to take that Sunday off. This balancing of work with social concerns demonstrates that slaves working within the confines of the internal economy determined how to order their time and labour and shows their priorities. Indeed, the structure of the slaves' internal economy, where they assumed the responsibility of deciding how to organize their work, resembled the economy of a landed peasantry.[65]

The processes by which slaves controlled their independent

economies doubtless proved cathartic. Although involvement had potentially deleterious effects, such as overwork and physical stress, slaves found independent production rewarding. They derived great satisfaction from working for themselves, pacing their work and organizing their own efforts, as well as controlling the disposal of, and profiting directly from, the fruits of their labour. The independent economic activities, moreover, established the material foundations for slave family and community life. Patterns of production and marketing permitted not only economic independence and distance from the planters' control but also helped establish unique patterns of life within slave communities, providing an independent material basis for their society and culture. The diversity and ubiquity of the economic activities of slaves in Louisiana testifies to their creative initiative. Although planters no doubt found benefits in the slaves' internal economy, this system of independent production prompted enterprise not subservience. Whereas the plantation economy followed the planters' will, the slaves' economy contradicted the very premises of chattel bondage and helped to shape patterns of African-American life, culture and economy that endured from slavery to freedom.

NOTES

1. J. Carlyle Sitterson, *Sugar Country: The Cane Sugar Industry in the South* (Lexington, 1953), 28–30, 60.
2. Ibid., 48; *Hunt's Merchant's Magazine and Commercial Review*, 7:2 (Aug. 1842), 133–47; 7:3 (Sept. 1842), 242; 30:4 (April 1854), 499; 31:6 (Dec. 1854), 675–91; 35:2 (Aug. 1856), 248–9; *De Bow's Review*, 1 (1846), 54–5; Joseph C.C. Kennedy, *Population of the United States in 1860; compiled from the Original Returns of the Eighth Census* (Washington, DC, 1864), 188–93. Here and subsequently numbers have been rounded off.
3. Sitterson, *Sugar Country*, 30, 48–50; *De Bow's*, 1 (1846), 54–5; 19 (1855), 354; *Hunt's*, 30:4 (April 1854), 499; 35:2 (Aug. 1856), 248–9; 42:2 (Feb. 1860), 163.
4. Sugar cane did not have to be replanted following each harvest since the stubble left after cutting sprouted new shoots or ratoons.
5. Captain Thomas Hamilton, *Men and Manners in America* (Edinburgh and London, 1833), 2: 229–30.
6. Ibid., 2: 229; Frances Milton Trollope, *Domestic Manners of the Americans*, ed. by Donald Smalley (New York, 1949), 246; E.S. Abdy, *Journal of a Residence and Tour in the United States of North America, from April 1833 to October 1834* (London, 1835), 3: 103–4.
7. T.B. Thorpe, 'Sugar and the Sugar Region of Louisiana', *Harper's New Monthly Magazine*, 7 (1853), 753; William Howard Russell, *My Diary North and South* (London, 1863), 371; Interview conducted under the auspices of the Slave Narrative Collection Project, Federal Writers' Project, Works Progress Administration. Interviewee – Elizabeth Ross Hite: Interviewer – Robert McKinney: Date – c. 1940, Louisiana Writers' Project File, Louisiana State Library, Baton Rouge, Louisiana (LWPF, LSL); Interview conducted under the auspices of a Slave Narrative Collection Project organized by Dillard University (DUSNCP) using only black interviewers. This project developed alongside the Federal Writers'

Project program. Interviewee – Catherine Cornelius: Interviewer – Octave Lilly Jr: Date – c. 1939, Archives and Manuscripts Department, Earl K. Long Library, University of New Orleans, New Orleans, Louisiana.

8. Interviewee – Melinda (last name unknown): Interviewer – Arguedas: Date – c. 1940: F.W.P. Interviews, Federal Writers' Project Files, Melrose Collection, Archives Division, Northwestern State University of Louisiana, Natchitoches, Louisiana (LWPF, NSU).
9. Russell, *My Diary*, 399; Interview with Elizabeth Ross Hite, LWPF, LSL; Plantation Diary, Vol. 1, 1838–40, Samuel McCutcheon Papers, Department of Archives and Manuscripts, Louisiana State University, Baton Rouge; Interview with Catherine Cornelius, DUSNCP.
10. Ashland Plantation Record Book, Archives, LSU.
11. Isaac Erwin Diary, Archives, LSU; Plantation Diary of Valcour Aime, Louisiana Historical Center, Louisiana State Museum, New Orleans.
12. Plantation Diary and Ledger, Elu Landry Estate, Archives, LSU.
13. Plantation Diary and Ledger, Landry Papers; Journal 6, Plantation Book 1853–63, John H. Randolph Papers, Archives, LSU.
14. *De Bow's Review*, 4 (1847), 393; 6 (1848), 436; 7 (1849), 420; 9 (1850), 456; 11 (1851), 496; 13 (1852), 512; 15 (1853), 528; 17 (1854), 530; 19 (1855), 458; 21 (1856), 368; 23 (1857), 365; 25 (1858), 469; 27 (1859), 477; 29 (1860), 521; Sam Bowers Hilliard, *Hog Meat and Hoecake* (Carbondale, Ill., 1972), 155.
15. 'Negroes Corn for 1857', Box 9, Folder 54; 'Negroes Corn 1859', Box 9, Folder 57, Lewis Stirling and Family Papers, Archives, LSU.
16. Ledger 1858–72, Benjamin Tureaud Papers, Archives, LSU; Daybook 1843–47 (Vol. 5), Edward J. Gay and Family Papers, Archives, LSU.
17. Plantation Diary of Valcour Aime; Daybook 1843–47 (Vol. 5), Gay Papers.
18. Thorpe, 'Sugar and the Sugar Region', 753; Russell, *My Diary*, 373; Thomas Haley to Mrs Mary Weeks, 11 April 1841, Box 9, Folder 29, David Weeks and Family Papers, Archives, LSU; Notebook 1853–57 (Vol. 9), The Weeks Hall Memorial Collection, David Weeks and Family Collection, Archives, LSU; Daybook 1843–47 (Vol. 5), Gay Papers; Ledger 1851–56 (Vol. 18), George Lanaux and Family Papers, Archives, LSU; Cashbook for Negroes 1848–55 (Vol. 6), W.W. Pugh Papers, Archives, LSU.
19. Russell, *My Diary*, 396.
20. 'Statements of the Sugar and Rice Crops Made in Louisiana', by L. Bouchereau (New Orleans, 1871) in Box 1, Folder 1, UU-211, No. 555, Pharr Family Papers, Archives, LSU; Box 7, Folder 39, Stirling Papers; Boxes 1 and 2, Uncle Sam Plantation Papers, Archives, LSU; Joseph K. Menn, *The Large Slaveholders of Louisiana – 1860* (New Orleans, 1964), 353–4; Plantation Record Book 1849–60 (Vol. 36), Gay Papers; Journal 1851–60 (Vol. 14), Lanaux Papers.
21. Plantation Diary 1842–59, 1867, William T. Palfrey & George D. Palfrey Account Books, Archives, LSU.
22. Diary 1847 (Vol. 1), Kenner Family Papers, Archives, LSU; Plantation Record Book 1849–60 (Vol. 36), Gay Papers; Cashbook for Negroes 1848–55 (Vol. 6), W.W. Pugh Papers.
23. Cashbook for Negroes 1848–55 (Vol. 6), W.W. Pugh Papers; Plantation Record Book 1849–60 (Vol. 36), Gay Papers.
24. Daybook 1843–47 (Vol. 5); Plantation Record Book 1849–60 (Vol. 36); 'Memorandum relative to payments to negroes Dec. 1844', Box 11, Folder 81, Gay Papers.
25. Ledger 1858–72, Tureaud Papers; S-124 (9) No. 2668, Bruce, Seddon and Wilkins Plantation Records, Archives, LSU.
26. Plantation Record Book, 1849–60 (Vol. 36), Gay Papers.
27. Journal 6, Plantation Book 1853–63, Randolph Papers.
28. Interviewee – Martha Stuart: Interviewer – Octave Lilly Jr: Date – c. 1938: DUSNCP; Interview with Elizabeth Ross Hite, LWPF, LSU.
29. Journal – Plantation Book 1847–52 (Vol. 5); Journal 6, Plantation Book 1853–63, Randolph Papers; Box 8, Folder 49; Box 8, Folder 51, Stirling Papers; Estate

Record Book 1832–45 (Vol. 8); Cashbook/Daybook 1837–43 (Vol. 18), Gay Papers.
30. Interviewee – Hunton Love: Interviewer – unknown: Date – c. 1940; LWPF, LSL.
31. J.L. Rogers to Robert Ruffin Barrow, 29 Oct. 1853, Box 2, Folder 1850 s–20; Residence Journal of R.R. Barrow, 1 Jan. 1857–13 June 1858, (copied from original manuscript in Southern Historical Collection, University of North Carolina, Chapel Hill, North Carolina), Department of Archives, Tulane University, New Orleans; Book of Accounts of the Magnolia Plantation 1829–53, Louisiana State Museum.
32. Edward Gay to Hynes and Craighead, 6 April 1844; 'Account 1844, Memorandum, Sale of moss for the negroes', Box 11, Folder 81, Gay Papers.
33. Moss Record Book 1849–61 (Vol. 35); Boxes 11–13, Folders 81–96, Gay Papers; Residence Journal of R.R. Barrow, 1857–58, Barrow Papers.
34. Moss Record Book 1849–61 (Vol. 35); Estate Record Book 1848–55 (Vol. 34), Gay Papers; Menn, *Large Slaveholders*, 244–5.
35. Ashland Plantation Record Book; Daybook 1843–47 (Vol. 5); Box 12, Folder 86; 'Sales of Moss & Molasses belonging to the Negroes', Box 13, Folder 100; Box 12, Folder 93; Box 13, Folder 96, Gay Papers.
36. Journal 6, Plantation Book 1853–63, Randolph Papers; Plantation Diary and Ledger, Landry Papers.
37. Rev. P.M. Goodwyn, to Edward Gay, 27 Aug. 1860, Box 29, Folder 255, Gay Papers.
38. Russell, *My Diary*, 396.
39. Ibid., 373; P.E. Jennings to Edward Gay, 25 Aug. 1858, Box 25, Folder 221, Gay Papers.
40. W.F. Weeks to Mary C. Moore, 31 Jan. 1853, Box 31, Folder 82, Weeks Papers.
41. Interviewee – Frances Doby: Interviewers – Arguedas–McKinney: Date – 1938: LWPF, NSU; Interview with Catherine Cornelius, DUSNCP; (William Kingsford), *Impressions of the West and South during a Six Weeks' Holiday* (Toronto, 1858), 47–8.
42. U.B. Phillips (comp.), *The Revised Statutes of Louisiana* (New Orleans, 1856), 48–65.
43. Maunsell White to G. Lanneau, 15 April 1859, Box 3, Folder 1, Lanaux Papers.
44. Frederick Law Olmsted, *A Journey in the Seaboard Slave States* (New York, 1856), 674.
45. Ibid., 675.
46. William F. Weeks to Mary C. Moore, 20 June 1860, Box 36, Folder 180, Weeks Papers.
47. Joseph Mather Diary 1852–59, Archives, LSU; Diary and Plantation Record of Ellen E. McCollam, Andrew and Ellen E. McCollam Papers, Archives, LSU; Maunsell White to James P. Bracewell, 10 Aug. 1859, Maunsell White Letterbook, Archives, LSU; J.E. Craighead to John B. Craighead, 11 Sept. 1847, Box 14, Folder 102, Gay Papers; Lyle Saxon (comp.), *Gumbo Ya-Ya* (Boston, 1945), 430.
48. Diary and Plantation Record of Ellen McCollam, McCollam Papers; Plantation Diary and Ledger, Landry Papers; Nicholas Phipps to Colonel Andrew Hynes, Feb. 1847, Box 13, Folder 97, Gay Papers.
49. F.D. Richardson to Moses Liddell, 18 July 1852, Safe 12, Folder 3, Moses and St John R. Liddell and Family Papers, Archives, LSU; Interview with Martha Stuart, DUSNCP.
50. Plantation Diary of Valcour Aime 1847–52; Boxes 1 and 2, Uncle Sam Papers.
51. T.B. Thorpe, 'Christmas in the South', *Frank Leslie's Illustrated Newspaper*, 5 (26 Dec. 1857), 62.
52. Ledger 1858–72, Tureaud Papers; Daybook 1843–47 (Vol. 5); Moss Record Book 1849–61 (Vol. 35), Gay Papers; 'List of Wood Cut by Slaves and Payment Made', Box 7, Folder 39; Box 8, Folder 39, Stirling Papers.
53. Ledger 1858–72, Tureaud Papers; Daybook 1843–47, Gay Papers; Journal – Plantation Book 1848–52, Randolph Papers; Plantation Record Book

1849–60, Gay Papers; Wilton Plantation Daily Journal 1853, Bruce, Seddon and Wilkins Records; Journal 1851–60, Journal 1851–56, Lanaux Papers; Cashbook for Negroes 1848–55, W.W. Pugh Papers.

54. P.O. Daigre to Edward J. Gay, 15 Aug. 1858, Box 25, Folder 221, Gay Papers.
55. Ledger 1858–72, Tureaud Papers; Notebook 1853–57 (Vol. 9), Weeks Collection.
56. Ledger 1858–72, Tureaud Papers; Daybook 1843–47, Gay Papers; T.B. Thorpe, 'Christmas', 62.
57. Ledger 1858–72, Tureaud Papers; Daybook 1843–47, Gay Papers.
58. Ledger 1858–72, Tureaud Papers; Daybook 1843–47, Gay Papers.
59. Ledger 1862–65 (Vol. 8), Randolph Papers; Memorandum Book 1840–41 (Vol. 28); Estate Record Book 1831–45 (Vol. 8), Gay Papers.
60. Cashbook for Negroes 1848–55, W.W. Pugh Papers; Daybook 1843–47, Gay Papers.
61. Estate Record Book 1831–45 (Vol. 8); Cashbook/Daybook 1837–43 (Vol. 18), Gay Papers.
62. Interview with Catherine Cornelius, DUSNCP.
63. Kingsford, *Impressions*, 47–8; V. Alton Moody, *Slavery on Louisiana Sugar Plantations* (New Orleans, 1924), 68. Slaves on the Gay family's estate, for example, were occasionally given whiskey. On 28 Dec. 1846 'whiskey for Negroes dinner' cost $1.50, and on 25 Dec. 1850 'Whiskey for Negroes' cost $2.50. The planter paid for these items. Estate Record Book 1842–47 (Vol. 12); Estate Record Book 1848–55 (Vol. 34), Gay Papers.
64. P.E. Jennings to Edward J. Gay, 25 Aug. 1858, Box 25, Folder 221, Gay Papers.
65. Journal of Mavis Grove Plantation 1856, Louisiana State Museum.

Notes on Contributors

Hilary McD. Beckles is a Reader in Caribbean Economic and Social History at University of the West Indies, Cave Hill Campus, Barbados. He is the author of a number of books including *White Servitude and Black Slavery in Barbados 1627–1755* (Tennessee Univ. Press, 1984); *Natural Rebels: A Social History of Enslaved Black Women in Barbados* (Rutgers Univ. Press, 1990); *A History of Barbados: from Amerindian Society to Nation-State* (Cambridge Univ. Press, 1990).

Ira Berlin is Professor of History and the Director of the Freedmen and Southern Society Project at the University of Maryland. He is the author of *Slaves Without Masters: The Free Negro in the Antebellum South* and an editor of *Freedom: A Documentary History of Emancipation*.

John Campbell teaches in the Department of History at the University of Arizona. He is currently writing a study of slave work and the slave family economy in the South Carolina cotton country, 1790–1860.

Woodville Marshall is Professor of History at University of the West Indies, Cave Hill Campus, Barbados. His research interests centre on post-slavery adjustments in the British Caribbean, and he has published several articles on labour systems, peasantries and villages in the British Windward Islands.

Roderick A. McDonald is an Associate Professor of History at Rider College, New Jersey. His book, *"Goods and Chattels": The Economy and Material Culture of Slaves on Sugar Plantations in Jamaica and Louisiana*, will soon be published, and at present he is working on *The Journal of John Anderson, St Vincent Special Magistrate, 1836–1839*.

Philip D. Morgan is Professor of History at Florida State University and an editor of *Colonial Chesapeake Society* and *Strangers Within the Realm* and the author of a forthcoming study of slavery in the colonial mainland North America, *Slave Counterpoint: Black Culture in the Eighteenth Century*.

Richard Price's most recent books are *Alabi's World* (Johns Hopkins, 1990) and, with Sally Price, a critical edition of John Gabriel

Stedman's *Narrative of a Five Years Expedition Against the Revolted Negroes of Surinam* (John Hopkins, 1988) and *Two Evenings in Saramaka* (Chicago, 1991). He resides in Anses d'Arlet, Martinique.

John T. Schlotterbeck is Associate Professor of History at DePauw University. He is currently working on a study of rural society and culture in the Virginia piedmont from the early eighteenth to the late nineteenth centuries.

Dale Tomich is Associate Professor of Sociology at State University of New York at Binghamton. He is currently engaged in a study of slavery in Cuba, Brazil, and the US South as part of the nineteenth-century world economy.

Mary Turner is Professor of Caribbean History at Dalhousie University, Nova Scotia and Visiting Fellow at the Institutes of Commonwealth and Latin America history, University of London. She is the author of *Slaves and Missionaries, the Disintegration of Jamaican Slave Society, 1787–1834* (University of Illinois, 1982), and articles dealing with the social and religious life of slave societies. She is currently preparing a comparative study of coerced labour systems in the Caribbean.

Index

211